Easy Diabetic

Cookbook for Beginners

2000+ Days Delicious, Low Carb & Low Sugar Recipes Book for Pre, Type 2 Diabetes, Newly Diagnosed | A Stress-Free 30-Day Meal Plan

Lorraine M. Malley

Table of Contents

Chapter 1   Introduction ·· 02

Chapter 2   Understanding Diabetes and Nutrition ········· 05

Chapter 3   Building a Diabetes-Friendly Kitchen ········· 09

Chapter 4   Breakfasts ·· 14

Chapter 5   Beans and Grains ································· 25

Chapter 6   Snacks and Appetizers ·························· 31

Chapter 7   Poultry ·· 38

Chapter 8   Beef, Pork, and Lamb ·························· 50

Chapter 9   Fish and Seafood ································· 61

Chapter 10   Vegetables and Sides ··························· 71

Chapter 11   Vegetarian Mains ································ 80

Chapter 12   Desserts ··· 89

Chapter 13   Stews and Soups ································· 97

Chapter 14   Salads ·· 106

Appendix 1:   Measurement Conversion Chart ············ 115

Appendix 2:   The Dirty Dozen and Clean Fifteen ········· 116

Appendix 3:   Recipe Index ······························· 117

Chapter 1

Introduction

Are you tired of constantly worrying about your blood sugar levels? Do you feel like you're always restricted when it comes to food choices because of your diabetes? Well, worry no more! The cookbook is here to help.

This cookbook is not just any ordinary cookbook. It's specifically designed for those with diabetes who want to enjoy delicious and nutritious meals without sacrificing taste or health. Our recipes are carefully crafted to ensure that they are low in sugar, carbohydrates, and unhealthy fats while still being packed with flavor and nutrients.

With so many recipes to choose from, you'll never run out of options. From breakfast to dinner, snacks to desserts, we've got you covered. And the best part? All of our recipes are easy to follow and can be made with ingredients that are easily accessible at your local grocery store.

But this cookbook isn't just about providing tasty recipes. We also provide helpful tips and information on how to manage your diabetes through proper nutrition. You'll learn about portion control, meal planning, and how to make healthier food choices.

Don't let diabetes control your life any longer. Take control of your health with this cookbook. Order your copy today and start enjoying delicious, healthy meals that will keep your blood sugar levels in check and your taste buds satisfied.

Importance of a Balanced Diet for Individuals with Diabetes

A balanced diet is crucial for individuals with diabetes as it can help them manage their blood sugar levels and reduce the risk of complications associated with the condition. Here are some reasons why a balanced diet is important for individuals with diabetes:

1. Blood sugar control: A balanced diet that includes the right balance of carbohydrates, proteins, and fats can help individuals with diabetes maintain stable blood sugar levels. This is because the body processes different types of nutrients differently, and a balanced diet can help regulate the amount of glucose in the bloodstream.

2. Weight management: Obesity and being overweight are major risk factors for developing type 2 diabetes. A balanced diet that is low in calories and high in fiber can help individuals with diabetes lose weight or maintain a healthy weight. This, in turn, can help improve insulin sensitivity and reduce the risk of complications associated with the condition.

3. Heart health: Individuals with diabetes are at an increased risk of developing heart disease. A balanced diet that is low in saturated and trans fats and high in fruits, vegetables, and whole grains can help lower cholesterol levels and reduce the risk of heart disease.

4. Overall health: A balanced diet that includes a variety of nutrient-rich foods can help individuals with diabetes maintain good overall health. This includes getting enough vitamins, minerals, and antioxidants that can help boost the immune system and reduce the risk of other health conditions.

In conclusion, a balanced diet is essential for individuals with diabetes as it can help manage blood sugar levels, promote weight loss, improve heart health, and maintain overall health. It's important to work with a healthcare provider or registered dietitian to develop a personalized meal plan that meets individual needs and preferences.

Understanding of the Diabetic Diet and Its Key Principles

The diabetic diet is a healthy eating plan that is specifically designed for individuals with diabetes. The goal of the diabetic diet is to help manage blood sugar levels and reduce the risk of complications associated with the condition. Here are some key principles of the diabetic diet:

1. Carbohydrate control: Carbohydrates are the main source of glucose in the body, which can cause blood sugar levels to rise. The diabetic diet emphasizes controlling the amount and type of carbohydrates consumed. This includes choosing complex carbohydrates that are high in fiber and have a lower glycemic index, such as whole grains, fruits, vegetables, and legumes.

2. Portion control: Eating too much food, even if it's healthy, can cause blood sugar levels to spike. The diabetic diet emphasizes portion control to help regulate blood sugar levels. This involves measuring and monitoring serving sizes, and spreading out meals and snacks throughout the day.

3. Healthy fats: The diabetic diet emphasizes consuming healthy fats, such as monounsaturated and polyunsaturated fats found in nuts, seeds, avocados, and fatty fish. These fats can help improve cholesterol levels and reduce the risk of heart disease.

4. Lean protein: Protein is an important nutrient for building and repairing tissues in the body. The diabetic diet emphasizes lean sources of protein, such as skinless chicken, fish, tofu, and legumes. It's important to avoid high-fat sources of protein, such as red meat and processed meats.

5. Limiting unhealthy foods: The diabetic diet emphasizes limiting or avoiding unhealthy foods that can cause blood sugar levels to spike, such as sugary drinks, candy, and desserts. It's also important to limit or avoid foods that are high in saturated and trans fats, such as fried foods and processed snacks.

In conclusion, the diabetic diet is a healthy eating plan that emphasizes carbohydrate control, portion control, healthy fats, lean protein, and limiting unhealthy foods. It's important to work with a healthcare provider or registered dietitian to develop a personalized meal plan that meets individual needs and preferences.

General Tips for Meal Planning and Portion Control

Meal planning and portion control are important aspects of managing diabetes and maintaining a healthy diet. Here are some general tips for meal planning and portion control:

1. Plan ahead: Take time to plan your meals and snacks in advance. This can help you make healthier choices and avoid impulse eating. Consider using a meal planning app or keeping a food journal to help you stay on track.

2. Use smaller plates: Using smaller plates can help you control portion sizes and reduce the amount of food you eat. Aim to fill half of your plate with non-starchy vegetables, one-quarter with lean protein, and one-quarter with complex carbohydrates.

3. Measure and weigh food: Measuring and weighing your food can help you accurately track portion sizes and ensure that you're not overeating. Use measuring cups, spoons, and a kitchen scale to help you portion out food.

4. Avoid distractions: Eating while distracted, such as watching TV or working on the computer, can cause you to eat more than you need. Focus on your food and enjoy the flavors and textures of each bite.

5. Snack wisely: Choose healthy snacks that are low in calories and high in fiber and protein. Some good options include raw vegetables with hummus, apple slices with almond butter, or a small handful of nuts.

6. Drink water: Drinking water before and during meals can help you feel full and reduce the amount of food you eat. Aim to drink at least 8-10 glasses of water per day.

7. Be mindful of restaurant portions: Restaurant portions are often much larger than what you need. Consider sharing a meal with a friend or taking half of it home for later.

In conclusion, meal planning and portion control are important aspects of managing diabetes and maintaining a healthy diet. By planning ahead, using smaller plates, measuring and weighing food, avoiding distractions, snacking wisely, drinking water, and being mindful of restaurant portions, you can control portion sizes and make healthier food choices.

Chapter 2

Understanding Diabetes and Nutrition

Overview of Different Types of Diabetes

There are several different types of diabetes, each with its own causes and risk factors. Here are the most common types of diabetes:

1. Type 1 diabetes: Type 1 diabetes is an autoimmune disease in which the body's immune system attacks and destroys the cells in the pancreas that produce insulin. This results in a lack of insulin production, which can cause high blood sugar levels. Type 1 diabetes is usually diagnosed in children and young adults.

2. Type 2 diabetes: Type 2 diabetes is the most common type of diabetes, accounting for about 90% of all cases. It occurs when the body becomes resistant to insulin or doesn't produce enough insulin to maintain normal blood sugar levels. Type 2 diabetes is often associated with obesity, sedentary lifestyle, and poor diet.

3. Gestational diabetes: Gestational diabetes is a type of diabetes that develops during pregnancy. It occurs when the hormones produced by the placenta interfere with the body's ability to use insulin effectively. Gestational diabetes usually goes away after delivery, but women who have had gestational diabetes are at a higher risk of developing type 2 diabetes later in life.

4. Prediabetes: Prediabetes is a condition in which blood sugar levels are higher than normal but not yet high enough to be diagnosed as type 2 diabetes. People with prediabetes are at a higher risk of developing type 2 diabetes if they don't make lifestyle changes, such as losing weight, eating a healthy diet, and exercising regularly.

5. Monogenic diabetes: Monogenic diabetes is a rare form of diabetes that is caused by a single gene mutation. It can be inherited from one or both parents and can occur at any age.

In conclusion, there are several different types of diabetes, each with its own causes and risk factors. It's important to work with a healthcare provider to determine the type of diabetes you have and develop a personalized treatment plan.

Basics of Blood Sugar Management

Blood sugar management is an important aspect of managing diabetes and maintaining good health. Here are some basics of blood sugar management:

1. Monitoring blood sugar levels: Regular monitoring of blood sugar levels is important for individuals with diabetes. This can help you identify patterns and make adjustments to your diet, exercise, and medication as needed.

2. Eating a healthy diet: A healthy diet that is low in sugar, saturated and trans fats, and high in fiber, lean protein, and complex carbohydrates can help regulate blood sugar levels. It's important to work with a registered dietitian to develop a personalized meal plan that meets individual needs and preferences.

3. Exercising regularly: Exercise can help improve insulin sensitivity and lower blood sugar levels. Aim for at least 30 minutes of moderate-intensity exercise most days of the week, such as brisk walking, cycling, or swimming.

4. Taking medication as prescribed: Medications, such as insulin or oral medications, can help manage blood sugar levels. It's important to take medication as prescribed and monitor blood sugar levels regularly to ensure that they are working effectively.

5. Managing stress: Stress can cause blood sugar levels to rise. Practice stress-reducing activities, such as yoga, meditation, or deep breathing exercises, to help manage stress levels.

6. Getting enough sleep: Lack of sleep can affect blood sugar levels and insulin sensitivity. Aim for at least 7-8 hours of sleep per night to help regulate blood sugar levels.

In conclusion, blood sugar management is an important aspect of managing diabetes and maintaining good health. By monitoring blood sugar levels, eating a healthy diet, exercising regularly, taking medication as prescribed, managing stress, and getting enough sleep, individuals with diabetes can help regulate blood sugar levels and reduce the risk of complications associated with the condition.

Nutritional Requirements for Individuals with Diabetes

Individuals with diabetes have unique nutritional requirements to help manage their blood sugar levels and reduce the risk of complications associated with the condition. Here are some key nutritional requirements for individuals with diabetes:

1. Carbohydrates: Carbohydrates are an important source of energy, but they can also cause blood sugar levels to rise. The recommended intake of carbohydrates for individuals with diabetes is about 45-60 grams per meal, or a total of 135-180 grams per day. Choose complex carbohydrates that are high in fiber and have a lower glycemic index, such as whole grains, fruits, vegetables, and legumes.

2. Protein: Protein is important for building and repairing tissues in the body. The recommended intake of protein for individuals with diabetes is about 15-20% of total daily calories. Choose lean sources of protein, such as skinless chicken, fish, tofu, and legumes.

3. Fats: Fats are an important source of energy and play a role in hormone production and absorption of vitamins. The recommended intake of fats for individuals with diabetes is about 20-35% of total daily calories. Choose healthy fats, such as monounsaturated and polyunsaturated fats found in nuts, seeds, avocados, and fatty fish.

4. Fiber: Fiber is important for maintaining good digestive health and regulating blood sugar levels. The recommended intake of fiber for individuals with diabetes is about 25-30 grams per day. Choose foods that are high in fiber, such as whole grains, fruits, vegetables, and legumes.

5. Micronutrients: Individuals with diabetes may be at risk of nutrient deficiencies, such as vitamin D, calcium, and magnesium. It's important to include a variety of nutrient-rich foods in the diet, such as leafy greens, dairy products, and fortified cereals.

In conclusion, individuals with diabetes have unique nutritional requirements to help manage their blood sugar levels and reduce the risk of complications associated with the condition. By choosing complex carbohydrates, lean protein, healthy fats, high-fiber foods, and nutrient-rich foods, individuals with diabetes can maintain a healthy diet and improve their overall health. It's important to work with a registered dietitian to develop a personalized meal plan that meets individual needs and preferences.

Key Nutrients to Focus on

Individuals with diabetes should focus on consuming nutrient-dense foods that provide important vitamins, minerals, and other key nutrients. Here are some key nutrients to focus on:

1. Omega-3 fatty acids: Omega-3 fatty acids are healthy fats that can help reduce inflammation, improve heart health, and lower triglyceride levels. Good sources of omega-3 fatty acids include fatty fish, such as salmon and tuna, flaxseed, chia seeds, and walnuts.

2. Magnesium: Magnesium is an important mineral that helps regulate blood sugar levels and improve insulin sensitivity. Good sources of magnesium include leafy greens, nuts, seeds, and whole grains.

3. Vitamin D: Vitamin D is important for bone health and immune function. Individuals with diabetes may be at risk of vitamin D deficiency, which can increase the risk of complications associated with the condition. Good sources of vitamin D include fortified dairy products, fatty fish, and exposure to sunlight.

4. Calcium: Calcium is important for bone health and muscle function. Good sources of calcium include dairy products, leafy greens, and fortified foods.

5. Chromium: Chromium is a mineral that can help improve insulin sensitivity and regulate blood sugar levels. Good sources of chromium include broccoli, grape juice, and whole grains.

In conclusion, individuals with diabetes should focus on consuming nutrient-dense foods that provide important vitamins, minerals, and other key nutrients. By including omega-3 fatty acids, magnesium, vitamin D, calcium, and chromium in the diet, individuals with diabetes can maintain good health and reduce the risk of complications associated with the condition.

Glycemic Index and Its Role in Meal Planning

The glycemic index (GI) is a measure of how quickly a carbohydrate-containing food raises blood sugar levels. Foods with a high GI value are rapidly digested and absorbed, causing a quick spike in blood sugar levels, while foods with a low GI value are digested more slowly and cause a slower rise in blood sugar levels. The GI can be an important tool for individuals with diabetes in meal planning. Here's how:

1. Choosing low GI foods: Choosing low GI foods can help regulate blood sugar levels and reduce the risk of complications associated with the condition. Good sources of low GI foods include whole grains, fruits, vegetables, legumes, and nuts.

2. Combining high GI foods with low GI foods: Combining high GI foods with low GI foods can help slow down the absorption of carbohydrates and prevent blood sugar spikes. For example, pairing a high GI food like white bread with a low GI food like avocado or peanut butter can help regulate blood sugar levels.

3. Timing of meals: The timing of meals can also affect blood sugar levels. Eating smaller, more frequent meals throughout the day can help regulate blood sugar levels and prevent spikes. It's also important to eat a balanced meal that includes protein, healthy fats, and complex carbohydrates to help slow down the absorption of carbohydrates.

4. Personalizing meal plans: The GI can be used to personalize meal plans for individuals with diabetes based on their individual needs and preferences. A registered dietitian can help develop a personalized meal plan that takes into account the GI of different foods and helps regulate blood sugar levels.

In conclusion, the glycemic index is a measure of how quickly a carbohydrate-containing food raises blood sugar levels. By choosing low GI foods, combining high GI foods with low GI foods, timing meals appropriately, and personalizing meal plans, individuals with diabetes can use the GI as a tool to help regulate blood sugar levels and reduce the risk of complications associated with the condition.

Chapter

3

Building a Diabetes-Friendly Kitchen

Essential Pantry Items for a Diabetic Diet

Having a well-stocked pantry is essential for maintaining a healthy diabetic diet. Here are some essential pantry items for individuals with diabetes:

1. Whole grains: Whole grains, such as brown rice, quinoa, and whole wheat pasta, are high in fiber and complex carbohydrates that can help regulate blood sugar levels.

2. Canned or dried beans: Beans are a good source of protein and fiber that can help regulate blood sugar levels. They can be added to soups, stews, salads, and side dishes.

3. Canned or frozen vegetables: Canned or frozen vegetables are convenient and can be used in a variety of dishes. Choose low-sodium canned vegetables and avoid those with added sauces or seasonings.

4. Nuts and seeds: Nuts and seeds are a good source of healthy fats, protein, and fiber. They can be added to salads, yogurt, or oatmeal for a nutrient boost.

5. Canned or dried fruit: Canned or dried fruit can be a convenient snack or addition to meals. Choose fruit packed in water or juice without added sugars.

6. Low-sugar cereal: Look for cereals that are high in fiber and low in sugar. Oatmeal, bran flakes, and shredded wheat are good options.

7. Spices and herbs: Spices and herbs can add flavor to meals without adding extra calories or sodium. Stock up on basics like salt-free seasoning blends, garlic powder, onion powder, and black pepper.

8. Cooking oils: Choose healthy cooking oils, such as olive oil, avocado oil, or canola oil, for cooking and baking.

9. Sugar substitutes: Sugar substitutes, such as stevia, monk fruit extract, or erythritol, can be used in place of sugar to sweeten foods and beverages without affecting blood sugar levels.

In conclusion, having a well-stocked pantry is essential for maintaining a healthy diabetic diet. By stocking up on whole grains, beans, vegetables, nuts and seeds, low-sugar cereal, spices and herbs, cooking oils, and sugar substitutes, individuals with diabetes can prepare nutritious meals and snacks that help regulate blood sugar levels and reduce the risk of complications associated with the condition.

Smart Ingredient Substitutions for Healthier Cooking

Making smart ingredient substitutions can help make cooking healthier without sacrificing flavor. Here are some ingredient substitutions that can be used to make recipes healthier:

1. Whole grains for refined grains: Replace refined grains, such as white flour and white rice, with whole grains, such as whole wheat flour and brown rice. Whole grains are higher in fiber and nutrients, and can help regulate blood sugar levels.

2. Greek yogurt for sour cream: Use Greek yogurt in place of sour cream in recipes. Greek yogurt is lower in fat and calories and higher in protein.

3. Unsweetened applesauce for oil or butter: Substitute unsweetened applesauce for oil or butter in baking recipes. Applesauce is lower in fat and calories and adds moisture to baked goods.

4. Avocado for mayonnaise: Use mashed avocado in place of mayonnaise in recipes. Avocado is a good source of healthy fats and can add creaminess to dishes.

5. Spices and herbs for salt: Use spices and herbs, such as garlic, onion powder, and black pepper, in place of salt to add flavor to dishes. This can help reduce sodium intake and promote heart health.

6. Nutritional yeast for cheese: Use nutritional yeast in place of cheese in recipes. Nutritional yeast is high in B vitamins and adds a cheesy flavor to dishes without the added fat and calories.

7. Honey or maple syrup for sugar: Use honey or maple syrup in place of sugar in recipes. They are natural sweeteners that are lower on the glycemic index and can help regulate blood sugar levels.

In conclusion, making smart ingredient substitutions can help make cooking healthier without sacrificing flavor. By using whole grains, Greek yogurt, unsweetened applesauce, avocado, spices and herbs, nutritional yeast, and natural sweeteners, individuals can prepare nutritious meals and snacks that promote good health and well-being.

Kitchen Tools and Equipment for Easy Meal Preparation

Having the right kitchen tools and equipment can make meal preparation easier and more efficient. Here are some essential kitchen tools and equipment for easy meal preparation:

1. Chef's knife: A good quality chef's knife is essential for cutting vegetables, fruits, and meats.

2. Cutting board: A sturdy cutting board is important for protecting countertops and making meal preparation easier.

3. Measuring cups and spoons: Accurate measurements are important for cooking and baking. Having a set of measuring cups and spoons can help ensure that recipes turn out correctly.

4. Mixing bowls: Mixing bowls come in handy for preparing ingredients and mixing batters and doughs.

5. Blender or food processor: A blender or food processor can be used for making smoothies, pureeing soups, and chopping vegetables.

6. Slow cooker: A slow cooker can be a convenient tool for preparing meals ahead of time or for busy days when there isn't time for hands-on cooking.

7. Non-stick cookware: Non-stick cookware can make cooking and cleaning up easier.

8. Oven-safe casserole dish: An oven-safe casserole dish can be used for baking casseroles, roasting vegetables, and making one-pot meals.

9. Instant-read thermometer: An instant-read thermometer can help ensure that meats are cooked to a safe temperature.

10. Vegetable peeler: A vegetable peeler can make peeling and preparing vegetables easier.

In conclusion, having the right kitchen tools and equipment can make meal preparation easier and more efficient. By having a good quality chef's knife, cutting board, measuring cups and spoons, mixing bowls, blender or food processor, slow cooker, non-stick cookware, oven-safe casserole dish, instant-read thermometer, and vegetable peeler, individuals can prepare nutritious meals with ease.

30-Day Meal Plan

DAYS	BREAKFAST	LUNCH	DINNER	SNACK/DESSERT
1	Seedy Muesli	Hoppin' John	Vegan Dal Makhani	Lemon Artichokes
2	Cocoa Carrot Muffins	Rice with Spinach and Feta	Stuffed Portobello Mushrooms	Peanut Butter Protein Bites
3	Instant Pot Hard-Boiled Eggs	Spicy Couscous and Chickpea Salad	Roasted Veggie Bowl	Cinnamon Toasted Pumpkin Seeds
4	Three-Berry Dutch Pancake	Sweet Potato Fennel Bake	Palak Tofu	Hummus
5	Cinnamon Overnight Oats	Farmers' Market Barley Risotto	Orange Tofu	Chilled Shrimp
6	Western Omelet	Sunshine Burgers	Crispy Eggplant Rounds	Chicken Kabobs
7	Breakfast Meatballs	Stewed Green Beans	Vegetable Burgers	Homemade Sun-Dried Tomato Salsa
8	High-Protein Oatmeal	Whole-Wheat Linguine with Kale Pesto	Chickpea-Spinach Curry	Creamy Cheese Dip
9	Griddle Corn Cakes	Edamame-Tabbouleh Salad	Gingered Tofu and Greens	Roasted Carrot and Herb Spread
10	Potato-Bacon Gratin	Herbed Beans and Brown Rice	Cheesy Zucchini Patties	Creamy Jalapeño Chicken Dip
11	Southwestern Egg Casserole	Cashew-Kale and Chickpeas	Mozzarella-Tomato Salad	Lemon Cream Fruit Dip
12	Shakshuka	Tofu and Bean Chili	Kidney Bean Salad	Instant Popcorn
13	Corn, Egg and Potato Bake	Veggie Fajitas	Edamame and Walnut Salad	Gruyere Apple Spread
14	Tomato and Chive Waffles	Quinoa–White Bean Loaf	Garden-Fresh Greek Salad	Guacamole with Jicama
15	Baked Avocado and Egg	Chickpea and Tofu Bolognese	Sunflower-Tuna-Cauliflower Salad	Creamy Spinach Dip
16	Vanilla Steel-Cut Oatmeal	Sautéed Spinach and Lima Beans	Three Bean and Basil Salad	Cucumber Roll-Ups
17	Baked Eggs	Chickpea Coconut Curry	Greek Rice Salad	Candied Pecans
18	Vegetable Frittata	No-Tuna Lettuce Wraps	Mediterranean Chicken Salad	Fresh Dill Dip
19	Biscuits	Stuffed Acorn Squash	Tu-No Salad	Oatmeal Chippers
20	Veggie-Stuffed Omelet	Italian Zucchini Boats	Cabbage Slaw Salad	Creamy Orange Cheesecake
21	Bran Apple Muffins	Summer Salad	Red Beans	Cream Cheese Swirl Brownies

DAYS	BREAKFAST	LUNCH	DINNER	SNACK/DESSERT
22	Shredded Potato Omelet	Chicken Salad with Apricots	Italian Bean Burgers	Banana Pudding
23	Breakfast Banana Barley	Nutty Deconstructed Salad	Veggie Unfried Rice	Broiled Pineapple
24	Cinnamon Bun Oatmeal	Italian Potato Salad	Southwestern Quinoa Salad	Apple Crunch
25	Orange Muffins	Three-Bean Salad with Black Bean Crumbles	Texas Caviar	Classic Crêpes
26	Lemon-Pineapple Muffins	Pasta Salad–Stuffed Tomatoes	Thai Red Lentils	Chocolate Cupcakes
27	Cheesy Quinoa-Crusted Spinach Frittata	Winter Chicken and Citrus Salad	Asian Fried Rice	Double-Ginger Cookies
28	Egg Bites with Sausage and Peppers	Wild Rice Salad3	Colorful Rice Casserole	Berry Smoothie Pops
29	Smoked Salmon and Asparagus Quiche Cups	Grilled Hearts of Romaine with Buttermilk Dressing	Green Chickpea Falafel	Ambrosia
30	Simple Grain-Free Biscuits	Sesame Chicken-Almond Slaw	Easy Lentil Burgers	Peach Shortcake

Chapter 4

Breakfasts

Whole Wheat Waffles with Honey–Peanut Butter Drizzle

Prep time: 35 minutes | Cook time: 5 minutes | Serves 8

Waffles

2 eggs or 4 egg whites

1 cup whole wheat flour

1 cup all-purpose flour

2 cups buttermilk

1 tablespoon sugar

3 tablespoons canola oil

2 teaspoons baking powder

¼ teaspoon salt

½ cup low-fat granola

Drizzle

½ cup honey

¼ cup creamy peanut butter

1. Heat waffle iron; brush with canola oil if necessary (or spray with cooking spray before heating). In medium bowl, beat eggs with fork or whisk until foamy. Beat in remaining waffle ingredients except granola just until smooth. 2. Pour about 1 cup batter onto center of hot waffle iron. (Check manufacturer's directions for recommended amount of batter.) Close lid of waffle iron. 3. Bake about 5 minutes or until steaming stops. Carefully remove waffle. Repeat with remaining batter. 4. Meanwhile, in small microwavable bowl, mix honey and peanut butter. Microwave uncovered on High 40 to 60 seconds or until warm; stir until smooth. Drizzle over waffles. Sprinkle with granola.

Per Serving:

calories: 360 | fat: 12g | protein: 10g | carbs: 52g | sugars: 25g | fiber: 3g | sodium: 320mg

Instant Pot Hard-Boiled Eggs

Prep time: 10 minutes | Cook time: 5 minutes | Serves 7

1 cup water

6 to 8 eggs

1. Pour the water into the inner pot. Place the eggs in a steamer basket or rack that came with pot. 2. Close the lid and secure to the locking position. Be sure the vent is turned to sealing. Set for 5 minutes on Manual at high pressure. (It takes about 5 minutes for pressure to build and then 5 minutes to cook.) 3. Let pressure naturally release for 5 minutes, then do quick pressure release. 4. Place hot eggs into cool water to halt cooking process. You can peel cooled eggs immediately or refrigerate unpeeled.

Per Serving:

calories: 72 | fat: 5g | protein: 6g | carbs: 0g | sugars: 0g | fiber: 0g | sodium: 71mg

Three-Berry Dutch Pancake

Prep time: 10 minutes | Cook time: 12 to 16 minutes | Serves 4

2 egg whites

1 egg

½ cup whole-wheat pastry flour

½ cup 2% milk

1 teaspoon pure vanilla extract

1 tablespoon unsalted butter, melted

1 cup sliced fresh strawberries

½ cup fresh blueberries

½ cup fresh raspberries

1. In a medium bowl, use an eggbeater or hand mixer to quickly mix the egg whites, egg, pastry flour, milk, and vanilla until well combined. 2. Use a pastry brush to grease the bottom of a baking pan with the melted butter. Immediately pour in the batter and put the basket back in the fryer. Bake at 330ºF (166ºC) for 12 to 16 minutes, or until the pancake is puffed and golden brown. 3. Remove the pan from the air fryer; the pancake will fall. Top with the strawberries, blueberries, and raspberries. Serve immediately.

Per Serving:

calories: 151 | fat: 5g | protein: 7g | carbs: 20g | sugars: 6g | fiber: 4g | sodium: 59mg

Seedy Muesli

Prep time: 5 minutes | Cook time: 0 minutes | Makes 6 cups

2 cups gluten-free rolled oats

1 cup roasted, slivered almonds

¾ cup raw sunflower seeds

½ cup raw pumpkin seeds

½ cup pistachios

½ cup apricots, sliced

¼ cup hemp seeds

¼ cup ground flaxseed

¼ cup toasted sesame seeds

1. In a medium bowl, combine the oats, almonds, sunflower seeds, pumpkin seeds, pistachios, apricots, hemp seeds, flaxseed, and sesame seeds. 2. Store the mixture in an airtight container at room temperature for up to 6 months.

Per Serving:

1 cup: calories: 494 | fat: 36g | protein: 23g | carbs: 38g | sugars: 5g | fiber: 14g | sodium: 9mg

Southwestern Egg Casserole

Prep time: 10 minutes | Cook time: 20 minutes | Serves 12

1 cup water

2½ cups egg substitute

½ cup flour

1 teaspoon baking powder

⅛ teaspoon salt

⅛ teaspoon pepper

2 cups fat-free cottage cheese

1½ cups shredded 75%-less-fat sharp cheddar cheese

¼ cup no-trans-fat tub margarine, melted

2 (4 ounces) cans chopped green chilies

1. Place the steaming rack into the bottom of the inner pot and pour in 1 cup of water. 2. Grease a round springform pan that will fit into the inner pot of the Instant Pot. 3. Combine the egg substitute, flour, baking powder, salt and pepper in a mixing bowl. It will be lumpy. 4. Stir in the cheese, margarine, and green chilies then pour into the springform pan. 5. Place the springform pan onto the steaming rack, close the lid, and secure to the locking position. Be sure the vent is turned to sealing. Set for 20 minutes on Manual at high pressure. 6. Let the pressure release naturally. 7. Carefully remove the springform pan with the handles of the steaming rack and allow to stand 10 minutes before cutting and serving.

Per Serving:

calories: 130 | fat: 4g | protein: 14g | carbs: 9g | sugars: 1g | fiber: 1g | sodium: 450mg

Cocoa Carrot Muffins

Prep time: 5 minutes | Cook time: 23 to 24 minutes | Makes 12 muffins

2 cups spelt flour (or 1¾ cups whole wheat pastry flour)

⅓ cup coconut sugar

¼ cup cocoa powder

1 teaspoon cinnamon

½ teaspoon nutmeg

¼ teaspoon sea salt

2 teaspoons baking powder

½ teaspoon baking soda

2 tablespoons nut butter, such as

almond or cashew butter (or 1½ tablespoons tahini mixed with 1 tablespoon maple syrup)

1 cup low-fat nondairy milk

¾ cup unsweetened applesauce

1 cup grated carrot

¼ cup raisins

2 tablespoons sugar-free nondairy chocolate chips (optional)

1. Preheat the oven to 350°F. Line a muffin pan with 12 parchment cupcake liners. 2. In a large bowl, combine the flour, sugar, cocoa, cinnamon, nutmeg, salt, baking powder, and baking soda, stirring well. In a medium bowl, combine the nut butter with a few tablespoons of the milk, whisking it to incorporate fully. Continue to add the remaining milk and then the applesauce, stirring thoroughly. Add this wet mixture to the dry, along with the carrot, raisins, and chips (if using). Fold and mix until just combined; do not overmix. Spoon the batter into the cupcake liners. Bake for 23 to 24 minutes, or until a toothpick inserted in the center comes out clean. Remove from the oven, let cool in the pan for a couple of minutes, then transfer to a cooling rack.

Per Serving:

1 muffin: calorie: 137 | fat: 2g | protein: 4g | carbs: 28g | sugars: 11g | fiber: 4g | sodium: 205mg

Vegetable Frittata

Prep time: 10 minutes | Cook time: 19 minutes | Serves 1 to 2

½ red or green bell pepper, cut into ½-inch chunks

4 button mushrooms, sliced

½ cup diced zucchini

½ teaspoon chopped fresh oregano or thyme

1 teaspoon olive oil

3 eggs, beaten

½ cup grated Cheddar cheese

Salt and freshly ground black pepper, to taste

1 teaspoon butter

1 teaspoon chopped fresh parsley

1. Preheat the air fryer to 400°F (204°C). 2. Toss the peppers, mushrooms, zucchini and oregano with the olive oil and air fry for 6 minutes, shaking the basket once or twice during the cooking process to redistribute the ingredients. 3. While the vegetables are cooking, beat the eggs well in a bowl, stir in the Cheddar cheese and season with salt and freshly ground black pepper. Add the air-fried vegetables to this bowl when they have finished cooking. 4. Place a cake pan into the air fryer basket with the butter using an aluminum sling to lower the pan into the basket. Air fry for 1 minute at 380°F (193°C) to melt the butter. Remove the cake pan and rotate the pan to distribute the butter and grease the pan. Pour the egg mixture into the cake pan and return the pan to the air fryer, using the aluminum sling. 5. Air fry at 380°F (193°C) for 12 minutes, or until the frittata has puffed up and is lightly browned. Let the frittata sit in the air fryer for 5 minutes to cool to an edible temperature and set up. Remove the cake pan from the air fryer, sprinkle with parsley and serve immediately.

Per Serving:

calories: 297 | fat: 21g | protein: 19g | carbs: 10g | sugars: 6g | fiber: 3g | sodium: 295mg

Western Omelet

Prep time: 5 minutes | Cook time: 10 minutes | Serves 2

1½ teaspoons canola oil

¾ cup egg whites

¼ cup minced lean ham

2 tablespoons minced green bell

pepper

2 tablespoons minced onion

⅛ teaspoon freshly ground black pepper

1. In a medium nonstick skillet over medium-low heat, heat the oil. 2. In a small mixing bowl, beat the egg whites slightly, and add the remaining ingredients along with a dash of salt, if desired. Pour the egg mixture into the heated skillet. 3. When the omelet begins to set, gently lift the edges of the omelet with a spatula, and tilt the skillet to allow the uncooked portion to flow underneath. Continue cooking until the eggs are firm. Then transfer to a serving platter.

Per Serving:

calories: 107 | fat: 4g | protein: 14g | carbs: 2g | sugars: 1g | fiber: 0g | sodium: 367mg

Shakshuka

Prep time: 5 minutes | Cook time: 25 minutes | Serves 4

2 tablespoons extra-virgin olive oil

1 onion, diced

2 tablespoons tomato paste

2 red bell peppers, diced

2 tablespoons harissa (optional)

4 garlic cloves, minced

2 teaspoons ground cumin

½ teaspoon ground coriander (optional)

1 teaspoon smoked paprika

2 (14 ounces) cans diced tomatoes

4 large eggs

½ cup plain Greek yogurt

Bread, for dipping (optional)

1. Heat the extra-virgin olive oil in a Dutch oven or large saucepan over medium heat. When it starts to shimmer, add the onion and cook until translucent, about 3 minutes. 2. Add the tomato paste, peppers, harissa (if using), garlic, cumin, coriander (if using), paprika, and tomatoes. Bring to a simmer and cook 10 to 15 minutes, until the peppers are cooked and the sauce is thick. Adjust the seasoning as desired. 3. Make four wells in the mixture with the back of a large spoon and gently break one egg into each well. Cover the saucepan and simmer gently until the egg whites are set but the yolks are still runny, 5 to 8 minutes. 4. Remove the saucepan from the heat and spoon the tomato mixture and one cooked egg into each of four bowls. Top with the Greek yogurt and serve with bread (if using).

Per Serving:

calories: 229 | fat: 13g | protein: 11g | carbs: 20g | sugars: 13g | fiber: 7g | sodium: 127mg

Breakfast Meatballs

Prep time: 10 minutes | Cook time: 15 minutes | Makes 18 meatballs

1 pound (454 g) ground pork
breakfast sausage
½ teaspoon salt
¼ teaspoon ground black pepper
½ cup shredded sharp Cheddar

cheese
1 ounce (28 g) cream cheese,
softened
1 large egg, whisked

1. Combine all ingredients in a large bowl. Form mixture into eighteen 1-inch meatballs. 2. Place meatballs into ungreased air fryer basket. Adjust the temperature to 400ºF (204ºC) and air fry for 15 minutes, shaking basket three times during cooking. Meatballs will be browned on the outside and have an internal temperature of at least 145ºF (63ºC) when completely cooked. Serve warm.

Per Serving:

1 meatball: calories: 106 | fat: 9g | protein: 5g | carbs: 0g | sugars: 0g | fiber: 0g | sodium: 284mg

High-Protein Oatmeal

Prep time: 2 minutes | Cook time: 8 minutes | Serves 1

8 ounces vanilla soy milk
½ cup oats
1 tablespoon chia seeds

¼ cup blueberries
1 tablespoon sliced and toasted
almonds

1. In a medium saucepan over medium-high heat, stir together the soy milk and oats. 2. Bring to a boil, reduce the heat to low, and simmer, stirring frequently, until cooked and tender, 5 to 8 minutes. 3. Remove the oatmeal from the heat and serve topped with chia seeds, blueberries, and almonds. 4. Store any leftovers in an airtight container in the refrigerator for up to 5 days.

Per Serving:

calories: 480 | fat: 14g | protein: 22g | carbs: 70g | sugars: 5g | fiber: 13g | sodium: 147mg

Griddle Corn Cakes

Prep time: 5 minutes | Cook time: 10 minutes | Serves 6

1 cup whole-wheat flour
2 teaspoons baking powder
1 tablespoon fructose
¾ cup low-fat buttermilk

1 egg white
2 tablespoons canola oil
1 cup corn kernels (frozen or
fresh; if frozen, defrost)

1. In a medium bowl, combine the flour, baking powder, and fructose. 2. In another bowl, combine the buttermilk, egg white, and oil. Stir in the corn kernels. Slowly add the wet mixture to the dry ingredients, just to blend. A few lumps will remain. 3. On a heated nonstick griddle, pour ¼ cup batter per cake. Cook cakes for about 3 minutes, flip them over, and cook 1–2 minutes more, until golden brown. Serve.

Per Serving:

calories: 160 | fat: 6g | protein: 5g | carbs: 25g | sugars: 5g | fiber: 3g | sodium: 71mg

Potato-Bacon Gratin

Prep time: 20 minutes | Cook time: 40 minutes | Serves 8

1 tablespoon olive oil
6 ounces bag fresh spinach
1 clove garlic, minced
4 large potatoes, peeled or
unpeeled, divided
6 ounces Canadian bacon slices,

divided
5 ounces reduced-fat grated
Swiss cheddar, divided
1 cup lower-sodium, lower-fat
chicken broth

1. Set the Instant Pot to Sauté and pour in the olive oil. Cook the spinach and garlic in olive oil just until spinach is wilted (5 minutes or less). Turn off the instant pot. 2. Cut potatoes into thin slices about ¼" thick. 3. In a springform pan that will fit into the inner pot of your Instant Pot, spray it with nonstick spray then layer ⅓ the potatoes, half the bacon, ⅓ the cheese, and half the wilted spinach. 4. Repeat layers ending with potatoes. Reserve ⅓ cheese for later. 5. Pour chicken broth over all. 6. Wipe the bottom of your Instant Pot to soak up any remaining oil, then add in 2 cups of water and the steaming rack. Place the springform pan on top. 7. Close the lid and secure to the locking position. Be sure the vent is turned to sealing. Set for 35 minutes on Manual at high pressure. 8. Perform a quick release. 9. Top with the remaining cheese, then allow to stand 10 minutes before removing from the Instant Pot, cutting and serving.

Per Serving:

calories: 220 | fat: 7g | protein: 14g | carbs: 28g | sugars: 2g | fiber: 3g | sodium: 415mg

Banana Protein Pancakes

Prep time: 10 minutes | Cook time: 10 minutes | Serves 4

Cooking oil spray, as needed
(optional)
2 medium bananas
1 large avocado, mashed
4 large eggs
½ cup (120 ml) egg whites
2 teaspoons (10 ml) pure vanilla
extract

2 teaspoons (8 g) baking powder
½ cup (50 g) whole-wheat flour
½ cup (56 g) coconut flour
1 teaspoon ground cinnamon
All-natural peanut butter, as
needed (see Tip)
Thawed frozen fruit, as needed

1. Heat a large nonstick skillet over medium heat until it is very hot. Spray the skillet lightly with the cooking oil spray (if using). 2. In a large bowl, mash the bananas. Whisk in the avocado, eggs, egg whites, and vanilla. Add the baking powder, whole-wheat flour, coconut flour, and cinnamon. Mix the batter until the ingredients are well combined. 3. Using a ¼-cup (60-ml) measuring cup, scoop the batter onto the skillet. Gently spread out the batter to create a circle if needed. Cook the pancakes for 3 minutes, flip them, and cook them for 2 to 3 minutes on the opposite side. The pancakes will be golden brown and ready to enjoy! 4. Drizzle the pancakes with the peanut butter and place the fruit on top just prior to serving.

Per Serving:

calorie: 357 | fat: 17g | protein: 15g | carbs: 39g | sugars: 9g | fiber: 12g | sodium: 158mg

Corn, Egg and Potato Bake

Prep time: 20 minutes | Cook time: 1 hour | Serves 8

Monterey Jack cheese (6 ounces)	cottage cheese
10 eggs or 2½ cups fat-free egg product	½ teaspoon dried oregano leaves
½ cup fat-free small-curd	¼ teaspoon garlic powder
	4 medium green onions, chopped (¼ cup)

1. Heat oven to 350°F. Spray 11x7-inch (2-quart) glass baking dish with cooking spray. In baking dish, layer potatoes, corn, bell peppers and 1 cup of the shredded cheese. 2. In medium bowl, beat eggs, cottage cheese, oregano and garlic powder with whisk until well blended. Slowly pour over potato mixture. Sprinkle with onions and remaining ½ cup shredded cheese. 3. Cover and bake 30 minutes. Uncover and bake about 30 minutes longer or until knife inserted in center comes out clean. Let stand 5 to 10 minutes before cutting.

Per Serving:

calories: 240 | fat: 11g | protein: 16g | carbs: 18g | sugars: 2g | fiber: 2g | sodium: 440mg

Coddled Huevos Rancheros

Prep time: 5 minutes | Cook time: 10 minutes | Serves 2

2 teaspoons unsalted butter	½ cup chunky tomato salsa (such as Pace brand)
4 large eggs	
1 cup drained cooked black beans, or two-thirds 15 ounces can black beans, rinsed and drained	2 cups shredded romaine lettuce
	1 tablespoon chopped fresh cilantro
Two 7-inch corn or whole-wheat tortillas, warmed	2 tablespoons grated Cotija cheese

1. Pour 1 cup water into the Instant Pot and place a long-handled silicone steam rack into the pot. (If you don't have the long-handled rack, use the wire metal steam rack and a homemade sling) 2. Coat each of four 4 ounces ramekins with ½ teaspoon butter. Crack an egg into each ramekin. Place the ramekins on the steam rack in the pot. 3. Secure the lid and set the Pressure Release to Sealing. Select the Steam setting and set the cooking time for 3 minutes at low pressure. (The pot will take about 5 minutes to come up to pressure before the cooking program begins.) 4. While the eggs are cooking, in a small saucepan over low heat, warm the beans for about 5 minutes, stirring occasionally. Cover the saucepan and remove from the heat. (Alternatively, warm the beans in a covered bowl in a microwave for 1 minute. Leave the beans covered until ready to serve.) 5. When the cooking program ends, let the pressure release naturally for 5 minutes, then move the Pressure Release to Venting to release any remaining steam. Open the pot and, wearing heat-resistant mitts, grasp the handles of the steam rack and carefully lift it out of the pot. 6. Place a warmed tortilla on each plate and spoon ½ cup of the beans onto each tortilla. Run a knife around the inside edge of each ramekin to loosen the egg and unmold two eggs onto the beans on each tortilla. Spoon the salsa over the eggs and top with the lettuce, cilantro, and cheese. Serve right away.

Per Serving:

calorie: 112 | fat: 8g | protein: 8g | carbs: 3g | sugars: 0g | fiber: 0g | sodium: 297mg

Tomato and Chive Waffles

Prep time: 15 minutes | Cook time: 40 minutes | Serves 8

2 cups low-fat buttermilk	½ cup almond flour
½ cup crushed tomato	½ cup coconut flour
1 medium egg	2 teaspoons baking powder
2 medium egg whites	½ teaspoon baking soda
1 cup gluten-free all-purpose flour	½ teaspoon dried chives
	Nonstick cooking spray

1. Heat a waffle iron. 2. In a medium bowl, whisk the buttermilk, tomato, egg, and egg whites together. 3. In another bowl, whisk the all-purpose flour, almond flour, coconut flour, baking powder, baking soda, and chives together. 4. Add the wet ingredients to the dry ingredients. 5. Lightly spray the waffle iron with cooking spray. 6. Gently pour ¼ to ½ cup portions of batter into the waffle iron. Cook time for waffles will vary depending on the kind of waffle iron you use, but it is usually 5 minutes per waffle. (Note: Once the waffle iron is hot, the cooking process is a bit faster.) Repeat until no batter remains. 7. Enjoy the waffles warm.

Per Serving:

calories: 128 | fat: 5g | protein: 7g | carbs: 18g | sugars: 4g | fiber: 1g | sodium: 167mg

Gluten-Free Carrot and Oat Pancakes

Prep time: 10 minutes | Cook time: 20 minutes | Serves 4

1 cup rolled oats	1 teaspoon baking powder
1 cup shredded carrots	½ teaspoon ground cinnamon
1 cup low-fat cottage cheese	2 tablespoons ground flaxseed
2 eggs	¼ cup plain nonfat Greek yogurt
½ cup unsweetened plain almond milk	1 tablespoon pure maple syrup
	2 teaspoons canola oil, divided

1. In a blender jar, process the oats until they resemble flour. Add the carrots, cottage cheese, eggs, almond milk, baking powder, cinnamon, and flaxseed to the jar. Process until smooth. 2. In a small bowl, combine the yogurt and maple syrup and stir well. Set aside. 3. In a large skillet, heat 1 teaspoon of oil over medium heat. Using a measuring cup, add ¼ cup of batter per pancake to the skillet. Cook for 1 to 2 minutes until bubbles form on the surface, and flip the pancakes. Cook for another minute until the pancakes are browned and cooked through. Repeat with the remaining 1 teaspoon of oil and remaining batter. 4. Serve warm topped with the maple yogurt.

Per Serving:

calories: 226 | fat: 8g | protein: 15g | carbs: 24g | sugars: 7g | fiber: 4g | sodium: 403mg

Cinnamon Overnight Oats

Prep timePrep Time: 5 Minutes | Cook Time: 0 Minutes | Serves 1

⅓ cup unsweetened almond milk

⅓ cup rolled oats (use gluten-free if necessary)

¼ apple, cored and finely chopped

2 tablespoons chopped walnuts

½ teaspoon cinnamon

Pinch sea salt

1. In a single-serving container or mason jar, combine all of the ingredients and mix well. 2. Cover and refrigerate overnight.

Per Serving:

calories: 358 | fat: 14g | protein: 13g | carbs: 47g | sugars: 10g | fiber: 9g | sodium: 213mg

Egg Bites with Sausage and Peppers

Prep time: 5 minutes | Cook time: 15 minutes | Serves 7

4 large eggs

¼ cup vegan cream cheese (such as Tofutti brand) or cream cheese

¼ teaspoon fine sea salt

¼ teaspoon freshly ground black pepper

3 ounces lean turkey sausage, cooked and crumbled, or 1 vegetarian sausage (such as

Beyond Meat brand), cooked and diced

½ red bell pepper, seeded and chopped

2 green onions, white and green parts, minced, plus more for garnish (optional)

¼ cup vegan cheese shreds or shredded sharp Cheddar cheese

1. In a blender, combine the eggs, cream cheese, salt, and pepper. Blend on medium speed for about 20 seconds, just until combined. Add the sausage, bell pepper, and green onions and pulse for 1 second once or twice. You want to mix in the solid ingredients without grinding them up very much. 2. Pour 1 cup water into the Instant Pot. Generously grease a 7 cups egg-bite mold or seven 2 ounces silicone baking cups with butter or coconut oil, making sure to coat each cup well. Place the prepared mold or cups on a long-handled silicone steam rack. (If you don't have the long-handled rack, use the wire metal steam rack and a homemade sling) 3. Pour ¼ cup of the egg mixture into each prepared mold or cup. Holding the handles of the steam rack, carefully lower the egg bites into the pot. 4. Secure the lid and set the Pressure Release to Sealing. Select the Steam setting and set the cooking time for 8 minutes at low pressure. (The pot will take about 5 minutes to come up to pressure before the cooking program begins.) 5. When the cooking program ends, let the pressure release naturally for 5 minutes, then move the Pressure Release to Venting to release any remaining steam. Open the pot. The egg muffins will have puffed up quite a bit during cooking, but they will deflate and settle as they cool. Wearing heat-resistant mitts, grasp the handles of the steam rack and carefully lift the egg bites out of the pot. Sprinkle the egg bites with the cheese, then let them cool for about 5 minutes, until the cheese has fully melted and you are able to handle the mold or cups comfortably. 6. Pull the sides of the egg mold or cups away from the egg bites, running a butter knife around the edge of each bite to loosen if necessary. Transfer the egg bites to plates, garnish with more green onions (if desired), and serve warm. To store, let cool to room temperature, transfer to an airtight container, and refrigerate for up to 3 days; reheat gently in the microwave for about 1 minute before serving.

Per Serving:

calories: 112 | fat: 8g | protein: 8g | carbs: 3g | sugars: 0g | fiber: 0g | sodium: 297mg

Baked Avocado and Egg

Prep time: 10 minutes | Cook time: 10 minutes | Serves 2

1 large avocado, halved and pitted

2 large eggs

2 tomato slices, divided

½ cup nonfat cottage cheese, divided

Fresh cilantro, for garnish

1. Preheat the oven to 425°F. 2. Slice a thin piece from the bottom of each avocado half so they sit flat. 3. Remove a small amount from each avocado half to make a bigger hole to hold the egg. 4. On a small foil-lined baking sheet, place the halves hollow-side up. 5. Break 1 egg into each half. 6. Top each with 1 slice of tomato and ¼ cup of cottage cheese. 7. Place the sheet in the preheated oven. Bake for 8 to 10 minutes for softboiled consistency, or longer for a firmer egg. 8. Garnish with fresh cilantro and serve.

Per Serving:

calories: 262 | fat: 20g | protein: 12g | carbs: 12g | sugars: 2g | fiber: 7g | sodium: 214mg

Baked Eggs

Prep time: 15 minutes | Cook time: 20 minutes | Serves 8

1 cup water

2 tablespoons no-trans-fat tub margarine, melted

1 cup reduced-fat buttermilk baking mix

1½ cups fat-free cottage cheese

2 teaspoons chopped onion

1 teaspoon dried parsley

½ cup grated reduced-fat cheddar cheese

1 egg, slightly beaten

1¼ cups egg substitute

1 cup fat-free milk

1. Place the steaming rack into the bottom of the inner pot and pour in 1 cup of water. 2. Grease a round springform pan that will fit into the inner pot of the Instant Pot. 3. Pour melted margarine into springform pan. 4. Mix together buttermilk baking mix, cottage cheese, onion, parsley, cheese, egg, egg substitute, and milk in large mixing bowl. 5. Pour mixture over melted margarine. Stir slightly to distribute margarine. 6. Place the springform pan onto the steaming rack, close the lid, and secure to the locking position. Be sure the vent is turned to sealing. Set for 20 minutes on Manual at high pressure. 7. Let the pressure release naturally. 8. Carefully remove the springform pan with the handles of the steaming rack and allow to stand 10 minutes before cutting and serving.

Per Serving:

calories: 155 | fat: 5g | protein: 12g | carbs: 15g | sugars: 4g | fiber: 0g | sodium: 460mg

Sausage, Sweet Potato, and Kale Hash

Prep time: 10 minutes | Cook time: 15 minutes | Serves 4

Avocado oil cooking spray
1⅓ cups peeled and diced sweet potatoes
8 cups roughly chopped kale, stemmed and loosely packed
(about 2 bunches)
4 links chicken or turkey breakfast sausage
4 large eggs
4 lemon wedges

1. Heat a large skillet over medium heat. When hot, coat the cooking surface with cooking spray. Cook the sweet potatoes for 4 minutes, stirring once halfway through. 2. Reduce the heat to medium-low and move the potatoes to one side of the skillet. Arrange the kale and sausage in a single layer. Cover and cook for 3 minutes. 3. Stir the vegetables and sausage together, then push them to one side of the skillet to create space for the eggs. Add the eggs and cook them to your liking. Cover the skillet and cook for 3 minutes. 4. Divide the sausage and vegetables into four equal portions and top with an egg and a squeeze of lemon.

Per Serving:

calories: 160 | fat: 8g | protein: 11g | carbs: 13g | sugars: 3g | fiber: 3g | sodium: 197mg

Cherry, Chocolate, and Almond Shake

Prep time: 5 minutes | Cook time: 0 minutes | Serves 2

10 ounces frozen cherries
2 tablespoons cocoa powder
2 tablespoons almond butter
2 tablespoons hemp seeds
8 ounces unsweetened almond milk

1. Combine the cherries, cocoa, almond butter, hemp seeds, and almond milk in a blender and blend on high speed until smooth. Use a spatula to scrape down the sides as needed. Serve immediately.

Per Serving:

calories: 243 | fat: 16g | protein: 8g | carbs: 24g | sugars: 13g | fiber: 7g | sodium: 85mg

Vanilla Steel-Cut Oatmeal

Prep time: 5 minutes | Cook time: 40 minutes | Serves 4

4 cups water
Pinch sea salt
1 cup steel-cut oats
¾ cup skim milk
2 teaspoons pure vanilla extract

1. In a large pot over high heat, bring the water and salt to a boil. 2. Reduce the heat to low and stir in the oats. 3. Cook the oats for about 30 minutes to soften, stirring occasionally. 4. Stir in the milk and vanilla and cook until your desired consistency is reached, about 10 more minutes. 5. Remove the cereal from the heat. Serve topped with sunflower seeds, chopped peaches, fresh berries, sliced almonds, or flaxseeds.

Per Serving:

calories: 79 | fat: 2g | protein: 6g | carbs: 18g | sugars: 3g | fiber: 4g | sodium: 25mg

Oat and Walnut Granola

Prep time: 10 minutes | Cook time: 30 minutes | Serves 16

4 cups rolled oats
1 cup walnut pieces
½ cup pepitas
¼ teaspoon salt
1 teaspoon ground cinnamon
1 teaspoon ground ginger
½ cup coconut oil, melted
½ cup unsweetened applesauce
1 teaspoon vanilla extract
½ cup dried cherries

1. Preheat the oven to 350°F. Line a baking sheet with parchment paper. 2. In a large bowl, toss the oats, walnuts, pepitas, salt, cinnamon, and ginger. 3. In a large measuring cup, combine the coconut oil, applesauce, and vanilla. Pour over the dry mixture and mix well. 4. Transfer the mixture to the prepared baking sheet. Cook for 30 minutes, stirring about halfway through. Remove from the oven and let the granola sit undisturbed until completely cool. Break the granola into pieces, and stir in the dried cherries. 5. Transfer to an airtight container, and store at room temperature for up to 2 weeks.

Per Serving:

calories: 224| fat: 15g | protein: 5g | carbs: 20g | sugars: 5g | fiber: 3g | sodium: 30mg

Cheesy Quinoa-Crusted Spinach Frittata

Prep time: 10 minutes | Cook time: 50 minutes | Serves 4

1 cup (170 g) uncooked quinoa
Cooking oil spray, as needed
½ cup (120 ml) egg whites
¾ cup (90 g) shredded Cheddar cheese
½ tablespoon (8 ml) cooking oil of choice
½ medium yellow onion, diced
5 ounces (142 g) baby spinach
6 large eggs
⅔ cup (160 ml) 2% milk
½ teaspoon mustard powder
½ teaspoon sea salt
¼ teaspoon black pepper

1. In a medium pot, cook the quinoa according to the package instructions. Set the quinoa aside to cool in the pot. 2. Preheat the oven to 375°F (191°C). Spray a 9-inch (23-cm) pie dish with the cooking oil spray. 3. Once the quinoa has cooled, add the egg whites and Cheddar cheese, stirring to combine the ingredients. Carefully press the quinoa mixture into the prepared pie dish. Bake the crust for 15 minutes. Remove the crust from the oven and allow it to cool. 4. While the crust is baking, heat the oil in a medium skillet over medium heat. Add the onion and spinach and sauté them for 10 to 15 minutes, until the onion is translucent and the spinach is wilted. Set the vegetables aside to cool. 5. Meanwhile, combine the eggs, milk, mustard powder, salt, and black pepper in a medium bowl and whisk to combine the ingredients. 6. Add the sautéed vegetables to the crust and spread them into an even layer. Pour the egg mixture over the vegetables. 7. Return the frittata to the oven and bake it for 35 to 40 minutes, or until the eggs have set in the middle.

Per Serving:

calorie: 414 | fat: 19g | protein: 26g | carbs: 33g | sugars: 4g | fiber: 4g | sodium: 624mg

Brussels Sprout Hash and Eggs

Prep time: 15 minutes | Cook time: 15 minutes | Serves 4

3 teaspoons extra-virgin olive oil, divided
1 pound Brussels sprouts, sliced
2 garlic cloves, thinly sliced
¼ teaspoon salt
Juice of 1 lemon
4 eggs

1. In a large skillet, heat 1½ teaspoons of oil over medium heat. Add the Brussels sprouts and toss. Cook, stirring regularly, for 6 to 8 minutes until browned and softened. Add the garlic and continue to cook until fragrant, about 1 minute. Season with the salt and lemon juice. Transfer to a serving dish. 2. In the same pan, heat the remaining 1½ teaspoons of oil over medium-high heat. Crack the eggs into the pan. Fry for 2 to 4 minutes, flip, and continue cooking to desired doneness. Serve over the bed of hash.

Per Serving:
calories: 158 | fat: 9g | protein: 10g | carbs: 12g | sugars: 4g | fiber: 4g | sodium: 234mg

BLT Breakfast Wrap

Prep time: 5 minutes | Cook time: 10 minutes | Serves 4

8 ounces (227 g) reduced-sodium bacon
8 tablespoons mayonnaise
8 large romaine lettuce leaves
4 Roma tomatoes, sliced
Salt and freshly ground black pepper, to taste

1. Arrange the bacon in a single layer in the air fryer basket. (It's OK if the bacon sits a bit on the sides.) Set the air fryer to 350°F (177°C) and air fry for 10 minutes. Check for crispiness and air fry for 2 to 3 minutes longer if needed. Cook in batches, if necessary, and drain the grease in between batches. 2. Spread 1 tablespoon of mayonnaise on each of the lettuce leaves and top with the tomatoes and cooked bacon. Season to taste with salt and freshly ground black pepper. Roll the lettuce leaves as you would a burrito, securing with a toothpick if desired.

Per Serving:
calorie: 465 | fat: 41g | protein: 14g | carbs: 8g | sugars: 4g | fiber: 3g | sodium: 861mg

Blueberry Oat Mini Muffins

Prep time: 12 minutes | Cook time: 10 minutes | Serves 7

½ cup rolled oats
¼ cup whole wheat pastry flour or white whole wheat flour
½ tablespoon baking powder
½ teaspoon ground cardamom or ground cinnamon
⅛ teaspoon kosher salt
2 large eggs
½ cup plain Greek yogurt
2 tablespoons pure maple syrup
2 teaspoons extra-virgin olive oil
½ teaspoon vanilla extract
½ cup frozen blueberries (preferably small wild blueberries)

1. In a large bowl, stir together the oats, flour, baking powder, cardamom, and salt. 2. In a medium bowl, whisk together the eggs, yogurt, maple syrup, oil, and vanilla. 3. Add the egg mixture to oat mixture and stir just until combined. Gently fold in the blueberries. 4. Scoop the batter into each cup of the egg bite mold. 5. Pour 1 cup of water into the electric pressure cooker. Place the egg bite mold on the wire rack and carefully lower it into the pot. 6. Close and lock the lid of the pressure cooker. Set the valve to sealing. 7. Cook on high pressure for 10 minutes. 8. When the cooking is complete, allow the pressure to release naturally for 10 minutes, then quick release any remaining pressure. Hit Cancel. 9. Lift the wire rack out of the pot and place on a cooling rack for 5 minutes. Invert the mold onto the cooling rack to release the muffins. 10. Serve the muffins warm or refrigerate or freeze.

Per Serving:
calories: 117 | fat: 4g | protein: 5g | carbs: 15g | sugars: 4g | fiber: 2g | sodium: 89mg

Simple Grain-Free Biscuits

Prep time: 10 minutes | Cook time: 15 minutes | Serves 4

2 tablespoons unsalted butter
Pinch salt
¼ cup plain low-fat Greek
yogurt
1½ cups finely ground almond flour

1. Preheat the oven to 375°F. 2. In a medium bowl, microwave the butter just enough to soften, 15 to 20 seconds. 3. Add the salt and yogurt to the butter and mix well. 4. Add the almond flour and mix. The dough will be crumbly at first, so continue to stir and mash it with a fork until there are no lumps and the mixture comes together. 5. Drop ¼ cup of dough on a baking sheet for each biscuit. Using your clean hand, flatten each biscuit until it is 1 inch thick. 6. Bake for 13 to 15 minutes.

Per Serving:
calories: 182 | fat: 15g | protein: 6g | carbs: 6g | sugars: 2g | fiber: 3g | sodium: 13mg
m: 415mg

Breakfast Banana Barley

Prep time: 5 minutes | Cook time: 10 minutes | Serves 2

3 cups water
Pinch kosher salt
1½ cups quick barley, rinsed and drained
3 tablespoons natural peanut butter
1 banana, sliced

1. In a small saucepan, bring the water and salt to a boil over high heat. 2. Stir in the barley, cover, reduce the heat, and simmer for 10 minutes or until tender. 3. Remove the saucepan from the heat and add the peanut butter, stirring to blend. Adjust the salt as desired, and divide the mixture between two bowls. 4. Top with the sliced bananas and serve. 5. Store any leftovers in an airtight container in the refrigerator for up to 5 days.

Per Serving:
calories: 721 | fat: 11g | protein: 23g | carbs: 139g | sugars: 11g | fiber: 26g | sodium: 160mg

Biscuits

Prep time: 15 minutes | Cook time: 15 minutes | Serves 12

1½ cups gluten-free all-purpose flour

½ cup split pea flour or chickpea flour

½ cup cornmeal

1 teaspoon baking powder

½ teaspoon salt

1 cup low-fat buttermilk

1 medium egg

2 medium egg whites

4 tablespoons (½ stick) unsalted non-hydrogenated plant-based butter, cold, cut into ¼-inch chunks

1. Preheat the oven to 400°F. Line a rimmed baking sheet with parchment paper. 2. In a medium bowl, whisk the gluten-free flour, split pea flour, cornmeal, baking powder, and salt together. 3. In a large bowl, beat the buttermilk, egg, and egg whites together. 4. Gently fold the dry ingredients into the wet ingredients until just combined, taking care not to overmix. 5. Add the butter to the mixture, gently working together with clean hands. Knead the dough only once or twice. 6. Transfer the dough to a clean workspace, and pat it to a 1-inch thickness. 7. Using a biscuit cutter, cut 12 biscuits, and place them, evenly spaced, onto the prepared baking sheet. 8. Transfer the baking sheet to the oven, and bake for 10 to 15 minutes, or until golden brown.

Per Serving:

calories: 139 | fat: 4g | protein: 5g | carbs: 21g | sugars: 2g | fiber: 1g | sodium: 138mg

Veggie-Stuffed Omelet

Prep time: 15 minutes | Cook time: 10 minutes | Serves 1

1 teaspoon olive or canola oil

2 tablespoons chopped red bell pepper

1 tablespoon chopped onion

¼ cup sliced fresh mushrooms

1 cup loosely packed fresh baby spinach leaves, rinsed

½ cup fat-free egg product or 2 eggs, beaten

1 tablespoon water

Pinch salt

Pinch pepper

1 tablespoon shredded reduced-fat Cheddar cheese

1. In 8-inch nonstick skillet, heat oil over medium-high heat. Add bell pepper, onion and mushrooms to oil. Cook 2 minutes, stirring frequently, until onion is tender. Stir in spinach; continue cooking and stirring just until spinach wilts. Transfer vegetables from pan to small bowl. 2. In medium bowl, beat egg product, water, salt and pepper with fork or whisk until well mixed. Reheat same skillet over medium-high heat. Quickly pour egg mixture into pan. While sliding pan back and forth rapidly over heat, quickly stir with spatula to spread eggs continuously over bottom of pan as they thicken. Let stand over heat a few seconds to lightly brown bottom of omelet. Do not overcook; omelet will continue to cook after folding. 3. Place cooked vegetable mixture over half of omelet; top with cheese. With spatula, fold other half of omelet over vegetables. Gently slide out of pan onto plate. Serve immediately.

Per Serving:

calorie: 140 | fat: 5g | protein: 16g | carbs: 6g | sugars: 3g | fiber: 2g | sodium: 470mg

Rice Breakfast Bake

Prep time: 10 minutes | Cook time: 20 minutes | Serves 4

1¼ cups vanilla low-fat nondairy milk

1 tablespoon ground chia seeds

2½ cups cooked short-grain brown rice

2 cups sliced ripe (but not overripe) banana (2–2½ medium bananas)

1 cup chopped apple

2 to 3 tablespoons raisins

(optional)

1 teaspoon cinnamon

½ teaspoon pure vanilla extract

¼ teaspoon freshly grated nutmeg (optional)

Rounded ⅛ teaspoon sea salt

2 tablespoons almond meal (or 1 tablespoon tigernut flour, for nut-free option)

2 tablespoons coconut sugar

1. Preheat the oven to 400°F. 2. In a blender or food processor, combine the milk, ground chia, and 1 cup of the rice. Puree until fairly smooth. In a large bowl, combine the blended mixture, bananas, apple, raisins (if using), cinnamon, vanilla, nutmeg (if using), salt, and the remaining 1½ cups rice. Stir to fully combine. Transfer the mixture to a baking dish (8" x 8" or similar size). In a small bowl, combine the almond meal and sugar, and sprinkle it over the rice mixture. Cover with foil and bake for 15 minutes, then remove the foil and bake for another 5 minutes. Remove, let cool for 5 to 10 minutes, then serve.

Per Serving:

calorie: 334 | fat: 5g | protein: 7g | carbs: 69g | sugars: 22g | fiber: 7g | sodium: 145mg

Bran Apple Muffins

Prep time: 10 minutes | Cook time: 20 minutes | Makes 18 muffins

2 cups whole-wheat flour

1 cup wheat bran

⅓ cup granulated sweetener

1 tablespoon baking powder

2 teaspoons ground cinnamon

½ teaspoon ground ginger

¼ teaspoon ground nutmeg

Pinch sea salt

2 eggs

1½ cups skim milk, at room temperature

½ cup melted coconut oil

2 teaspoons pure vanilla extract

2 apples, peeled, cored, and diced

1. Preheat the oven to 350°F. 2. Line 18 muffin cups with paper liners and set the tray aside. 3. In a large bowl, stir together the flour, bran, sweetener, baking powder, cinnamon, ginger, nutmeg, and salt. 4. In a small bowl, whisk the eggs, milk, coconut oil, and vanilla until blended. 5. Add the wet ingredients to the dry ingredients, stirring until just blended. 6. Stir in the apples and spoon equal amounts of batter into each muffin cup. 7. Bake the muffins until a toothpick inserted in the center of a muffin comes out clean, about 20 minutes. 8. Cool the muffins completely and serve. 9. Store leftover muffins in a sealed container in the refrigerator for up to 3 days or in the freezer for up to 1 month.

Per Serving:

calories: 145 | fat: 7g | protein: 4g | carbs: 19g | sugars: 6g | fiber: 4g | sodium: 17mg

Lemon-Pineapple Muffins

Prep time: 5 minutes | Cook time: 26 to 28 minutes | Makes 12 muffins

2 cups oat flour

1 cup spelt flour

⅓ cup coconut sugar

2½ teaspoons baking powder

½ teaspoon baking soda

½ teaspoon cinnamon

¼ teaspoon nutmeg

Generous ¼ teaspoon sea salt

1 to 1½ teaspoons lemon zest

¾ cup plain nondairy yogurt

¼ cup coconut nectar or maple syrup

1½ tablespoons freshly squeezed lemon juice

1 cup plain low-fat nondairy milk

1 cup diced fresh, frozen, or canned pineapple

1. Preheat the oven to 350°F. Line a muffin pan with 12 parchment cupcake liners. In a large bowl, combine the oat flour, spelt flour, and sugar. Sift in the baking powder and baking soda, then add the cinnamon, nutmeg, salt, and lemon zest. Stir to combine. In a small bowl, combine the yogurt with the nectar or syrup, lemon juice, and milk. Add the wet mixture to the dry, stirring until just combined, and then gently fold in the pineapple. Pour the mixture into the muffin cups. Bake for 26 to 28 minutes, or until a toothpick inserted in the center of a muffin comes out clean. Remove from the oven, cool for a couple of minutes in the pan, and then transfer the muffins to a cooling rack.

Per Serving:

1 muffin: calorie: 175 | fat: 2g | protein: 5g | carbs: 36g | sugars: 13g | fiber: 4g | sodium: 240mg

Quinoa Breakfast Bake with Pistachios and Plums

Prep time: 10 minutes | Cook time: 1 hour | Serves 2

Extra-virgin olive oil cooking spray

⅓ cup dry quinoa, thoroughly rinsed

1 teaspoon vanilla extract

1 teaspoon cinnamon

½ teaspoon nutmeg

Stevia, for sweetening

2 large egg whites

1 cup nonfat milk

2 plums, chopped, divided

4 tablespoons chopped unsalted pistachios, divided

1. Preheat the oven to 350°F. 2. Spray two mini loaf pans with cooking spray. Set aside. 3. In a medium bowl, stir together the quinoa, vanilla, cinnamon, nutmeg, and stevia until the quinoa is coated with the spices. 4. Pour half of the quinoa mixture into each loaf pan. 5. In the same medium bowl, beat the egg whites and thoroughly whisk in the milk. 6. Evenly scatter half of the plums and 2 tablespoons of pistachios in each pan. 7. Pour half of the egg mixture over each loaf. Stir lightly to partially submerge the plums. 8. Place the pans in the preheated oven. Bake for 1 hour, or until the loaves are set, with only a small amount of liquid remaining. 9. Remove from the pans and enjoy hot!

Per Serving:

calories: 295 | fat: 9g | protein: 16g | carbs: 38g | sugars: 14g | fiber: 5g | sodium: 122mg

Shredded Potato Omelet

Prep time: 15 minutes | Cook time: 20 minutes | Serves 6

3 slices bacon, cooked and crumbled

2 cups shredded cooked potatoes

¼ cup minced onion

¼ cup minced green bell pepper

1 cup egg substitute

¼ cup fat-free milk

¼ teaspoon salt

⅛ teaspoon black pepper

1 cup 75%-less-fat shredded cheddar cheese

1 cup water

1. With nonstick cooking spray, spray the inside of a round baking dish that will fit in your Instant Pot inner pot. 2. Sprinkle the bacon, potatoes, onion, and bell pepper around the bottom of the baking dish. 3. Mix together the egg substitute, milk, salt, and pepper in mixing bowl. Pour over potato mixture. 4. Top with cheese. 5. Add water, place the steaming rack into the bottom of the inner pot and then place the round baking dish on top. 6. Close the lid and secure to the locking position. Be sure the vent is turned to sealing. Set for 20 minutes on Manual at high pressure. 7. Let the pressure release naturally. 8. Carefully remove the baking dish with the handles of the steaming rack and allow to stand 10 minutes before cutting and serving.

Per Serving:

calories: 130 | fat: 3g | protein: 12g | carbs: 13g | sugars: 2g | fiber: 2g | sodiu

Smoked Salmon and Asparagus Quiche Cups

Prep time: 15 minutes | Cook time: 15 minutes | Serves 2

Nonstick cooking spray

4 asparagus spears, cut into ½-inch pieces

2 tablespoons finely chopped onion

3 ounces (85 g) smoked salmon

(skinless and boneless), chopped

3 large eggs

2 tablespoons 2% milk

¼ teaspoon dried dill

Pinch ground white pepper

1. Pour 1½ cups of water into the electric pressure cooker and insert a wire rack or trivet. 2. Lightly spray the bottom and sides of the ramekins with nonstick cooking spray. Divide the asparagus, onion, and salmon between the ramekins. 3. In a measuring cup with a spout, whisk together the eggs, milk, dill, and white pepper. Pour half of the egg mixture into each ramekin. Loosely cover the ramekins with aluminum foil. 4. Carefully place the ramekins inside the pot on the rack. 5. Close and lock the lid of the pressure cooker. Set the valve to sealing. 6. Cook on high pressure for 15 minutes. 7. When the cooking is complete, hit Cancel and quick release the pressure. 8. Once the pin drops, unlock and remove the lid. 9. Carefully remove the ramekins from the pot. Cool, covered, for 5 minutes. 10. Run a small silicone spatula or a knife around the edge of each ramekin. Invert each quiche onto a small plate and serve.

Per Serving:

calories: 180 | fat: 9g | protein: 20g | carbs: 3g | sugars: 1g | fiber: 1g | sodium: 646mg

Pumpkin–Peanut Butter Single-Serve Muffins

Prep time: 10 minutes | Cook time: 25 minutes | Serves 2

2 tablespoons powdered peanut butter

2 tablespoons coconut flour

2 tablespoons finely ground flaxseed

1 teaspoon pumpkin pie spice

½ teaspoon baking powder

1 tablespoon dried cranberries

½ cup water

1 cup canned pumpkin

2 large eggs

½ teaspoon vanilla extract

Extra-virgin olive oil cooking spray

1. Preheat the oven to 350°F. 2. In a medium bowl, stir together the powdered peanut butter, coconut flour, flaxseed, pumpkin pie spice, baking powder, dried cranberries, and water. 3. In a separate medium bowl, whisk together the pumpkin and eggs until smooth. 4. Add the pumpkin mixture to the dry ingredients. Stir to combine. 5. Add the vanilla. Mix together well. 6. Spray 2 (8 ounces) ramekins with cooking spray. 7. Spoon half of the batter into each ramekin. 8. Place the ramekins on a baking and carefully transfer the sheet to the preheated oven. Bake for 25 minutes, or until a toothpick in the center comes out clean. Enjoy immediately!

Per Serving:

calories: 286 | fat: 16g | protein: 15g | carbs: 24g | sugars: 9g | fiber: 7g | sodium: 189mg

Cinnamon Bun Oatmeal

Prep time: 5 minutes | Cook time: 15 minutes | Serves 3

1½ cups rolled oats

⅓ cup chopped dates

1 teaspoon cinnamon

Pinch of sea salt (optional)

2 cups water

3 tablespoons raisins

¾ cup + 1 to 2 tablespoons low-fat nondairy milk

Sprinkle of cinnamon

3 teaspoons coconut sugar (optional)

1. In a pot over high heat, combine the oats, dates, cinnamon, salt, and water, and bring to a boil. Reduce the heat to low and let simmer for 7 to 8 minutes, until the water is absorbed and the oats are softening. Add the raisins and ¾ cup of the milk, and cook for another 6 to 7 minutes, or until the raisins have softened. Remove from the heat and let stand for a few minutes. The oatmeal will thicken more as it sits, so add the remaining 1 to 2 tablespoons of milk if needed to thin. Top each serving with the cinnamon and 1 teaspoon of the coconut sugar (if using).

Per Serving:

calorie: 251 | fat: 3 | protein: 7g | carbs: 51g | sugars: 18g | fiber: 7g | sodium: 34mg

Greek Yogurt Cinnamon Pancakes

Prep time: 5 minutes | Cook time: 20 minutes | Serves 4

1 cup 2 percent plain Greek yogurt

3 eggs

1½ teaspoons pure vanilla extract

1 cup rolled oats

1 tablespoon granulated sweetener

1 teaspoon baking powder

1 teaspoon ground cinnamon

Pinch ground cloves

Nonstick cooking spray

1. Place the yogurt, eggs, and vanilla in a blender and pulse to combine. 2. Add the oats, sweetener, baking powder, cinnamon, and cloves to the blender and blend until the batter is smooth. 3. Place a large nonstick skillet over medium heat and lightly coat it with cooking spray. 4. Spoon ¼ cup of batter per pancake, 4 at a time, into the skillet. Cook the pancakes until the bottoms are firm and golden, about 4 minutes. 5. Flip the pancakes over and cook the other side until they are cooked through, about 3 minutes. 6. Remove the pancakes to a plate and repeat with the remaining batter. 7. Serve with fresh fruit.

Per Serving:

calories: 34 | fat: 7g | protein: 14g | carbs: 34g | sugars: 7g | fiber: 5g | sodium: 92mg

Orange Muffins

Prep time: 15 minutes | Cook time: 15 minutes | Serves 9

2½ cups finely ground almond flour

¾ teaspoon ground cinnamon

½ teaspoon baking powder

½ teaspoon ground cardamom

¼ teaspoon salt

4 tablespoons avocado or

coconut oil

2 large eggs

Grated zest and juice of 1 medium orange

1 tablespoon raw honey or 100% pure maple syrup

¼ teaspoon vanilla extract

1. Preheat the oven to 375°F. 2. In a large bowl, whisk together the almond flour, cinnamon, baking powder, cardamom, and salt. Set aside. 3. In a medium bowl, whisk together the oil, eggs, zest, juice, honey, and vanilla. Add this mixture to the dry ingredients, and stir until well combined. 4. In a nonstick muffin tin, fill each muffin cup until nearly full. 5. Bake for 15 minutes, or until the top center is firm.

Per Serving:

calories: 208 | fat: 17g | protein: 6g | carbs: 8g | sugars: 4g | fiber: 3g | sodium: 81mg

Chapter 5

Beans and Grains

Hoppin' John

Prep time: 15 minutes | Cook time: 50 minutes | Serves 12

1 tablespoon canola oil	2 cups brown rice, rinsed
2 celery stalks, thinly sliced	5 cups store-bought low-sodium
1 small yellow onion, chopped	vegetable broth, divided
1 medium green bell pepper,	2 bay leaves
chopped	1 teaspoon smoked paprika
1 tablespoon tomato paste	1 teaspoon Creole seasoning
2 garlic cloves, minced	1¼ cups frozen black-eyed peas

1. In a Dutch oven, heat the canola oil over medium heat. 2. Add the celery, onion, bell pepper, tomato paste, and garlic and cook, stirring often, for 3 to 5 minutes, or until the vegetables are softened. 3. Add the rice, 4 cups of broth, bay leaves, paprika, and Creole seasoning. 4. Reduce the heat to low, cover, and cook for 30 minutes, or until the rice is tender. 5. Add the black-eyed peas and remaining 1 cup of broth. Mix well, cover, and cook for 12 minutes, or until the peas soften. Discard the bay leaves. 6. Enjoy.

Per Serving:

calorie: 155 | fat: 2g | protein: 4g | carbs: 30g | sugars: 1g | fiber: 2g | sodium: 24mg

Whole-Wheat Linguine with Kale Pesto

Prep time: 10 minutes | Cook time: 20 minutes | Serves 6

½ cup shredded kale	oil
½ cup fresh basil	8 ounces dry whole-wheat
½ cup sun-dried tomatoes	linguine
¼ cup chopped almonds	½ cup grated Parmesan cheese
2 tablespoons extra-virgin olive	

1. Put the bell peppers, chickpeas, jalapeño pepper, oil, water, lime juice, salt, garlic powder, cumin, and black pepper into a food processor or blender and blend until smooth. The sauce will have texture, but it shouldn't be chunky.

Per Serving:

calorie: 365 | fat: 19g | protein: 15g | carbs: 38g | sugars: 3g | fiber: 7g | sodium: 299mg

Edamame-Tabbouleh Salad

Prep time: 20 minutes | Cook time: 10 minutes | Serves 6

Salad	2 medium tomatoes, seeded,
1 package (5.8 ounces) roasted	chopped (1½ cups)
garlic and olive oil couscous	1 small cucumber, peeled,
mix	chopped (1 cup)
1¼ cups water	¼ cup chopped fresh parsley
1 teaspoon olive or canola oil	Dressing
1 bag (10 ounces) refrigerated	1 teaspoon grated lemon peel
fully cooked ready-to-eat	2 tablespoons lemon juice
shelled edamame (green	1 teaspoon olive or canola oil
soybeans)	

1. Make couscous mix as directed on package, using the water and oil. 2. In large bowl, mix couscous and remaining salad ingredients. In small bowl, mix dressing ingredients. Pour dressing over salad; mix well. Serve immediately, or cover and refrigerate until serving time.

Per Serving:

calorie: 200 | fat: 5g | protein: 10g | carbs: 28g | sugars: 3g | fiber: 4g | sodium: 270mg

Rice with Spinach and Feta

Prep time: 10 minutes | Cook time: 15 minutes | Serves 4

¾ cup uncooked brown rice	½ teaspoon dried oregano
1½ cups water	9 cups fresh spinach, stems
1 tablespoon extra-virgin olive	trimmed, washed, patted dry,
oil	and coarsely chopped
1 medium onion, diced	⅓ cup crumbled fat-free feta
1 cup sliced mushrooms	cheese
2 garlic cloves, minced	⅛ teaspoon freshly ground black
1 tablespoon lemon juice	pepper

1. In a medium saucepan over medium heat, combine the rice and water. Bring to a boil, cover, reduce heat, and simmer for 15 minutes. Transfer to a serving bowl. 2. In a skillet, heat the oil. Sauté the onion, mushrooms, and garlic for 5 to 7 minutes. Stir in the lemon juice and oregano. Add the spinach, cheese, and pepper, tossing until the spinach is slightly wilted. 3. Toss with rice and serve.

Per Serving:

calorie: 205 | fat: 5g | protein: 7g | carbs: 34g | sugars: 2g | fiber: 4g | sodium: 129mg

Sweet Potato Fennel Bake

Prep time: 15 minutes | Cook time: 45 minutes | Serves 4

1 teaspoon butter	to taste
1 fennel bulb, trimmed and	½ teaspoon ground cinnamon
thinly sliced	¼ teaspoon ground nutmeg
2 sweet potatoes, peeled and	1 cup low-sodium vegetable
thinly sliced	broth
Freshly ground black pepper,	

1. Preheat the oven to 375°F. 2. Lightly butter a 9-by-11-inch baking dish. 3. Arrange half the fennel in the bottom of the dish and top with half the sweet potatoes. 4. Season the potatoes with black pepper. Sprinkle half the cinnamon and nutmeg on the potatoes. 5. Repeat the layering to use up all the fennel, sweet potatoes, cinnamon, and nutmeg. 6. Pour in the vegetable broth and cover the dish with aluminum foil. 7. Bake until the vegetables are very tender, about 45 minutes. 8. Serve immediately.

Per Serving:

calorie: 118 | fat: 1g | protein: 2g | carbs: 28g | sugars: 7g | fiber: 5g | sodium: 127mg

Spicy Couscous and Chickpea Salad

Prep time: 20 minutes | Cook time: 10 minutes | Serves 4

alad
½ cup uncooked whole wheat couscous
1½ cups water
¼ teaspoon salt
1 can (15 ounces) chickpeas (garbanzo beans), drained, rinsed
1 can (14½ ounces) diced tomatoes with green chiles, undrained
½ cup frozen shelled edamame

(green soybeans) or lima beans, thawed
2 tablespoons chopped fresh cilantro
Green bell peppers, halved, if desired
Dressing
2 tablespoons olive oil
1 teaspoon ground coriander
½ teaspoon ground cumin
½ teaspoon ground cinnamon

1. Cook couscous in the water and salt as directed on package. 2. Meanwhile, in medium bowl, mix chickpeas, tomatoes, edamame and cilantro. In small bowl, mix dressing ingredients until well blended. 3. Add cooked couscous to salad; mix well. Pour dressing over salad; stir gently to mix. Spoon salad mixture into halved bell peppers. Serve immediately, or cover and refrigerate until serving time.

Per Serving:

calorie: 370 | fat: 11g | protein: 16g | carbs: 53g | sugars: 6g | fiber: 10g | sodium: 460mg

Farmers' Market Barley Risotto

Prep time: 30 minutes | Cook time: 15 minutes | Serves 4

1 tablespoon olive oil
1 medium onion, chopped (½ cup)
1 medium bell pepper, coarsely chopped (1 cup)
2 cups chopped fresh mushrooms (4 ounces)
1 cup frozen whole-kernel corn
1 cup uncooked medium pearled barley
¼ cup dry white wine or

chicken broth
2 cups reduced-sodium chicken broth
3 cups water
1½ cups grape tomatoes, cut in half (if large, cut into quarters)
⅔ cup shredded Parmesan cheese
3 tablespoons chopped fresh or
1 teaspoon dried basil leaves
½ teaspoon pepper

1. In 4-quart Dutch oven or saucepan, heat oil over medium heat. Cook onion, bell pepper, mushrooms and corn in oil about 5 minutes, stirring frequently, until onion is crisp-tender. Add barley, stirring about 1 minute to coat. 2. Stir in wine and ½ cup of the broth. Cook 5 minutes, stirring frequently, until liquid is almost absorbed. Repeat with remaining broth and 3 cups water, adding ½ to ¾ cup of broth or water at a time and stirring frequently, until absorbed. 3. Stir in tomatoes, ¼ cup of the cheese, the basil and pepper. Cook until thoroughly heated. Sprinkle with remaining ¼ cup cheese.

Per Serving:

calorie: 370 | fat: 8g | protein: 15g | carbs: 55g | sugars: 6g | fiber: 11g | sodium: 520mg

Sunshine Burgers

Prep time: 10 minutes | Cook time: 18 to 20 minutes | Makes 10 burgers

2 cups sliced raw carrots
1 large clove garlic, sliced or quartered
2 cans (15 ounces each) chickpeas, rinsed and drained
¼ cup sliced dry-packed sun-dried tomatoes
2 tablespoons tahini

1 teaspoon red wine vinegar or apple cider vinegar
1 teaspoon smoked paprika
½ teaspoon dried rosemary
½ teaspoon ground cumin
½ teaspoon sea salt
1 cup rolled oats

1. In a food processor, combine the carrots and garlic. Pulse several times to mince. Add the chickpeas, tomatoes, tahini, vinegar, paprika, rosemary, cumin, and salt. Puree until well combined, scraping down the sides of the bowl once or twice. Add the oats, and pulse briefly to combine. Refrigerate the mixture for 30 minutes, if possible. 2. Preheat the oven to 400°F. Line a baking sheet with parchment paper. 3. Use an ice cream scoop to scoop the mixture onto the prepared baking sheet, flattening to shape it into patties. Bake for 18 to 20 minutes, flipping the burgers halfway through. Alternatively, you can cook the burgers in a nonstick skillet over medium heat for 6 to 8 minutes Per side, or until golden brown. Serve.

Per Serving:

calorie: 137 | fat: 4 | protein: 6g | carbs: 21g | sugars: 4g | fiber: 6g | sodium: 278mg

Veggie Unfried Rice

Prep time: 15 minutes | Cook time: 25 minutes | Serves 4

1 tablespoon extra-virgin olive oil
1 bunch collard greens, stemmed and cut into chiffonade
½ cup store-bought low-sodium vegetable broth
1 carrot, cut into 2-inch matchsticks

1 red onion, thinly sliced
1 garlic clove, minced
2 tablespoons coconut aminos
1 cup cooked brown rice
1 large egg
1 teaspoon red pepper flakes
1 teaspoon paprika

1. In a large Dutch oven, heat the olive oil over medium heat. 2. Add the collard greens and cook for 3 to 5 minutes, or until the greens are wilted. 3. Add the broth, carrot, onion, garlic, and coconut aminos, then cover and cook for 5 to 7 minutes, or until the carrot softens and the onion and garlic are translucent. 4. Uncover, add the rice, and cook for 3 to 5 minutes, gently mixing all the ingredients together until well combined but not mushy. 5. Crack the egg over the pot and gently scramble the egg. Cook for 2 to 5 minutes, or until the eggs are no longer runny. 6. Remove from the heat and season with the red pepper flakes and paprika.

Per Serving:

calorie: 164 | fat: 4g | protein: 9g | carbs: 26g | sugars: 3g | fiber: 9g | sodium: 168mg

Stewed Green Beans

Prep time: 5 minutes | Cook time: 10 minutes | Serves 4

1 pound green beans, trimmed
1 medium tomato, chopped
½ yellow onion, chopped
1 garlic clove, minced

1 teaspoon Creole seasoning
¼ cup store-bought low-sodium vegetable broth

1. In an electric pressure cooker, combine the green beans, tomato, onion, garlic, Creole seasoning, and broth. 2. Close and lock the lid, and set the pressure valve to sealing. 3. Select the Manual/Pressure Cook setting, and cook for 10 minutes. 4. Once cooking is complete, quick-release the pressure. Carefully remove the lid. 5. Transfer the beans to a serving dish. Serve warm.

Per Serving:
calorie: 58 | fat: 0g | protein: 3g | carbs: 13g | sugars: 7g | fiber: 4g | sodium: 98mg

Herbed Beans and Brown Rice

Prep time: 15 minutes | Cook time: 15 minutes | Serves 8

2 teaspoons extra-virgin olive oil
½ sweet onion, chopped
1 teaspoon minced jalapeño pepper
1 teaspoon minced garlic
1 (15 ounces) can sodium-free

red kidney beans, rinsed and drained
1 large tomato, chopped
1 teaspoon chopped fresh thyme
Sea salt
Freshly ground black pepper
2 cups cooked brown rice

1. Put the bell peppers, chickpeas, jalapeño pepper, oil, water, lime juice, salt, garlic powder, cumin, and black pepper into a food processor or blender and blend until smooth. The sauce will have texture, but it shouldn't be chunky.

Per Serving:
calorie: 97 | fat: 2g | protein: 3g | carbs: 18g | sugars: 2g | fiber: 4g | sodium: 20mg

Wild Rice with Blueberries and Pumpkin Seeds

Prep time: 15 minutes | Cook time: 45 minutes | Serves 4

1 tablespoon extra-virgin olive oil
½ sweet onion, chopped
2½ cups sodium-free chicken broth
1 cup wild rice, rinsed and

drained
Pinch sea salt
½ cup toasted pumpkin seeds
½ cup blueberries
1 teaspoon chopped fresh basil

1. Put the bell peppers, chickpeas, jalapeño pepper, oil, water, lime juice, salt, garlic powder, cumin, and black pepper into a food processor or blender and blend until smooth. The sauce will have texture, but it shouldn't be chunky.

Per Serving:

calorie: 306 | fat: 15g | protein: 12g | carbs: 37g | sugars: 7g | fiber: 6g | sodium: 12mg

Coconut-Ginger Rice

Prep time: 10 minutes | Cook time: 20 minutes | Serves 8

2½ cups reduced-sodium chicken broth
⅔ cup reduced-fat (lite) coconut milk (not cream of coconut)
1 tablespoon grated gingerroot
½ teaspoon salt
1⅓ cups uncooked regular long-

grain white rice
1 teaspoon grated lime peel
3 medium green onions, chopped (3 tablespoons)
3 tablespoons flaked coconut, toasted
Lime slices

1. In 3-quart saucepan, heat broth, coconut milk, gingerroot and salt to boiling over medium-high heat. Stir in rice. Return to boiling. Reduce heat; cover and simmer about 15 minutes or until rice is tender and liquid is absorbed. Remove from heat. 2. Add lime peel and onions; fluff rice mixture lightly with fork to mix. Garnish with coconut and lime slices.

Per Serving:
calorie: 150 | fat: 2g | protein: 3g | carbs: 30g | sugars: 1g | fiber: 0g | sodium: 340mg

Italian Bean Burgers

Prep time: 10 minutes | Cook time: 20 minutes | Makes 9 burgers

2 cans (14 or 15 ounces each) chickpeas, drained and rinsed
1 medium–large clove garlic, cut in half
2 tablespoons tomato paste
1½ tablespoons red wine vinegar (can substitute apple cider vinegar)
1 tablespoon tahini
1 teaspoon Dijon mustard
½ teaspoon onion powder

Scant ½ teaspoon sea salt
2 tablespoons chopped fresh oregano
⅓ cup roughly chopped fresh basil leaves
1 cup rolled oats
⅓ cup chopped sun-dried tomatoes (not packed in oil)
½ cup roughly chopped kalamata or green olives

1. In a food processor, combine the chickpeas, garlic, tomato paste, vinegar, tahini, mustard, onion powder, and salt. Puree until fully combined. Add the oregano, basil, and oats, and pulse briefly. (You want to combine the ingredients but retain some of the basil's texture.) Finally, pulse in the sun-dried tomatoes and olives, again maintaining some texture. Transfer the mixture to a bowl and refrigerate, covered, for 30 minutes or longer. 2. Preheat the oven to 400°F. Line a baking sheet with parchment paper. Use an ice cream scoop to scoop the mixture onto the prepared baking sheet, flattening to shape into patties. Bake for about 20 minutes, flipping the burgers halfway through. Alternatively, you can cook the burgers in a nonstick skillet over medium heat for 6 to 8 minutes Per side, or until golden brown. Serve.

Per Serving:
calorie: 148 | fat: 4g | protein: 6g | carbs: 23g | sugars: 4g | fiber: 6g | sodium: 387mg

Chicken and Vegetables with Quinoa

Prep time: 25 minutes | Cook time: 25 minutes | Serves 4

1⅓ cups uncooked quinoa
2⅔ cups water
⅔ cup chicken broth
2 cups 1-inch pieces fresh green beans
½ cup ready-to-eat baby-cut carrots, cut in half lengthwise
1 tablespoon olive oil
½ lb boneless skinless chicken

breasts, cut into bite-size pieces
½ cup bite-size strips red bell pepper
½ cup sliced fresh mushrooms
½ teaspoon dried rosemary leaves
¼ teaspoon salt
2 cloves garlic, finely chopped

1. Rinse quinoa thoroughly by placing in a fine-mesh strainer and holding under cold running water until water runs clear; drain well. 2. In 2-quart saucepan, heat water to boiling. Add quinoa; return to boiling. Reduce heat to low. Cover; cook 12 to 16 minutes or until liquid is absorbed. 3 Meanwhile, in 12-inch nonstick skillet, heat broth to boiling over high heat. Add green beans and carrots. Reduce heat to medium-high. Cover; cook 5 to 7 minutes or until vegetables are crisp-tender. 4. Stir oil, chicken, bell pepper, mushrooms, rosemary, salt and garlic into vegetables. Cook over medium-high heat 8 to 9 minutes, stirring frequently, until chicken is no longer pink in center. Serve over quinoa.

Per Serving:

calorie: 350 | fat: 9g | protein: 22g | carbs: 46g | sugars: 6g | fiber: 6g | sodium: 380mg

Southwestern Quinoa Salad

Prep time: 15 minutes | Cook time: 25 minutes | Serves 6

Salad
1 cup uncooked quinoa
1 large onion, chopped (1 cup)
1½ cups reduced-sodium chicken broth
1 cup packed fresh cilantro leaves
¼ cup raw unsalted hulled pumpkin seeds (pepitas)
2 cloves garlic, sliced
⅛ teaspoon ground cumin
2 tablespoons chopped green

chiles (from 4.5-oz can)
1 tablespoon olive oil
1 can (15 ounces) no-salt-added black beans, drained, rinsed
6 medium plum (Roma) tomatoes, chopped (2 cups)
2 tablespoons lime juice
Garnish
1 avocado, pitted, peeled, thinly sliced
4 small cilantro sprigs

1. Rinse quinoa thoroughly by placing in a fine-mesh strainer and holding under cold running water until water runs clear; drain well. 2. Spray 3-quart saucepan with cooking spray. Heat over medium heat. Add onion to pan; cook 6 to 8 minutes, stirring occasionally, until golden brown. Stir in quinoa and chicken broth. Heat to boiling; reduce heat. Cover and simmer 10 to 15 minutes or until all liquid is absorbed; remove from heat. 3. Meanwhile, in small food processor, place cilantro, pumpkin seeds, garlic and cumin. Cover; process 5 to 10 seconds, using quick on-and-off motions; scrape side. Add chiles and oil. Cover; process, using quick on-and-off motions, until paste

forms. 4. To cooked quinoa, add pesto mixture and the remaining salad ingredients. Refrigerate at least 30 minutes to blend flavors. 5. To serve, divide salad evenly among 4 plates; top each serving with 3 or 4 slices avocado and 1 sprig cilantro.

Per Serving:

calorie: 310 | fat: 12g | protein: 13g | carbs: 38g | sugars: 5g | fiber: 9g | sodium: 170mg

Red Beans

Prep time: 10 minutes | Cook time: 45 minutes | Serves 8

1 cup crushed tomatoes
1 medium yellow onion, chopped
2 garlic cloves, minced
2 cups dried red kidney beans

1 cup roughly chopped green beans
4 cups store-bought low-sodium vegetable broth
1 teaspoon smoked paprika

1. Select the Sauté setting on an electric pressure cooker, and combine the tomatoes, onion, and garlic. Cook for 3 to 5 minutes, or until softened. 2. Add the kidney beans, green beans, broth, and paprika. Stir to combine. 3. Close and lock the lid, and set the pressure valve to sealing. 4. Change to the Manual/Pressure Cook setting, and cook for 35 minutes. 5. Once cooking is complete, quick-release the pressure. Carefully remove the lid. 6. Serve.

Per Serving:

calorie: 73 | fat: 0g | protein: 4g | carbs: 14g | sugars: 4g | fiber: 4g | sodium: 167mg

Green Chickpea Falafel

Prep time: 10 minutes | Cook time: 11 to 12 minutes | Serves 4

1 bag (14 ounces) green chickpeas, thawed (about 3½ cups)
½ cup fresh flat-leaf parsley leaves
½ cup fresh cilantro leaves
1½ tablespoons freshly squeezed lemon juice

2 medium-large cloves garlic
2 teaspoons ground cumin
½ teaspoon turmeric
1 teaspoon ground coriander
1 teaspoon sea salt
¼ to ½ teaspoon crushed red-pepper flakes
1 cup rolled oats

1. In a food processor, combine the chickpeas, parsley, cilantro, lemon juice, garlic, cumin, turmeric, coriander, salt, and red-pepper flakes. (Use ¼ teaspoon if you like it mild and ½ teaspoon if you like it spicier.) Process until the mixture breaks down and begins to smooth out. Add the oats and pulse a few times to work them in. Refrigerate for 30 minutes, if possible. 2. Preheat the oven to 400°F. Line a baking sheet with parchment paper. 3. Use a cookie scoop to take small scoops of the mixture, 1 to 1½ tablespoons each. Place falafel balls on the prepared baking sheet. Bake for 11 to 12 minutes, until the falafel balls begin to firm (they will still be tender inside) and turn golden in spots.

Per Serving:

calorie: 253 | fat: 4g | protein: 12g | carbs: 43g | sugars: 5g | fiber: 10g | sodium: 601mg

Texas Caviar

Prep time: 10 minutes | Cook time: 0 minutes | Serves 6

1 cup cooked black-eyed peas	½ red onion, chopped
1 cup cooked lima beans	3 tablespoons apple cider
1 ear fresh corn, kernels	vinegar
removed	2 tablespoons extra-virgin olive
2 celery stalks, chopped	oil
1 red bell pepper, chopped	1 teaspoon paprika

1. In a large bowl, combine the black-eyed peas, lima beans, corn, celery, bell pepper, and onion. 2. In a small bowl, to make the dressing, whisk the vinegar, oil, and paprika together. 3. Pour the dressing over the bean mixture, and gently mix. Set aside for 15 to 30 minutes, allowing the flavors to come together.

Per Serving:
calorie: 142 | fat: 5g | protein: 6g | carbs: 19g | sugars: 3g | fiber: 6g | sodium: 10mg

Thai Red Lentils

Prep time: 5 minutes | Cook time: 25 minutes | Serves 4

2 cups dried red lentils	¼ to ½ teaspoon sea salt (use
1 can (13½ ounces) lite coconut	less if using more curry paste)
milk	2 to 2¼ cups water
2 tablespoons red or yellow	⅓ cup finely chopped fresh basil
Thai curry paste	3 to 4 tablespoons lime juice

1. In a large saucepan over high heat, combine the lentils, coconut milk, curry paste, salt, and 2 cups of the water. Stir and bring to a boil. Reduce the heat to low, cover, and cook for 20 minutes, or until the lentils are fully softened. Add the basil and 3 tablespoons of the lime juice, and stir. Season to taste with more salt and the remaining 1 tablespoon lime juice, if desired. Add the remaining ¼ cup water to thin, if desired.

Per Serving:
calorie: 389 | fat: 8g | protein: 25g | carbs: 58g | sugars: 4g | fiber: 16g | sodium: 441mg

Easy Lentil Burgers

Prep time: 10 minutes | Cook time: 20 minutes | Serves 5

1 medium-large clove garlic	2 teaspoons onion powder
2 tablespoons tamari	¼ teaspoon sea salt
2 tablespoons tomato paste	Few pinches freshly ground
1 tablespoon red wine vinegar	black pepper
1½ tablespoons tahini	3 cups cooked brown lentils
2 tablespoons fresh thyme or	1 cup toasted breadcrumbs
oregano	½ cup rolled oats

1. In a food processor, combine the garlic, tamari, tomato paste, vinegar, tahini, thyme or oregano, onion powder, salt, pepper, and 1½ cups of the lentils. Puree until fairly smooth. Add the breadcrumbs, rolled oats, and the remaining 1½ cups of lentils. Pulse a few times. At this stage you're looking for a sticky texture that will hold together when pressed. If the mixture is still a little crumbly, pulse a few more times. 2. Preheat the oven to 400°F. Line a baking sheet with parchment paper. 3. Use an ice cream scoop to scoop the mixture onto the prepared baking sheet, flattening to shape into patties. Bake for about 20 minutes, flipping the burgers halfway through. Alternatively, you can cook the burgers in a nonstick skillet over medium heat for 4 to 5 minutes Per side, or until golden brown.

Per Serving:
calorie: 148 | fat: 2g | protein: 8g | carbs: 24g | sugars: 1g | fiber: 5g | sodium: 369mg

Colorful Rice Casserole

Prep time: 5 minutes | Cook time: 20 minutes | Serves 12

1 tablespoon extra-virgin olive	added chopped tomatoes,
oil	undrained
1½ pounds zucchini, thinly	¼ cup chopped parsley
sliced	1 teaspoon oregano
¾ cup chopped scallions	3 cups cooked brown (or white)
2 cups corn kernels (frozen or	rice
fresh; if frozen, defrost)	⅛ teaspoon freshly ground black
One 14.5 ounces can no-salt-	pepper

1. In a large skillet, heat the oil. Add the zucchini and scallions, and sauté for 5 minutes. 2. Add the remaining ingredients, cover, reduce heat, and simmer for 10–15 minutes or until the vegetables are heated through. Season with salt, if desired, and pepper. Transfer to a bowl, and serve.

Per Serving:
calorie: 109 | fat: 2g | protein: 3g | carbs: 21g | sugars: 4g | fiber: 3g | sodium: 14mg

Asian Fried Rice

Prep time: 5 minutes | Cook time: 20 minutes | Serves 4

2 tablespoons peanut oil	½ cup water chestnuts, drained
¼ cup chopped onion	½ cup sliced mushrooms
1 cup sliced carrot	1 tablespoon light soy sauce
1 green bell pepper, diced	2 egg whites
1 tablespoon grated fresh ginger	½ cup sliced scallions
2 cups cooked brown rice, cold	

1. In a large skillet, heat the oil. Sauté the onion, carrot, green pepper, and ginger for 5 to 6 minutes. 2. Stir in the rice, water chestnuts, mushrooms, and soy sauce, and stir-fry for 8 to 10 minutes. 3. Stir in the egg whites, and continue to stir-fry for another 3 minutes. Top with the sliced scallions to serve.

Per Serving:
calorie: 223 | fat: 9g | protein: 6g | carbs: 32g | sugars: 5g | fiber: 4g | sodium: 151mg

Chapter 6

Snacks and Appetizers

Vietnamese Meatball Lollipops with Dipping Sauce

Prep time: 30 minutes | Cook time: 20 minutes | Serves 12

Meatballs
1¼ pounds lean (at least 90%) ground turkey
¼ cup chopped water chestnuts (from 8 ounces can), drained
¼ cup chopped fresh cilantro
1 tablespoon cornstarch
2 tablespoons fish sauce
½ teaspoon pepper
3 cloves garlic, finely chopped
Dipping Sauce
¼ cup water

¼ cup reduced-sodium soy sauce
2 tablespoons packed brown sugar
2 tablespoons chopped fresh chives or green onions
2 tablespoons lime juice
2 cloves garlic, finely chopped
½ teaspoon crushed red pepper
About 24 (6-inch) bamboo skewers

1. Heat oven to 400°F. Line cookie sheet with foil; spray with cooking spray (or use nonstick foil). 2. In large bowl, combine all meatball ingredients until well mixed. Shape into 1¼-inch meatballs. On cookie sheet, place meatballs 1 inch apart. Bake 20 minutes, turning halfway through baking, until thermometer inserted in center of meatballs reads at least 165°F. 3. Meanwhile, in 1-quart saucepan, heat all dipping sauce ingredients over low heat until sugar is dissolved; set aside. 4. Insert bamboo skewers into cooked meatballs; place on serving plate. Serve with warm dipping sauce.

Per Serving:

calorie: 80 | fat: 2g | protein: 10g | carbs: 5g | sugars: 3g | fiber: 0g | sodium: 440mg

Roasted Carrot and Chickpea Dip

Prep time: 10 minutes | Cook time: 15 minutes | Makes 4 cups

4 medium carrots, quartered lengthwise
¼ cup plus 2 teaspoons extra-virgin olive oil, divided
Pinch kosher salt
Pinch freshly ground black pepper
1 (15 ounces) can chickpeas, drained and rinsed
1 garlic clove, minced

1 red chile (optional)
Zest and juice of 1 lemon
2 tablespoons tahini
1 tablespoon harissa
½ teaspoon ground cumin
¼ teaspoon ground coriander
Pomegranate arils (seeds) (optional)
Cilantro, chopped (optional)

1. Preheat the oven to 425°F. Line a baking sheet with parchment paper. 2. In a medium bowl, toss the carrots with 2 teaspoons of extra-virgin olive oil, the salt, and the pepper. Spread them in a single layer on the prepared baking sheet and roast until tender, about 15 minutes. Turn the carrots over halfway through. 3. Meanwhile, place the chickpeas, garlic, chile, lemon zest and juice, tahini, harissa, cumin, and coriander in a food processor. Set aside. Add the carrots to the processor when they are cooked. Pulse until the mixture is coarse. Scrape the bowl down, then turn the processor back on while you drizzle the remaining ¼ cup of extra-virgin olive oil through

the feed tube of the machine. Adjust the seasonings as desired. If it's too thick, add water to thin. 4. Top with pomegranate seeds and chopped cilantro (if using,) and Serve with cut vegetables. 5. Store any leftovers in an airtight container in the refrigerator for up to 4 days.

Per Serving:

calorie: 141 | fat: 10g | protein: 3g | carbs: 12g | sugars: 3g | fiber: 3g | sodium: 93mg

Fresh Dill Dip

Prep time: 5 minutes | Cook time: 5 minutes | Serves 6

1 cup plain fat-free yogurt
¼ teaspoon salt
¼ teaspoon freshly ground black pepper
¼ cup minced parsley

2 tablespoons finely chopped fresh chives
1 tablespoon finely chopped fresh dill
1 tablespoon apple cider vinegar

1. In a small bowl, combine all the ingredients. Chill for 2 to 4 hours. Serve with fresh cut vegetables.

Per Serving:

calorie: 20 | fat: 0g | protein: 2g | carbs: 3g | sugars: 2g | fiber: 0g | sodium: 120mg

Peanut Butter Protein Bites

Prep time: 10 minutes | Cook time: 0 minutes | Makes 16 Balls

½ cup sugar-free peanut butter
¼ cup (1 scoop) sugar-free peanut butter powder or sugar-free protein powder
2 tablespoons unsweetened

cocoa powder
2 tablespoons canned coconut milk (or more to adjust consistency)

1. In a bowl, mix all ingredients until well combined. 2. Roll into 16 balls. Refrigerate before serving.

Per Serving:

calorie: 59 | fat: 5g | protein: 3g | carbs: 2g | sugars: 1g | fiber: 1g | sodium: 4mg

Cinnamon Toasted Pumpkin Seeds

Prep time: 5 minutes | Cook time: 45 minutes | Serves 4

1 cup pumpkin seeds
2 tablespoons canola oil
1 teaspoon cinnamon

2 (1-gram) packets stevia
¼ teaspoon sea salt

1. Preheat the oven to 300°F. 2. In a bowl, toss the pumpkin seeds with the oil, cinnamon, stevia, and salt. 3. Spread the seeds in a single layer on a rimmed baking sheet. Bake until browned and fragrant, stirring once or twice, about 45 minutes.

Per Serving:

calorie: 233 | fat: 21g | protein: 9g | carbs: 5g | sugars: 0g | fiber: 2g | sodium: 151mg

Lemon Artichokes

Prep time: 5 minutes | Cook time: 5 to 15 minutes | Serves 4

4 artichokes

1 cup water

2 tablespoons lemon juice

1 teaspoon salt

1. Wash and trim artichokes by cutting off the stems flush with the bottoms of the artichokes and by cutting ¾–1 inch off the tops. Stand upright in the bottom of the inner pot of the Instant Pot. 2. Pour water, lemon juice, and salt over artichokes. 3. Secure the lid and make sure the vent is set to sealing. On Manual, set the Instant Pot for 15 minutes for large artichokes, 10 minutes for medium artichokes, or 5 minutes for small artichokes. 4. When cook time is up, perform a quick release by releasing the pressure manually.

Per Serving:

calories: 60 | fat: 0g | protein: 4g | carbs: 13g | sugars: 1g | fiber: 6g | sodium: 397mg

Turkey Rollups with Veggie Cream Cheese

Prep time: 10 minutes | Cook time: 0 minutes | Serves 2

¼ cup cream cheese, at room temperature

2 tablespoons finely chopped red onion

2 tablespoons finely chopped red bell pepper

1 tablespoon chopped fresh chives

1 teaspoon Dijon mustard

1 garlic clove, minced

¼ teaspoon sea salt

6 slices deli turkey

1. In a small bowl, mix the cream cheese, red onion, bell pepper, chives, mustard, garlic, and salt. 2. Spread the mixture on the turkey slices and roll up.

Per Serving:

calorie: 146 | fat: 1g | protein: 24g | carbs: 8g | sugars: 6g | fiber: 1g | sodium: 572mg

Hummus

Prep time: 5 minutes | Cook time: 5 minutes | Serves 12

One 15 ounces can chickpeas, drained (reserve a little liquid)

3 cloves garlic

Juice of 1 lemon

Juice of 1 lime

1 teaspoon extra-virgin olive oil

1 teaspoon ground cumin

1. In a blender or food processor, combine all the ingredients until smooth, adding chickpea liquid or water if necessary to blend, and create a creamy texture. Refrigerate until ready to serve. Serve with crunchy vegetables, crackers, or pita bread.

Per Serving:

calorie: 56 | fat: 1g | protein: 3g | carbs: 9g | sugars: 2g | fiber: 2g | sodium: 76mg

Chilled Shrimp

Prep time: 5 minutes | Cook time: 5 minutes | Serves 20

5 pounds jumbo shrimp, unshelled

¼ cup plus 2 tablespoons extra-virgin olive oil, divided

4 medium lemons, thinly sliced

3 tablespoons minced garlic

3 medium red onions, thinly sliced

½ cup minced parsley

Parsley sprigs (for garnish)

1. Preheat the oven to 400 degrees. Peel, and devein shrimp, leaving the tails intact. 2. Arrange the shrimp on a baking sheet and brush with 2 tablespoons of the olive oil. Bake the shrimp for 3 minutes or until they turn bright pink. 3. Place the lemon slices in a large bowl. Add the remaining ¼ cup of olive oil, garlic, onions, and minced parsley. Add the shrimp and toss vigorously to coat. Cover, and let marinate, refrigerated, for 6–8 hours. 4. Just before serving, arrange the shrimp on a serving platter. Garnish with parsley sprigs and some of the red onions and lemons from the bowl.

Per Serving:

calorie: 127 | fat: 3g | protein: 23g | carbs: 2g | sugars: 0g | fiber: 0g | sodium: 136mg

Creamy Cheese Dip

Prep time: 5 minutes | Cook time: 5 minutes | Serves 40

1 cup plain fat-free yogurt, strained overnight in cheesecloth over a bowl set in

the refrigerator

1 cup fat-free ricotta cheese

1 cup low-fat cottage cheese

1. Combine all the ingredients in a food processor; process until smooth. Place in a covered container, and refrigerate until ready to use (this cream cheese can be refrigerated for up to 1 week).

Per Serving:

calorie: 21 | fat: 1g | protein: 2g | carbs: 1g | sugars: 1g | fiber: 0g | sodium: 81mg

Lemon Cream Fruit Dip

Prep time: 5 minutes | Cook time: 0 minutes | Serves 4

1 cup (200 g) plain nonfat Greek yogurt

¼ cup (28 g) coconut flour 1 tablespoon (15 ml) pure maple syrup

½ teaspoon pure vanilla extract

½ teaspoon pure almond extract

Zest of 1 medium lemon

Juice of ½ medium lemon

1. In a medium bowl, whisk together the yogurt, coconut flour, maple syrup, vanilla, almond extract, lemon zest, and lemon juice. Serve the dip with fruit or crackers.

Per Serving:

calorie: 80 | fat: 1g | protein: 7g | carbs: 10g | sugars: 6g | fiber: 3g | sodium: 37mg

Creamy Apple-Cinnamon Quesadilla

Prep time: 15 minutes | Cook time: 10 minutes | Serves 4

1 tablespoon granulated sugar	sugar
½ teaspoon ground cinnamon	2 whole wheat tortillas (8 inch)
¼ cup reduced-fat cream cheese	½ small apple, cut into ¼-inch
(from 8 ounces container)	slices (½ cup)
1 tablespoon packed brown	Cooking spray

1. In small bowl, mix granulated sugar and ¼ teaspoon of the cinnamon; set aside. In another small bowl, mix cream cheese, brown sugar and remaining ¼ teaspoon cinnamon with spoon. 2. Spread cream cheese mixture over tortillas. Place apple slices on cream cheese mixture on 1 tortilla. Top with remaining tortilla, cheese side down. Spray both sides of quesadilla with cooking spray; sprinkle with cinnamon-sugar mixture. 3. Heat 10-inch nonstick skillet over medium heat. Add quesadilla; cook 2 to 3 minutes or until bottom is brown and crisp. Turn quesadilla; cook 2 to 3 minutes longer or until bottom is brown and crisp. 4. Transfer quesadilla from skillet to cutting board; let stand 2 to 3 minutes. Cut into 8 wedges to serve.

Per Serving:

calories: 110 | fat: 3g | protein: 3g | carbs: 19g | sugars: 9g | fiber: 2g | sodium: 170mg

Instant Popcorn

Prep time: 1 minutes | Cook time: 5 minutes | Serves 5

2 tablespoons coconut oil	optional
½ cup popcorn kernels	Sea salt to taste
¼ cup margarine spread, melted,	

1. Set the Instant Pot to Sauté. 2. Melt the coconut oil in the inner pot, then add the popcorn kernels and stir. 3. Press Adjust to bring the temperature up to high. 4. When the corn starts popping, secure the lid on the Instant Pot. 5. When you no longer hear popping, turn off the Instant Pot, remove the lid, and pour the popcorn into a bowl. 6. Top with the optional melted margarine and season the popcorn with sea salt to your liking.

Per Serving:

calories: 161 | fat: 12g | protein: 1g | carbs: 13g | sugars: 0g | fiber: 3g | sodium: 89mg

Gruyere Apple Spread

Prep time: 5 minutes | Cook time: 5 minutes | Serves 20

4 ounces fat-free cream cheese,	pepper
softened	½ cup shredded apple
½ cup low-fat cottage cheese	(unpeeled)
4 ounces Gruyere cheese	2 tablespoons finely chopped
¼ teaspoon dry mustard	pecans
⅛ teaspoon freshly ground black	2 teaspoons minced fresh chives

1. Place the cheeses in a food processor, and blend until smooth. Add

the mustard and pepper, and blend for 30 seconds. 2. Transfer the mixture to a serving bowl, and fold in the apple and pecans. Sprinkle the dip with chives. 3. Cover, and refrigerate the mixture for 1 to 2 hours. Serve chilled with crackers, or stuff into celery stalks.

Per Serving:

calorie: 46 | fat: 3g | protein: 4g | carbs: 1g | sugars: 1g | fiber: 0g | sodium: 107mg

Chicken Kabobs

Prep time: 5 minutes | Cook time: 20 minutes | Serves 6

1 pound boneless, skinless	oil
chicken breast	3 tablespoons dry vermouth
3 tablespoons light soy sauce	1 large clove garlic, finely
One 1-inch cube of fresh ginger	chopped
root, finely chopped	12 watercress sprigs
3 tablespoons extra-virgin olive	2 large lemons, cut into wedges

1. Cut the chicken into 1-inch cubes and place in a shallow bowl. 2. In a small bowl, combine the soy sauce, ginger root, oil, vermouth, and garlic and pour over the chicken. Cover the chicken, and let marinate for at least 1 hour (or overnight). 3. Thread the chicken onto 12 metal or wooden skewers (remember to soak wooden skewers in water before using). Grill or broil 6 inches from the heat source for 8 minutes, turning frequently. 4. Arrange the skewers on a platter and garnish with the watercress and lemon wedges. Serve hot with additional soy sauce, if desired.

Per Serving:

calorie: 187 | fat: 10g | protein: 18g | carbs: 4g | sugars: 2g | fiber: 1g | sodium: 158mg

Caramelized Onion–Shrimp Spread

Prep time: 30 minutes | Cook time: 20 minutes | Serves 18

1 tablespoon butter (do not use	fat cream cheese, softened
margarine)	1 bag (4 ounces) frozen cooked
½ medium onion, thinly sliced	salad shrimp, thawed, well
(about ½ cup)	drained (about 1 cup)
1 clove garlic, finely chopped	1 teaspoon chopped fresh chives
¼ cup apple jelly	36 whole-grain crackers
1 container (8 ounces) reduced-	

1. In 1-quart saucepan, melt butter over medium-low heat. Add onion; cook 15 minutes, stirring frequently. Add garlic; cook 1 minute, stirring occasionally, until onion and garlic are tender and browned. Stir in apple jelly. Cook, stirring constantly, until melted. Remove from heat. Let stand 5 minutes to cool. 2. Meanwhile, in small bowl, stir together cream cheese and shrimp. On 8-inch plate, spread shrimp mixture into a 5-inch round. 3. Spoon onion mixture over shrimp mixture. Sprinkle with chives. Serve with crackers.

Per Serving:

calories: 90| fat: 4g | protein: 3g | carbs: 10g | sugars: 3g | fiber: 1g | sodium: 140mg

Homemade Sun-Dried Tomato Salsa

Prep time: 5 minutes | Cook time: 0 minutes | Serves 4

½ (15 ounces [425 g]) can no-salt-added diced tomatoes, drained
6 tablespoons (20 g) julienned sun-dried tomatoes (see Tip)
1½ cups (330 g) canned artichoke hearts, drained

1 clove garlic
⅛ cup (3 g) fresh basil leaves
1 teaspoon balsamic vinegar
2 tablespoons (30 ml) olive oil
Sea salt, as needed
Black pepper, as needed

1. In a food processor or blender, combine the diced tomatoes, sun-dried tomatoes, artichoke hearts, garlic, basil, vinegar, oil, sea salt, and black pepper. Process or blend the ingredients to the desired consistency.

Per Serving:

calorie: 131 | fat: 7g | protein: 2g | carbs: 13g | sugars: 3g | fiber: 4g | sodium: 279mg

Roasted Carrot and Herb Spread

Prep time: 20 minutes | Cook time: 1 hour | Serves 16

1 pound ready-to-eat baby-cut carrots
1 dark orange sweet potato, peeled, cut into 1-inch pieces (2½ cups)
1 small onion, cut into 8 wedges, separated
2 tablespoons olive oil

1 clove garlic, finely chopped
1 tablespoon chopped fresh or 1 teaspoon dried thyme leaves
¼ teaspoon salt
⅛ teaspoon freshly ground pepper
Assorted whole-grain crackers or vegetable chips

1. Heat oven to 350°F. Spray 15x10x1-inch pan with cooking spray. Place carrots, sweet potato and onion in pan; drizzle with oil. Sprinkle with garlic, thyme, salt and pepper; stir to coat. 2. Bake uncovered about 1 hour, stirring occasionally, until vegetables are tender. 3. In food processor, place vegetable mixture. Cover; process until blended. Spoon into serving bowl. Serve warm, or cover and refrigerate until serving. Serve with crackers.

Per Serving:

calories: 90 | fat: 4g | protein: 1g | carbs: 12g | sugars: 3g | fiber: 2g | sodium: 125mg

Creamy Jalapeño Chicken Dip

Prep time: 5 minutes | Cook time: 12 minutes | Serves 10

1 pound boneless chicken breast
8 ounces low-fat cream cheese
3 jalapeños, seeded and sliced
½ cup water

8 ounces reduced-fat shredded cheddar cheese
¾ cup low-fat sour cream

1. Place the chicken, cream cheese, jalapeños, and water in the inner pot of the Instant Pot. 2. Secure the lid so it's locked and turn the vent to sealing. 3. Press Manual and set the Instant Pot for 12 minutes on high pressure. 4. When cooking time is up, turn off Instant Pot, do a quick release of the remaining pressure, then remove lid. 5. Shred the chicken between 2 forks, either in the pot or on a cutting board, then place back in the inner pot. 6. Stir in the shredded cheese and sour cream.

Per Serving:

calories: 238 | fat: 13g | protein: 24g | carbs: 7g | sugars: 5g | fiber: 1g | sodium: 273mg

Low-Sugar Blueberry Muffins

Prep time: 5 minutes | Cook time: 20 to 25 minutes | Makes 12 muffins

2 large eggs
1½ cups (144 g) almond flour
1 cup (80 g) gluten-free rolled oats
½ cup (120 ml) pure maple syrup
½ cup (120 ml) avocado oil

1 teaspoon baking powder
1 teaspoon ground cinnamon
½ teaspoon pure vanilla extract
½ teaspoon pure almond extract
1 cup (150 g) fresh or frozen blueberries

1. Preheat the oven to 350°F (177°C). Line a 12-well muffin pan with paper liners or spray the wells with cooking oil spray. 2. In a blender, combine the eggs, almond flour, oats, maple syrup, oil, baking powder, cinnamon, vanilla, and almond extract. Blend the ingredients on high for 20 to 30 seconds, until the mixture is homogeneous. 3. Transfer the batter to a large bowl and gently stir in the blueberries. 4. Divide the batter evenly among the muffin wells. Bake the muffins for 20 to 25 minutes, until a toothpick inserted in the middle comes out clean. 5. Let the muffins rest for 5 minutes, then transfer them to a cooling rack.

Per Serving:

calorie: 240 | fat: 18g | protein: 5g | carbs: 19g | sugars: 10g | fiber: 3g | sodium: 19mg

Creamy Spinach Dip

Prep time: 13 minutes | Cook time: 5 minutes | Serves 11

8 ounces low-fat cream cheese
1 cup low-fat sour cream
½ cup finely chopped onion
½ cup no-sodium vegetable broth
5 cloves garlic, minced
½ teaspoon salt

¼ teaspoon black pepper
10 ounces frozen spinach
12 ounces reduced-fat shredded Monterey Jack cheese
12 ounces reduced-fat shredded Parmesan cheese

1. Add cream cheese, sour cream, onion, vegetable broth, garlic, salt, pepper, and spinach to the inner pot of the Instant Pot. 2. Secure lid, make sure vent is set to sealing, and set to the Bean/Chili setting on high pressure for 5 minutes. 3. When done, do a manual release. 4. Add the cheeses and mix well until creamy and well combined.

Per Serving:

calorie: 274 | fat: 18g | protein: 19g | carbs: 10g | sugars: 3g | fiber: 1g | sodium: 948mg

Smoky Spinach Hummus with Popcorn Chips

Prep time: 10 minutes | Cook time: 0 minutes | Serves 12

1 can (15 ounces) chickpeas (garbanzo beans), drained, liquid reserved

1 cup chopped fresh spinach leaves

2 tablespoons lemon juice

2 tablespoons sesame tahini paste (from 16 ounces. jar)

2 teaspoons smoked Spanish paprika

1 teaspoon ground cumin

½ teaspoon salt

2 tablespoons chopped red bell pepper, if desired

6 ounces popcorn snack chips

1. In food processor, place chickpeas, ¼ cup of the reserved liquid, spinach, lemon juice, tahini paste, paprika, cumin and salt. Cover; process 30 seconds, using quick on-and-off motions; scrape side. 2. Add additional reserved bean liquid, 1 tablespoon at a time, covering and processing, using quick on-and-off motions, until smooth and desired dipping consistency. Garnish with bell pepper. Serve with popcorn snack chips.

Per Serving:

calories: 140 | fat: 4g | protein: 4g | carbs: 22g | sugars: 0g | fiber: 3g | sodium: 270mg

Veggies with Cottage Cheese Ranch Dip

Prep time: 10 minutes | Cook time: 0 minutes | Serves 4

1 cup cottage cheese

2 tablespoons mayonnaise

Juice of ½ lemon

2 tablespoons chopped fresh chives

2 tablespoons chopped fresh dill

2 scallions, white and green parts, finely chopped

1 garlic clove, minced

½ teaspoon sea salt

2 zucchinis, cut into sticks

8 cherry tomatoes

1. In a small bowl, mix the cottage cheese, mayonnaise, lemon juice, chives, dill, scallions, garlic, and salt. 2. Serve with the zucchini sticks and cherry tomatoes for dipping.

Per Serving:

calorie: 88 | fat: 3g | protein: 6g | carbs: 10g | sugars: 4g | fiber: 2g | sodium: 495mg

Crab-Filled Mushrooms

Prep time: 5 minutes | Cook time: 25 minutes | Serves 10

20 large fresh mushroom caps

6 ounces canned crabmeat, rinsed, drained, and flaked

½ cup crushed whole-wheat crackers

2 tablespoons chopped fresh parsley

2 tablespoons finely chopped

green onion

⅛ teaspoon freshly ground black pepper

¼ cup chopped pimiento

3 tablespoons extra-virgin olive oil

10 tablespoons wheat germ

1. Preheat the oven to 350 degrees. Clean the mushrooms by dusting off any dirt on the cap with a mushroom brush or paper towel; remove the stems. 2. In a small mixing bowl, combine the crabmeat, crackers, parsley, onion, and pepper. 3. Place the mushroom caps in a 13-x-9-x-2-inch baking dish, crown side down. Stuff some of the crabmeat filling into each cap. Place a little pimiento on top of the filling. 4. Drizzle the olive oil over the caps and sprinkle each cap with ½ tablespoon wheat germ. Bake for 15–17 minutes. Transfer to a serving platter, and serve hot.

Per Serving:

calorie: 113 | fat: 6g | protein: 7g | carbs: 9g | sugars: 1g | fiber: 2g | sodium: 77mg

Vegetable Kabobs with Mustard Dip

Prep time: 35 minutes | Cook time: 10 minutes | Serves 9

Dip

⅔ cup plain fat-free yogurt

⅓ cup fat-free sour cream

1 tablespoon finely chopped fresh parsley

1 teaspoon onion powder

1 teaspoon garlic salt

1 tablespoon Dijon mustard

Kabobs

1 medium bell pepper, cut into 6 strips, then cut into thirds

1 medium zucchini, cut diagonally into ½-inch slices

1 package (8 ounces) fresh whole mushrooms

9 large cherry tomatoes

2 tablespoons olive or vegetable oil

1. In small bowl, mix dip ingredients. Cover; refrigerate at least 1 hour. 2. Heat gas or charcoal grill. On 5 (12-inch) metal skewers, thread vegetables so that one kind of vegetable is on the same skewer (use 2 skewers for mushrooms); leave space between each piece. Brush vegetables with oil. 3. Place skewers of bell pepper and zucchini on grill over medium heat. Cover grill; cook 2 minutes. Add skewers of mushrooms and tomatoes. Cover grill; cook 4 to 5 minutes, carefully turning every 2 minutes, until vegetables are tender. Transfer vegetables from skewers to serving plate. Serve with dip.

Per Serving:

calories: 60 | fat: 4g | protein: 2g | carbs: 6g | sugars: 3g | fiber: 1g | sodium: 180mg

Guacamole with Jicama

Prep time: 5 minutes | Cook time: 0 minutes | Serves 4

1 avocado, cut into cubes

Juice of ½ lime

2 tablespoons finely chopped red onion

2 tablespoons chopped fresh

cilantro

1 garlic clove, minced

¼ teaspoon sea salt

1 cup sliced jicama

1. In a small bowl, combine the avocado, lime juice, onion, cilantro, garlic, and salt. Mash lightly with a fork. 2. Serve with the jicama for dipping.

Per Serving:

calorie: 97 | fat: 7g | protein: 1g | carbs: 8g | sugars: 1g | fiber: 5g | sodium: 151mg

No-Bake Coconut and Cashew Energy Bars

Prep time: 5 minutes | Cook time: 0 minutes | Makes 12 energy bars

1 cup (110 g) raw cashews
1 cup (80 g) unsweetened shredded coconut
½ cup (120 g) unsweetened nut

butter of choice
2 tablespoon (30 ml) pure maple syrup

1. Line an 8 x 8–inch (20 x 20–cm) baking pan with parchment paper. 2. In a large food processor, combine the cashews and coconut. Pulse them for 15 to 20 seconds to form a powder. 3. Add the nut butter and maple syrup and process until a doughy paste is formed, scraping down the sides if needed. 4. Spread the dough into the prepared baking pan. Cover the dough with another sheet of parchment paper and press it flat. 5. Freeze the dough for 1 hour. Cut the dough into bars.

Per Serving:

calorie: 169 | fat: 14g | protein: 4g | carbs: 10g | sugars: 3g | fiber: 2g | sodium: 6mg

Candied Pecans

Prep time: 5 minutes | Cook time: 20 minutes | Serves 10

4 cups raw pecans
1½ teaspoons liquid stevia
½ cup plus 1 tablespoon water, divided
1 teaspoon vanilla extract

1 teaspoon cinnamon
¼ teaspoon nutmeg
⅛ teaspoon ground ginger
⅛ teaspoon sea salt

1. Place the raw pecans, liquid stevia, 1 tablespoon water, vanilla, cinnamon, nutmeg, ground ginger, and sea salt into the inner pot of the Instant Pot. 2. Press the Sauté button on the Instant Pot and sauté the pecans and other ingredients until the pecans are soft. 3. Pour in the ½ cup water and secure the lid to the locked position. Set the vent to sealing. 4. Press Manual and set the Instant Pot for 15 minutes. 5. Preheat the oven to 350°F. 6. When cooking time is up, turn off the Instant Pot, then do a quick release. 7. Spread the pecans onto a greased, lined baking sheet. 8. Bake the pecans for 5 minutes or less in the oven, checking on them frequently so they do not burn.

Per Serving:

calories: 275 | fat: 28g | protein: 4g | carbs: 6g | sugars: 2g | fiber: 4g | sodium: 20mg

Broiled Shrimp with Garlic

Prep time: 5 minutes | Cook time: 10 minutes | Serves 12

2 pounds large shrimp, unshelled
⅓ cup extra-virgin olive oil
1 tablespoon lemon juice
¼ cup chopped scallions
1 tablespoon chopped garlic

2 teaspoons freshly ground black pepper
1 large lemon, sliced
4 tablespoons chopped fresh parsley

1. Set the oven to broil. Shell the uncooked shrimp, but do not remove the tails. With a small knife, split the shrimp down the back, and remove the vein. Wash the shrimp with cool water, and pat dry with paper towels. 2. In a medium skillet, over medium heat, heat the olive oil. Add the lemon juice, scallions, garlic, and pepper. Heat the mixture for 3 minutes. Set aside. 3. In a baking dish, arrange the shrimp and pour the olive oil mixture over the shrimp. Broil the shrimp 4–5 inches from the heat for 2 minutes per side, just until the shrimp turns bright pink. Transfer the shrimp to a platter and garnish with lemon slices and parsley. Pour the juices from the pan over the shrimp.

Per Serving:

calorie: 92 | fat: 3g | protein: 15g | carbs: 1g | sugars: 0g | fiber: 0g | sodium: 142mg

Cucumber Roll-Ups

Prep time: 5 minutes | Cook time: 0 minutes | Serves 2 to 4

2 (6-inch) gluten-free wraps
2 tablespoons cream cheese
1 medium cucumber, cut into

long strips
2 tablespoons fresh mint

1. Place the wraps on your work surface and spread them evenly with the cream cheese. Top with the cucumber and mint. 2. Roll the wraps up from one side to the other, kind of like a burrito. Slice into 1-inch bites or keep whole. 3. Serve. 4. Store any leftovers in an airtight container in the refrigerator for 1 to 2 days.

Per Serving:

calorie: 70 | fat: 1g | protein: 4g | carbs: 12g | sugars: 3g | fiber: 2g | sodium: 183mg

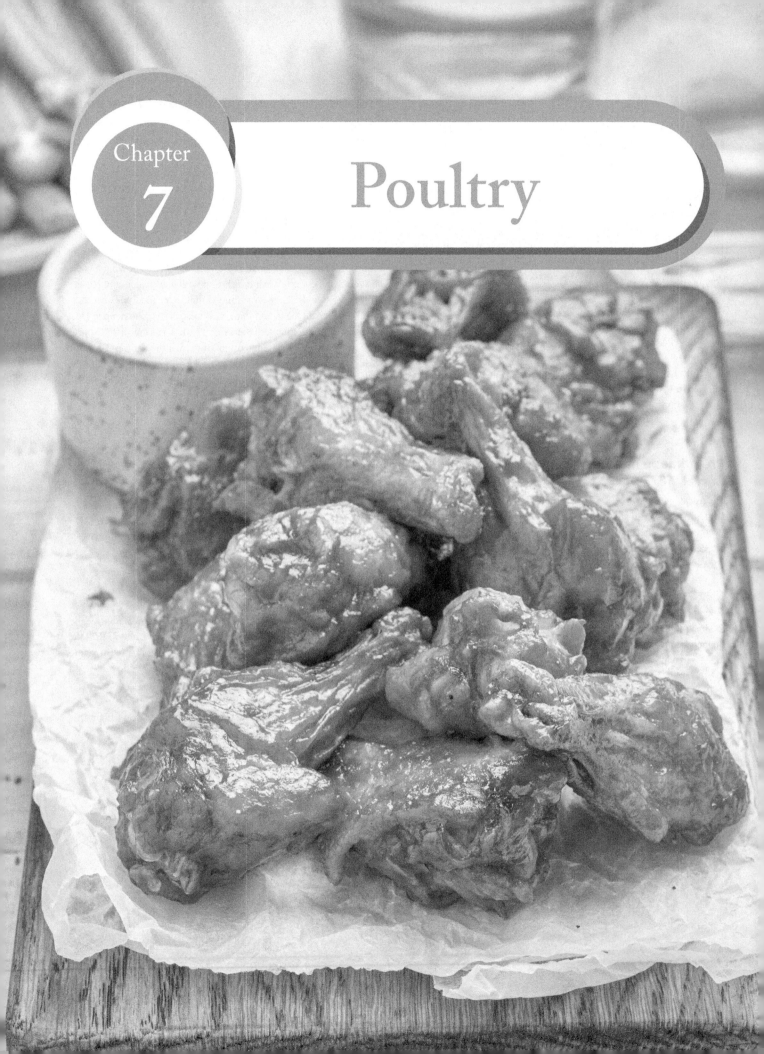

Poultry

Chicken in Mushroom Gravy

Prep time: 10 minutes | Cook time: 10 minutes | Serves 6

6 (5 ounces each) boneless, skinless chicken-breast halves
Salt and pepper to taste
¼ cup dry white wine or low-sodium chicken broth

10¾ ounces can 98% fat-free, reduced-sodium cream of mushroom soup
4 ounces sliced mushrooms

1. Place chicken in the inner pot of the Instant Pot. Season with salt and pepper. 2. Combine wine and soup in a bowl, then pour over the chicken. Top with the mushrooms. 3. Secure the lid and make sure the vent is set to sealing. Set on Manual mode for 10 minutes. 4. When cooking time is up, let the pressure release naturally.

Per Serving:
calories: 204 | fat: 4g | protein: 34g | carbs: 6g | sugars: 1g | fiber: 1g | sodium: 320mg

Thai Yellow Curry with Chicken Meatballs

Prep time: 5 minutes | Cook time: 30 minutes | Serves 4

1 pound 95 percent lean ground chicken
⅓ cup gluten-free panko (Japanese bread crumbs)
1 egg white
1 tablespoon coconut oil
1 yellow onion, cut into 1-inch pieces
One 14 ounces can light coconut milk
3 tablespoons yellow curry paste
¾ cup water
8 ounces carrots, halved lengthwise, then cut crosswise

into 1-inch lengths (or quartered if very large)
8 ounces zucchini, quartered lengthwise, then cut crosswise into 1-inch lengths (or cut into halves, then thirds if large)
8 ounces cremini mushrooms, quartered
Fresh Thai basil leaves for serving (optional)
Fresno or jalapeño chile, thinly sliced, for serving (optional)
1 lime, cut into wedges
Cooked cauliflower "rice" for serving

1. In a medium bowl, combine the chicken, panko, and egg white and mix until evenly combined. Set aside. 2. Select the Sauté setting on the Instant Pot and heat the oil for 2 minutes. Add the onion and sauté for 5 minutes, until it begins to soften and brown. Add ½ cup of the coconut milk and the curry paste and sauté for 1 minute more, until bubbling and fragrant. Press the Cancel button to turn off the pot, then stir in the water. 3. Using a 1½-tablespoon cookie scoop, shape and drop meatballs into the pot in a single layer. 4. Secure the lid and set the Pressure Release to Sealing. Select the Pressure Cook or Manual setting and set the cooking time for 5 minutes at high pressure. (The pot will take about 5 minutes to come up to pressure before the cooking program begins.) 5. When the cooking program ends, perform a quick pressure release by moving the Pressure Release to Venting, or let the pressure release naturally. Open the pot and stir in the carrots, zucchini, mushrooms, and remaining 1¼ cups coconut milk. 6. Press the Cancel button to reset the cooking program, then select the Sauté setting. Bring the curry to a simmer (this will take about 2 minutes), then let cook, uncovered, for about 8 minutes, until the carrots are fork-tender. Press the Cancel button to turn off the pot. 7. Ladle the curry into bowls. Serve piping hot, topped with basil leaves and chile slices, if desired, and the lime wedges and cauliflower "rice" on the side.

Per Serving:
calories: 349 | fat: 15g | protein: 30g | carbs: 34g | sugars: 8g | fiber: 5g | sodium: 529mg

Peppered Chicken with Balsamic Kale

Prep time: 5 minutes | Cook time: 15 minutes | Serves 4

4 (4 ounces) boneless, skinless chicken breasts
¼ teaspoon salt
1 tablespoon freshly ground black pepper
2 tablespoons unsalted butter
1 tablespoon extra-virgin olive

oil
8 cups stemmed and roughly chopped kale, loosely packed (about 2 bunches)
½ cup balsamic vinegar
20 cherry tomatoes, halved

1. Season both sides of the chicken breasts with the salt and pepper. 2. Heat a large skillet over medium heat. When hot, heat the butter and oil. Add the chicken and cook for 8 to 10 minutes, flipping halfway through. When cooked all the way through, remove the chicken from the skillet and set aside. 3. Increase the heat to medium-high. Put the kale in the skillet and cook for 3 minutes, stirring every minute. 4. Add the vinegar and the tomatoes and cook for another 3 to 5 minutes. 5. Divide the kale and tomato mixture into four equal portions, and top each portion with 1 chicken breast.

Per Serving:
calorie: 383 | fat: 12g | protein: 34g | carbs: 38g | sugars: 25g | fiber: 11g | sodium: 256mg

Pizza in a Pot

Prep time: 25 minutes | Cook time: 15 minutes | Serves 8

1 pound bulk lean sweet Italian turkey sausage, browned and drained
28 ounces can crushed tomatoes
15½ ounces can chili beans
2¼ ounces can sliced black olives, drained
1 medium onion, chopped

1 small green bell pepper, chopped
2 garlic cloves, minced
¼ cup grated Parmesan cheese
1 tablespoon quick-cooking tapioca
1 tablespoon dried basil
1 bay leaf

1. Set the Instant Pot to Sauté, then add the turkey sausage. Sauté until browned. 2. Add the remaining ingredients into the Instant Pot and stir. 3. Secure the lid and make sure the vent is set to sealing. Cook on Manual for 15 minutes. 4. When cook time is up, let the pressure release naturally for 5 minutes then perform a quick release. Discard bay leaf.

Per Serving:
calorie: 251 | fat: 10g | protein: 18g | carbs: 23g | sugars: 8g | fiber: 3g | sodium: 936mg

Herbed Buttermilk Chicken

Prep time: 5 minutes | Cook time: 25 minutes | Serves 4

1½ pounds boneless, skinless chicken breasts	pepper
4 cups buttermilk	1 cup thinly sliced yellow onion
Pinch kosher salt	2 tablespoons canola oil
Pinch freshly ground black	¼ cup Italian seasoning
	1 lemon, cut into wedges

1. In a large bowl or sealable plastic bag, combine the chicken, buttermilk, salt, and pepper. Cover or seal and refrigerate for at least 1 hour and up to 24 hours. 2. When the chicken is ready to cook, preheat the oven to 425°F. Line a baking sheet with parchment paper. 3. Remove the chicken from the buttermilk brine and pat it dry. Place the chicken on the prepared baking sheet along with the onion, and drizzle everything with the canola oil. Toss together on the baking sheet (this will save you a bowl) to coat the chicken and onion evenly. 4. Bake for 25 minutes or until the chicken is cooked through. (If the chicken is thick, you can cut the breasts in half lengthwise. It will cut down on your cook time by half or less. Check the chicken after it's cooked for 8 minutes if the breasts are thin.) 5. Allow the chicken to rest and sprinkle it and the onions with the Italian seasoning. 6. Serve with a squeeze of lemon juice.

Per Serving:

calorie: 380 | fat: 14g | protein: 47g | carbs: 16g | sugars: 13g | fiber: 1g | sodium: 543mg

Herbed Cornish Hens

Prep time: 5 minutes | Cook time: 30 minutes | Serves 8

4 Cornish hens, giblets removed (about 1¼ pound each)	½ teaspoon poultry seasoning
2 cups white wine, divided	½ teaspoon paprika
2 garlic cloves, minced	½ teaspoon dried oregano
1 small onion, minced	¼ teaspoon freshly ground black pepper
½ teaspoon celery seeds	

1. Using a long, sharp knife, split each hen lengthwise. You may also buy precut hens. 2. Place the hens, cavity side up, on a rack in a shallow roasting pan. Pour 1½ cups of the wine over the hens; set aside. 3. In a shallow bowl, combine the garlic, onion, celery seeds, poultry seasoning, paprika, oregano, and pepper. Sprinkle half of the combined seasonings over the cavity of each split half. Cover, and refrigerate. Allow the hens to marinate for 2–3 hours. 4. Preheat the oven to 350 degrees. Bake the hens uncovered for 1 hour. Remove from the oven, turn breast side up, and remove the skin. Pour the remaining ½ cup of wine over the top, and sprinkle with the remaining seasonings. 5. Continue to bake for an additional 25–30 minutes, basting every 10 minutes until the hens are done. Transfer to a serving platter, and serve hot.

Per Serving:

calorie: 383 | fat: 10g | protein: 57g | carbs: 3g | sugars: 1g | fiber: 0g | sodium: 197mg

Chicken Provençal

Prep time: 5 minutes | Cook time: 25 minutes | Serves 4

2 tablespoons extra-virgin olive oil	½ cup dry white wine
Two 8 ounces boneless, skinless chicken breasts, halved	1 cup canned diced tomatoes
1 medium garlic clove, minced	¼ cup pitted Kalamata olives
¼ cup minced onion	¼ cup finely chopped fresh basil
¼ cup minced green bell pepper	⅛ teaspoon freshly ground black pepper

1. Heat the oil in a skillet over medium heat. Add the chicken, and brown about 3–5 minutes. 2. Add the remaining ingredients, and cook uncovered over medium heat for 20 minutes or until the chicken is no longer pink. Transfer to a serving platter and season with additional pepper to taste, if desired, before serving.

Per Serving:

calorie: 245 | fat: 11g | protein: 26g | carbs: 5g | sugars: 2g | fiber: 2g | sodium: 121mg

Roast Chicken with Pine Nuts and Fennel

Prep time: 20 minutes | Cook time: 30 minutes | Serves 2

For the herb paste	2 teaspoons extra-virgin olive oil
2 tablespoons fresh rosemary leaves	For the vegetables
1 tablespoon freshly grated lemon zest	1 large fennel bulb, cored and chopped (about 3 cups)
2 garlic cloves, quartered	1 cup sliced fresh mushrooms
½ teaspoon freshly ground black pepper	½ cup sliced carrots
¼ teaspoon salt	¼ cup chopped sweet onion
1 teaspoon extra-virgin olive oil	2 teaspoons extra-virgin olive oil
For the chicken	2 tablespoons pine nuts
4 (6 ounces) skinless chicken drumsticks	2 teaspoons white wine vinegar

To make the vegetables 1. Preheat the oven to 450°F. 2. In a 9-by-13-inch baking dish, toss together the fennel, mushrooms, carrots, onion, and olive oil. Place the dish in the preheated oven. Bake for 10 minutes. 3. Stir in the pine nuts. 4. Top with the browned drumsticks. Return the dish to the oven. Bake for 15 to 20 minutes more, or until the fennel is golden and an instant-read thermometer inserted into the thickest part of a drumstick without touching the bone registers 165°F. 5. Remove the chicken from the pan. 6. Stir the white wine vinegar into the pan. Toss the vegetables to coat, scraping up any browned bits. 7. Serve the chicken with the vegetables and enjoy!

Per Serving:

calorie: 316 | fat: 15g | protein: 35g | carbs: 10g | sugars: 4g | fiber: 3g | sodium: 384mg

Tantalizing Jerked Chicken

Prep time: 10 minutes | Cook time: 20 minutes | Serves 4

4 (5 ounces) boneless, skinless chicken breasts

½ sweet onion, cut into chunks

2 habanero chile peppers, halved lengthwise, seeded

¼ cup freshly squeezed lime juice

2 tablespoons extra-virgin olive oil

1 tablespoon minced garlic

1 tablespoon ground allspice

2 teaspoons chopped fresh thyme

1 teaspoon freshly ground black pepper

½ teaspoon ground nutmeg

¼ teaspoon ground cinnamon

2 cups fresh greens (such as arugula or spinach)

1 cup halved cherry tomatoes

1. Place two chicken breasts in each of two large resealable plastic bags. Set them aside. 2. Place the onion, habaneros, lime juice, olive oil, garlic, allspice, thyme, black pepper, nutmeg, and cinnamon in a food processor and pulse until very well blended. 3. Pour half the marinade into each bag with the chicken breasts. Squeeze out as much air as possible, seal the bags, and place them in the refrigerator for 4 hours. 4. Preheat a barbecue to medium-high heat. 5. Let the chicken sit at room temperature for 15 minutes and then grill, turning at least once, until cooked through, about 15 minutes total. 6. Let the chicken rest for about 5 minutes before serving. Divide the greens and tomatoes among four serving plates, and top with the chicken.

Per Serving:

calorie: 268 | fat: 10g | protein: 33g | carbs: 9g | sugars: 4g | fiber: 2g | sodium: 74mg

Mediterranean-Style Chicken Scaloppine

Prep time: 15 minutes | Cook time: 1 hour | Serves

Six 3-ounce boneless, skinless chicken breast halves

2 cups fat-free Greek yogurt

¼ cup lemon juice

Zest of 1 lemon

¼ cup freshly chopped baby dill

2 teaspoons paprika

2 garlic cloves, minced

¼ teaspoon salt

¼ teaspoon freshly ground black

pepper

1 cup dried whole-wheat bread crumbs

2½ cups frozen artichoke hearts, thawed

2 tablespoons extra-virgin olive oil

¼ cup finely chopped fresh parsley

1 lemon, sliced

1. Wash chicken breasts under cold running water, and pat dry. 2. In a medium bowl, combine the yogurt, lemon juice, lemon zest, baby dill, paprika, garlic, salt, and pepper. Measure out ½ cup of this marinade, and reserve the rest in the refrigerator. 3. Add the chicken to the ½ cup of marinade, and coat each piece well. Refrigerate overnight. 4. Preheat the oven to 350 degrees. 5. Remove the chicken from the marinade, discard the marinade, and roll the chicken in bread crumbs, coating evenly. 6. Arrange the chicken in a single layer in a large baking pan. Add the artichoke hearts in with the chicken. Drizzle the olive oil over the chicken and artichokes. Bake at 350 degrees, uncovered, for 45 minutes, or until the chicken is

no longer pink. 7. Transfer to a serving platter, and serve with the remaining marinade as a sauce and parsley and lemon slices as a garnish.

Per Serving:

calorie: 344 | fat: 11g | protein: 40g | carbs: 23g | sugars: 11g | fiber: 6g | sodium: 502mg

Chicken Satay Stir-Fry

Prep time: 10 minutes | Cook time: 15 minutes | Serves 4

3 tablespoons extra-virgin olive oil

1 pound chicken breasts or thighs, cut into ¾-inch pieces

½ teaspoon sea salt

2 cups broccoli florets

1 red bell pepper, seeded and

chopped

6 scallions, green and white parts, sliced on the bias (cut diagonally into thin slices)

1 head cauliflower, riced

Peanut Sauce

1. In a large skillet over medium-high heat, heat the olive oil until it shimmers. 2. Season the chicken with the salt. Add the chicken to the oil and cook, stirring occasionally, until opaque, about 5 minutes. Remove the chicken from the oil with a slotted spoon and set it aside on a plate. Return the pan to the heat. 3. Add the broccoli, bell pepper, and scallions. Cook, stirring, until the vegetables are crisp-tender, 3 to 5 minutes. Add the cauliflower and cook for 3 minutes more. 4. Return the chicken to the skillet. Stir in the Peanut Sauce. Bring to a simmer and reduce heat to medium-low. Simmer to heat through, about 2 minutes more.

Per Serving:

calorie: 283 | fat: 15g | protein: 26g | carbs: 11g | sugars: 4g | fiber: 4g | sodium: 453mg

Baked Turkey Spaghetti

Prep time: 5 minutes | Cook time: 20 minutes | Serves 4

1 (10-ounce) package zucchini noodles

2 tablespoons extra-virgin olive oil, divided

1 pound 93% lean ground turkey

½ teaspoon dried oregano

2 cups low-sodium spaghetti sauce

½ cup shredded sharp Cheddar cheese

1. Pat zucchini noodles dry between two paper towels. 2. In an oven-safe medium skillet, heat 1 tablespoon of olive oil over medium heat. When hot, add the zucchini noodles. Cook for 3 minutes, stirring halfway through. 3. Add the remaining 1 tablespoon of oil, ground turkey, and oregano. Cook for 7 to 10 minutes, stirring and breaking apart, as needed. 4. Add the spaghetti sauce to the skillet and stir. 5. If your broiler is in the top of your oven, place the oven rack in the center position. Set the broiler on high. 6. Top the mixture with the cheese, and broil for 5 minutes or until the cheese is bubbly.

Per Serving:

calorie: 365 | fat: 23g | protein: 27g | carbs: 13g | sugars: 9g | fiber: 3g | sodium: 214mg

Tangy Barbecue Strawberry-Peach Chicken

Prep time: 20 minutes | Cook time: 40 minutes | Serves 4

For the barbecue sauce	1 teaspoon garlic powder
1 cup frozen peaches	½ teaspoon cayenne pepper
1 cup frozen strawberries	½ teaspoon onion powder
¼ cup tomato purée	½ teaspoon freshly ground black
½ cup white vinegar	pepper
1 tablespoon yellow mustard	1 teaspoon celery seeds
1 teaspoon mustard seeds	For the chicken
1 teaspoon turmeric	4 boneless, skinless chicken
1 teaspoon sweet paprika	thighs

Make The Barbecue Sauce: 1. In a stockpot, combine the peaches, strawberries, tomato purée, vinegar, mustard, mustard seeds, turmeric, paprika, garlic powder, cayenne, onion powder, black pepper, and celery seeds. Cook over low heat for 15 minutes, or until the flavors come together. 2. Remove the sauce from the heat, and let cool for 5 minutes. 3. Transfer the sauce to a blender, and purée until smooth. Make The Chicken 1. Preheat the oven to 350°F. 2. Put the chicken in a medium bowl. Coat well with ½ cup of barbecue sauce. 3. Place the chicken on a rimmed baking sheet. 4. Place the baking sheet on the middle rack of the oven, and bake for about 20 minutes (depending on the thickness of thighs), or until the juices run clear. 5. Brush the chicken with additional sauce, return to the oven, and broil on high for 3 to 5 minutes, or until a light crust forms. 6. Serve.

Per Serving:

calorie: 389 | fat: 8g | protein: 63g | carbs: 13g | sugars: 7g | fiber: 3g | sodium: 175mg

Grain-Free Parmesan Chicken

Prep time: 5 minutes | Cook time: 20 minutes | Serves 4

1½ cups (144 g) almond flour	mm]-thick) boneless, skinless
½ cup (50 g) grated Parmesan	chicken breasts
cheese	½ cup (120 ml) no-added-sugar
1 tablespoon (3 g) Italian	marinara sauce
seasoning	½ cup (56 g) shredded
1 teaspoon garlic powder	mozzarella cheese
½ teaspoon black pepper	2 tablespoons (8 g) minced fresh
2 large eggs	herbs of choice (optional)
4 (6 ounces [170 g], ½-inch [13	

1. Preheat the oven to 375°F (191°C). Line a large, rimmed baking sheet with parchment paper. 2. In a shallow dish, mix together the almond flour, Parmesan cheese, Italian seasoning, garlic powder, and black pepper. In another shallow dish, whisk the eggs. Dip a chicken breast into the egg wash, then gently shake off any extra egg. Dip the chicken breast into the almond flour mixture, coating it well. Place the chicken breast on the prepared baking sheet. Repeat this process with the remaining chicken breasts. 3. Bake the chicken for 15 to 20 minutes, or until the meat is no longer pink in the center. 4. Remove the chicken from the oven and flip each breast. Top each breast with

2 tablespoons (30 ml) of marinara sauce and 2 tablespoons (14 g) of mozzarella cheese. 5. Increase the oven temperature to broil and place the chicken back in the oven. Broil it until the cheese is melted and just starting to brown. Carefully remove the chicken from the oven, top it with the herbs (if using), and let it rest for about 10 minutes before serving.

Per Serving:

calorie: 572 | fat: 32g | protein: 60g | carbs: 13g | sugars: 4g | fiber:5g | sodium: 560mg

Kung Pao Chicken and Zucchini Noodles

Prep time: 15 minutes | Cook time: 15 minutes | Serves 2

For the noodles	Freshly ground black pepper, to
2 medium zucchini, ends	season
trimmed	1 teaspoon extra-virgin olive oil
For the sauce	1 teaspoon sesame oil
1½ tablespoons low-sodium soy	2 garlic cloves, minced
sauce	1 tablespoon chopped fresh
1 tablespoon balsamic vinegar	ginger
1 teaspoon hoisin sauce	½ red bell pepper, cut into
2½ tablespoons water	½-inch pieces
1½ teaspoons red chili paste	½ (8 ounces) can water
2 teaspoons granulated stevia	chestnuts, drained and sliced
2 teaspoons cornstarch	1 celery stalk, cut into ¾-inch
For the chicken	dice
6 ounces boneless skinless	2 tablespoons crushed dry-
chicken breast, cut into ½-inch	roasted peanuts, divided
pieces	2 tablespoons scallions, divided
Salt, to season	

To make the noodles: 1. With a spiralizer or julienne peeler, cut the zucchini lengthwise into spaghetti-like strips. Set aside. To make the sauce: 2. In a small bowl, whisk together the soy sauce, balsamic vinegar, hoisin sauce, water, red chili paste, stevia, and cornstarch. Set aside. To make the chicken: 3. Season the chicken with salt and pepper. 4. In a large, deep nonstick pan or wok set over medium-high heat, heat the olive oil. 5. Add the chicken. Cook for 4 to 5 minutes, stirring, or until browned and cooked through. Transfer the chicken to a plate. Set aside. 6. Return the pan to the stove. Reduce the heat to medium. 7. Add the sesame oil, garlic, and ginger. Cook for about 30 seconds, or until fragrant. 8. Add the red bell pepper, water chestnuts, and celery. 9. Stir in the sauce. Bring to a boil. Reduce the heat to low. Simmer for 1 to 2 minutes, until thick and bubbling. 10. Stir in the zucchini noodles. Cook for about 2 minutes, tossing, until just tender and mixed with the sauce. 11. Add the chicken and any accumulated juices. Stir to combine. Cook for about 2 minutes, or until heated through. 12. Divide the mixture between 2 bowls. Top each serving with 1 tablespoon of peanuts and 1 tablespoon of scallions. Enjoy!

Per Serving:

calorie: 322 | fat: 13g | protein: 29g | carbs: 28g | sugars: 12g | fiber: 8g | sodium: 553mg

Wine-Poached Chicken with Herbs and Vegetables

Prep time: 5 minutes | Cook time: 1 hour | Serves 8

4 quarts low-sodium chicken broth

2 cups dry white wine

4 large bay leaves

4 sprigs fresh thyme

¼ teaspoon freshly ground black pepper

4-pound chicken, giblets removed, washed and patted dry

½ pound carrots, peeled and julienned

½ pound turnips, peeled and julienned

½ pound parsnips, peeled and julienned

4 small leeks, washed and trimmed

1. In a large stockpot, combine the broth, wine, bay leaves, thyme, dash salt (optional), and pepper. Let simmer over medium heat while you prepare the chicken. 2. Stuff the cavity with ⅓ each of the carrots, turnips, and parsnips; then truss. Add the stuffed chicken to the stockpot, and poach, covered, over low heat for 30 minutes. 3. Add the remaining vegetables with the leeks, and continue to simmer for 25 to 30 minutes, or until juices run clear when the chicken is pierced with a fork. 4. Remove the chicken and vegetables to a serving platter. Carve the chicken, remove the skin, and surround the sliced meat with poached vegetables to serve.

Per Serving:

calorie: 476 | fat: 13g | protein: 57g | carbs: 24g | sugars: 6g | fiber: 4g | sodium: 387mg

Turkey with Almond Duxelles

Prep time: 5 minutes | Cook time:35 minutes | Serves 8

2 tablespoons extra-virgin olive oil

¼ cup dry sherry

¾ pound diced fresh mushrooms

4 medium shallots, finely minced

2 garlic cloves, minced

1 teaspoon minced fresh thyme

Dash cayenne pepper

½ cup ground almonds

¼ teaspoon freshly ground black pepper

2 pounds turkey breast cutlets, pounded to ¼-inch thickness and cut into 8 portions

Paprika, for garnish

½ cup low-fat plain Greek yogurt

1. Preheat the oven to 350 degrees. 2. In a large skillet over medium heat, heat the olive oil and sherry. Add the mushrooms, shallots, garlic, thyme, and cayenne pepper. Cook, stirring often, until the mushrooms turn dark. Add the ground almonds, dash salt (optional), and pepper, and sauté for 2–3 minutes. 3. Divide the mixture into 8 portions, and place each portion in the center of each turkey portion. Fold the edges over, roll up, and place in a baking dish, seam side down, 1 inch apart. 4. Place about 1 tablespoon Greek yogurt over each turkey roll, and sprinkle with paprika. Bake at 350 degrees for 25–30 minutes or until the turkey is tender. Transfer to a serving platter, and serve.

Per Serving:

calorie: 216 | fat: 9g | protein: 30g | carbs: 5g | sugars: 2g | fiber: 1g | sodium: 97mg

Juicy Turkey Burgers

Prep time: 10 minutes | Cook time: 20 minutes | Serves 4

1½ pounds lean ground turkey

½ cup bread crumbs

½ sweet onion, chopped

1 carrot, peeled, grated

1 teaspoon minced garlic

1 teaspoon chopped fresh thyme

Sea salt

Freshly ground black pepper

Nonstick cooking spray

1. In a large bowl, mix together the turkey, bread crumbs, onion, carrot, garlic, and thyme until very well mixed. 2. Season the mixture lightly with salt and pepper. 3. Shape the turkey mixture into 4 equal patties. 4. Place a large skillet over medium-high heat and coat it lightly with cooking spray. 5. Cook the turkey patties until golden and completely cooked through, about 10 minutes per side. 6. Serve the burgers plain or with your favorite toppings on a whole-wheat bun.

Per Serving:

calorie: 330 | fat: 15g | protein: 34g | carbs: 15g | sugars: 4g | fiber: 1g | sodium: 230mg

Asian Mushroom-Chicken Soup

Prep time: 30 minutes | Cook time: 15 minutes | Serves 6

1½ cups water

1 package (1 ounce) dried portabella or shiitake mushrooms

1 tablespoon canola oil

¼ cup thinly sliced green onions (4 medium)

2 tablespoons gingerroot, peeled, minced

3 cloves garlic, minced

1 jalapeño chile, seeded, minced

1 cup fresh snow pea pods, sliced diagonally

3 cups reduced-sodium chicken broth

1 can (8 ounces) sliced bamboo shoots, drained

2 tablespoons low-sodium soy sauce

½ teaspoon sriracha sauce

1 cup shredded cooked chicken breast

1 cup cooked brown rice

4 teaspoons lime juice

½ cup thinly sliced fresh basil leaves

1. In medium microwavable bowl, heat water uncovered on High 30 seconds or until hot. Add mushrooms; let stand 5 minutes or until tender. Drain mushrooms (reserve liquid). Slice any mushrooms that are large. Set aside. 2. In 4-quart saucepan, heat oil over medium heat. Add 2 tablespoons of the green onions, the gingerroot, garlic and chile to oil. Cook about 3 minutes, stirring occasionally, until vegetables are tender. Add snow pea pods; cook 2 minutes, stirring occasionally. Stir in mushrooms, reserved mushroom liquid and the remaining ingredients, except lime juice and basil. Heat to boiling; reduce heat. Cover and simmer 10 minutes or until hot. Stir in lime juice. 3. Divide soup evenly among 6 bowls. Top servings with basil and remaining green onions.

Per Serving:

calories: 150 | fat: 4g | protein: 11g | carbs: 16g | sugars: 3g | fiber: 3g | sodium: 490mg

Saffron-Spiced Chicken Breasts

Prep time: 10 minutes | Cook time: 10 minutes | Serves 4

Pinch saffron (3 or 4 threads)
½ cup plain nonfat yogurt
2 tablespoons water
½ onion, chopped
3 garlic cloves, minced
2 tablespoons chopped fresh cilantro
Juice of ½ lemon
½ teaspoon salt
1 pound boneless, skinless chicken breasts, cut into 2-inch strips
1 tablespoon extra-virgin olive oil

1. In a blender jar, combine the saffron, yogurt, water, onion, garlic, cilantro, lemon juice, and salt. Pulse to blend. 2. In a large mixing bowl, combine the chicken and the yogurt sauce, and stir to coat. Cover and refrigerate for at least 1 hour or up to overnight. 3. In a large skillet, heat the oil over medium heat. Add the chicken pieces, shaking off any excess marinade. Discard the marinade. Cook the chicken pieces on each side for 5 minutes, flipping once, until cooked through and golden brown.

Per Serving:

calories: 155 | fat: 5g | protein: 26g | carbs: 3g | sugars: 1g | fiber: 0g | sodium: 501mg

Speedy Chicken Cacciatore

Prep time: 5 minutes | Cook time: 30 minutes | Serves 6

2 pounds boneless, skinless chicken thighs
1½ teaspoons fine sea salt
½ teaspoon freshly ground black pepper
2 tablespoons extra-virgin olive oil
3 garlic cloves, chopped
2 large red bell peppers, seeded and cut into ¼ by 2-inch strips
2 large yellow onions, sliced
½ cup dry red wine
1½ teaspoons Italian seasoning
½ teaspoon red pepper flakes (optional)
One 14½ ounces can diced tomatoes and their liquid
2 tablespoons tomato paste
Cooked brown rice or whole-grain pasta for serving

1. Season the chicken thighs on both sides with 1 teaspoon of the salt and the black pepper. 2. Select the Sauté setting on the Instant Pot and heat the oil and garlic for 2 minutes, until the garlic is bubbling but not browned. Add the bell peppers, onions, and remaining ½ teaspoon salt and sauté for 3 minutes, until the onions begin to soften. Stir in the wine, Italian seasoning, and pepper flakes (if using). Using tongs, add the chicken to the pot, turning each piece to coat it in the wine and spices and nestling them in a single layer in the liquid. Pour the tomatoes and their liquid on top of the chicken and dollop the tomato paste on top. Do not stir them in. 3. Secure the lid and set the Pressure Release to Sealing. Press the Cancel button to reset the cooking program, then select the Poultry, Pressure Cook, or Manual setting and set the cooking time for 12 minutes at high pressure. (The pot will take about 15 minutes to come up to pressure before the cooking program begins.) 4. When the cooking program ends, perform a quick pressure release by moving the Pressure Release to Venting, or let the pressure release naturally. Open the pot and, using tongs, transfer the chicken and vegetables to a serving dish. 5. Spoon some of the sauce over the chicken and serve hot, with the rice on the side.

Per Serving:

calories: 297 | fat: 11g | protein: 32g | carbs: 16g | sugars: 3g | fiber: 3g | sodium: 772mg

Coconut Chicken Curry

Prep time: 15 minutes | Cook time: 35 minutes | Serves 4

2 teaspoons extra-virgin olive oil
3 (5 ounces) boneless, skinless chicken breasts, cut into 1-inch chunks
1 tablespoon grated fresh ginger
1 tablespoon minced garlic
2 tablespoons curry powder
2 cups low-sodium chicken broth
1 cup canned coconut milk
1 carrot, peeled and diced
1 sweet potato, diced
2 tablespoons chopped fresh cilantro

1. Place a large saucepan over medium-high heat and add the oil. 2. Sauté the chicken until lightly browned and almost cooked through, about 10 minutes. 3. Add the ginger, garlic, and curry powder, and sauté until fragrant, about 3 minutes. 4. Stir in the chicken broth, coconut milk, carrot, and sweet potato and bring the mixture to a boil. 5. Reduce the heat to low and simmer, stirring occasionally, until the vegetables and chicken are tender, about 20 minutes. 6. Stir in the cilantro and serve.

Per Serving:

calorie: 327 | fat: 18g | protein: 29g | carbs: 14g | sugars: 2g | fiber: 3g | sodium: 122mg

Turkey Cabbage Soup

Prep time: 15 minutes | Cook time: 30 minutes | Serves 4

1 tablespoon extra-virgin olive oil
1 sweet onion, chopped
2 celery stalks, chopped
2 teaspoons minced fresh garlic
4 cups finely shredded green cabbage
1 sweet potato, peeled, diced
8 cups chicken or turkey broth
2 bay leaves
1 cup chopped cooked turkey
2 teaspoons chopped fresh thyme
Sea salt
Freshly ground black pepper

1. Place a large saucepan over medium-high heat and add the olive oil. 2. Sauté the onion, celery, and garlic until softened and translucent, about 3 minutes. 3. Add the cabbage and sweet potato and sauté for 3 minutes. 4. Stir in the chicken broth and bay leaves and bring the soup to a boil. 5. Reduce the heat to low and simmer until the vegetables are tender, about 20 minutes. 6. Add the turkey and thyme and simmer until the turkey is heated through, about 4 minutes. 7. Remove the bay leaves and season the soup with salt and pepper.

Per Serving:

calorie: 444 | fat: 14g | protein: 38g | carbs: 46g | sugars: 17g | fiber: 7g | sodium: 427mg

Coconut Lime Chicken

Prep time: 5 minutes | Cook time: 15 minutes | Serves 4

1 tablespoon coconut oil
4 (4 ounces) boneless, skinless chicken breasts
½ teaspoon salt
1 red bell pepper, cut into ¼-inch-thick slices
16 asparagus spears, bottom ends trimmed

1 cup unsweetened coconut milk
2 tablespoons freshly squeezed lime juice
½ teaspoon garlic powder
¼ teaspoon red pepper flakes
¼ cup chopped fresh cilantro

1. In a large skillet, heat the oil over medium-low heat. When hot, add the chicken. 2. Season the chicken with the salt. Cook for 5 minutes, then flip. 3. Push the chicken to the side of the skillet, and add the bell pepper and asparagus. Cook, covered, for 5 minutes. 4. Meanwhile, in a small bowl, whisk together the coconut milk, lime juice, garlic powder, and red pepper flakes. 5. Add the coconut milk mixture to the skillet, and boil over high heat for 2 to 3 minutes. 6. Top with the cilantro.

Per Serving:

calorie: 319 | fat: 21g | protein: 28g | carbs: 7g | sugars: 4g | fiber: 2g | sodium: 353mg

Herb-Roasted Turkey and Vegetables

Prep time: 20 minutes | Cook time: 2 hours | Serves 6

2 teaspoons minced garlic
1 tablespoon chopped fresh parsley
1 teaspoon chopped fresh thyme
1 teaspoon chopped fresh rosemary
2 pounds boneless, skinless whole turkey breast
3 teaspoons extra-virgin olive oil, divided

Sea salt
Freshly ground black pepper
2 sweet potatoes, peeled and cut into 2-inch chunks
2 carrots, peeled and cut into 2-inch chunks
2 parsnips, peeled and cut into 2-inch chunks
1 sweet onion, peeled and cut into eighths

1. Preheat the oven to 350°F. 2. Line a large roasting pan with aluminum foil and set it aside. 3. In a small bowl, mix together the garlic, parsley, thyme, and rosemary. 4. Place the turkey breast in the roasting pan and rub it all over with 1 teaspoon of olive oil. 5. Rub the garlic-herb mixture all over the turkey and season lightly with salt and pepper. 6. Place the turkey in the oven and roast for 30 minutes. 7. While the turkey is roasting, toss the sweet potatoes, carrots, parsnips, onion, and the remaining 2 teaspoons of olive oil in a large bowl. 8. Remove the turkey from the oven and arrange the vegetables around it. 9. Roast until the turkey is cooked through (170°F internal temperature) and the vegetables are lightly caramelized, about 1 ½ hours.

Per Serving:

calorie: 267 | fat: 4g | protein: 35g | carbs: 25g | sugars: 8g | fiber: 5g | sodium: 379mg

Chicken with Lemon Caper Pan Sauce

Prep time: 10 minutes | Cook time: 15 minutes | Serves 4

3 tablespoons extra-virgin olive oil
4 chicken breast halves or thighs, pounded slightly to even thickness
½ teaspoon sea salt
⅛ teaspoon freshly ground black

pepper
¼ cup freshly squeezed lemon juice
¼ cup dry white wine
2 tablespoons capers, rinsed
2 tablespoons salted butter, very cold, cut into pieces

1. In a large skillet over medium-high heat, heat the olive oil until it shimmers. 2. Season the chicken with the salt and pepper. Add it to the hot oil and cook until opaque with an internal temperature of 165°F, about 5 minutes per side. Transfer the chicken to a plate and tent loosely with foil to keep warm. Keep the pan on the heat. 3. Add the lemon juice and wine to the pan, using the side of a spoon to scrape any browned bits from the bottom of the pan. Add the capers. Simmer until the liquid is reduced by half, about 3 minutes. Reduce the heat to low. 4. Whisk in the butter, one piece at a time, until incorporated. 5. Return the chicken to the pan, turning once to coat with the sauce. Serve with additional sauce spooned over the top.

Per Serving:

calorie: 367 | fat: 23g | protein: 37g | carbs: 2g | sugars: 1g | fiber: 0g | sodium: 591mg

Jerk Chicken Casserole

Prep time: 15 minutes | Cook time: 45 minutes | Serves 6

1¼ teaspoons salt
½ teaspoon pumpkin pie spice
¾ teaspoon ground allspice
¾ teaspoon dried thyme leaves
¼ teaspoon ground red pepper (cayenne)
6 boneless skinless chicken thighs
1 tablespoon vegetable oil

1 can (15 ounces) black beans, drained, rinsed
1 large sweet potato (1 lb), peeled, cubed (3 cups)
¼ cup honey
¼ cup lime juice
2 teaspoons cornstarch
2 tablespoons sliced green onions (2 medium)

1. Heat oven to 375°F. Spray 8-inch square (2-quart) glass baking dish with cooking spray. In small bowl, mix salt, pumpkin pie spice, allspice, thyme and red pepper. Rub mixture on all sides of chicken. In 12-inch nonstick skillet, heat oil over medium-high heat. Cook chicken in oil 2 to 3 minutes per side, until brown. 2. In baking dish, layer beans and sweet potato. Top with browned chicken. In small bowl, mix honey, lime juice and cornstarch; add to skillet. Heat to boiling, stirring constantly. Pour over chicken in baking dish. 3. Bake 35 to 45 minutes or until juice of chicken is clear when center of thickest part is cut (165°F) and sweet potatoes are fork-tender. Sprinkle with green onions.

Per Serving:

calories: 330 | fat: 8g | protein: 21g | carbs: 43g | sugars: 16g | fiber: 9g | sodium: 550mg

Turkey Chili

Prep time: 15 minutes | Cook time: 30 minutes | Serves 6

1 tablespoon extra-virgin olive oil

1 pound lean ground turkey

1 large onion, diced

3 garlic cloves, minced

1 red bell pepper, seeded and diced

1 cup chopped celery

2 tablespoons chili powder

1 tablespoon ground cumin

1 (28 ounces) can reduced-salt diced tomatoes

1 (15 ounces) can low-sodium kidney beans, drained and rinsed

2 cups low-sodium chicken broth

½ teaspoon salt

Shredded cheddar cheese, for serving (optional)

1. In a large pot, heat the oil over medium heat. Add the turkey, onion, and garlic, and cook, stirring regularly, until the turkey is cooked through. 2. Add the bell pepper, celery, chili powder, and cumin. Stir well and continue to cook for 1 minute. 3. Add the tomatoes with their liquid, kidney beans, and chicken broth. Bring to a boil, reduce the heat to low, and simmer for 20 minutes. 4. Season with the salt and serve topped with cheese (if using).

Per Serving:

calorie: 276 | fat: 10g | protein: 23g | carbs: 27g | sugars: 7g | fiber: 8g | sodium: 556mg

Orange Chicken Thighs with Bell Peppers

Prep time: 15 to 20 minutes | Cook time: 7 minutes | Serves 4 to 6

6 boneless skinless chicken thighs, cut into bite-sized pieces

2 packets crystallized True Orange flavoring

½ teaspoon True Orange Orange Ginger seasoning

½ teaspoon coconut aminos

¼ teaspoon Worcestershire sauce

Olive oil or cooking spray

2 cups bell pepper strips, any color combination (I used red)

1 onion, chopped

1 tablespoon green onion, chopped fine

3 cloves garlic, minced or chopped

½ teaspoon pink salt

½ teaspoon black pepper

1 teaspoon garlic powder

1 teaspoon ground ginger

¼ to ½ teaspoon red pepper flakes

2 tablespoons tomato paste

½ cup chicken bone broth or water

1 tablespoon brown sugar substitute (I use Sukrin Gold)

½ cup Seville orange spread (I use Crofter's brand)

1. Combine the chicken with the 2 packets of crystallized orange flavor, the orange ginger seasoning, the coconut aminos, and the Worcestershire sauce. Set aside. 2. Turn the Instant Pot to Sauté and add a touch of olive oil or cooking spray to the inner pot. Add in the orange ginger marinated chicken thighs. 3. Sauté until lightly browned. Add in the peppers, onion, green onion, garlic, and seasonings. Mix well. 4. Add the remaining ingredients; mix to combine. 5. Lock the lid, set the vent to sealing, set to 7 minutes. 6. Let the pressure release naturally for 2 minutes, then manually release the rest when cook time is up.

Per Serving:

calories: 120| fat: 2g | protein: 12g | carbs: 8g | sugars: 10g | fiber: 1.6g | sodium: 315mg

One-Pan Chicken Dinner

Prep time: 5 minutes | Cook time: 35 minutes | Serves 4

3 tablespoons extra-virgin olive oil

1 tablespoon red wine vinegar or apple cider vinegar

¼ teaspoon garlic powder

3 tablespoons Italian seasoning

4 (4 ounces) boneless, skinless chicken breasts

2 cups cubed sweet potatoes

20 Brussels sprouts, halved lengthwise

1. Preheat the oven to 400ºF. 2. In a large bowl, whisk together the oil, vinegar, garlic powder, and Italian seasoning. 3. Add the chicken, sweet potatoes, and Brussels sprouts, and coat thoroughly with the marinade. 4. Remove the ingredients from the marinade and arrange them on a baking sheet in a single layer. Roast for 15 minutes. 5. Remove the baking sheet from the oven, flip the chicken over, and bake for another 15 to 20 minutes.

Per Serving:

calorie: 346 | fat: 13g | protein: 30g | carbs: 26g | sugars: 6g | fiber: 7g | sodium: 575mg

Chicken Enchilada Spaghetti Squash

Prep time: 5 minutes | Cook time: 40 minutes | Serves 4

1 (3 pounds) spaghetti squash, halved lengthwise and seeded

1½ teaspoons ground cumin, divided

Avocado oil cooking spray

4 (4 ounces) boneless, skinless

chicken breasts

1 large zucchini, diced

¾ cup canned red enchilada sauce

¾ cup shredded Cheddar or mozzarella cheese

1. Preheat the oven to 400ºF. 2. Season both halves of the squash with ½ teaspoon of cumin, and place them cut-side down on a baking sheet. Bake for 25 to 30 minutes. 3. Meanwhile, heat a large skillet over medium-low heat. When hot, spray the cooking surface with cooking spray and add the chicken breasts, zucchini, and 1 teaspoon of cumin. Cook the chicken for 4 to 5 minutes per side. Stir the zucchini when you flip the chicken. 4. Transfer the zucchini to a medium bowl and set aside. Remove the chicken from the skillet, and let it rest for 10 minutes or until it's cool enough to handle. Shred or dice the cooked chicken. 5. Place the chicken and zucchini in a large bowl, and add the enchilada sauce. 6. Remove the squash from the oven, flip it over, and comb through it with a fork to make thin strands. 7. Scoop the chicken mixture on top of the squash halves and top with the cheese. Return the squash to the oven and broil for 2 to 5 minutes, or until the cheese is bubbly.

Per Serving:

calorie: 391 | fat: 12g | protein: 35g | carbs: 40g | sugars: 3g | fiber: 7g | sodium: 368mg

Spicy Chicken Drumsticks

Prep time: 5 minutes | Cook time: 50 minutes | Serves 2

¼ cup plain low-fat yogurt
2 tablespoons hot pepper sauce
Crushed red pepper flakes, to taste

4 chicken drumsticks, skinned (about 1 pound)
¼ cup dried bread crumbs

1. In a shallow dish, combine the yogurt, hot pepper sauce, and crushed red pepper flakes, mixing well. Add the drumsticks, turning to coat. Cover, and marinate in the refrigerator for 2 to 4 hours. 2. Preheat the oven to 350 degrees. 3. Remove the drumsticks from the marinade, dredge in the bread crumbs, and place in a baking dish. Bake at 350 degrees for 40 to 50 minutes. Transfer to a serving platter, and serve.

Per Serving:

calorie: 337 | fat: 10g | protein: 48g | carbs: 12g | sugars: 3g | fiber: 1g | sodium: 501mg

Chicken Reuben Bake

Prep time: 10 minutes | Cook time: 6 to 8 hours | Serves 6

4 boneless, skinless chicken-breast halves
¼ cup water
1-pound bag sauerkraut, drained and rinsed
4 to 5 (1 ounce each) slices

Swiss cheese
¾ cup fat-free Thousand Island salad dressing
2 tablespoons chopped fresh parsley

1. Place chicken and water in inner pot of the Instant Pot along with ¼ cup water. Layer sauerkraut over chicken. Add cheese. Top with salad dressing. Sprinkle with parsley. 2. Secure the lid and cook on the Slow Cook setting on low 6 to 8 hours.

Per Serving:

calories: 217 | fat: 5g | protein: 28g | carbs: 13g | sugars: 6g | fiber: 2g | sodium: 693mg

Garlic Dill Wings

Prep time: 5 minutes | Cook time: 25 minutes | Serves 4

2 pounds (907 g) bone-in chicken wings, separated at joints
½ teaspoon salt

½ teaspoon ground black pepper
½ teaspoon onion powder
½ teaspoon garlic powder
1 teaspoon dried dill

1. In a large bowl, toss wings with salt, pepper, onion powder, garlic powder, and dill until evenly coated. Place wings into ungreased air fryer basket in a single layer, working in batches if needed. 2. Adjust the temperature to 400°F (204°C) and air fry for 25 minutes, shaking the basket every 7 minutes during cooking. Wings should have an internal temperature of at least 165°F (74°C) and be golden brown when done. Serve warm.

Per Serving:

calorie: 340 | fat: 24g | protein: 27g | carbs: 2g | sugars: 0g | fiber: 0g | sodium: 642mg

Chicken Casablanca

Prep time: 20 minutes | Cook time: 12 minutes | Serves 8

2 large onions, sliced
1 teaspoon ground ginger
3 garlic cloves, minced
2 tablespoons canola oil, divided
3 pounds skinless chicken pieces
3 large carrots, diced
2 large potatoes, unpeeled, diced
½ teaspoon ground cumin

½ teaspoon salt
½ teaspoon pepper
¼ teaspoon cinnamon
2 tablespoons raisins
14½-ounce can chopped tomatoes
3 small zucchini, sliced
15 ounces can garbanzo beans, drained
2 tablespoons chopped parsley

1. Using the Sauté function of the Instant Pot, cook the onions, ginger, and garlic in 1 tablespoon of the oil for 5 minutes, stirring constantly. Remove onions, ginger, and garlic from pot and set aside. 2. Brown the chicken pieces with the remaining oil, then add the cooked onions, ginger and garlic back in as well as all of the remaining ingredients, except the parsley. 3. Secure the lid and make sure vent is in the sealing position. Cook on Manual mode for 12 minutes. 4. When cook time is up, let the pressure release naturally for 5 minutes and then release the rest of the pressure manually.

Per Serving:

calories: 395 | fat: 10g | protein: 36g | carbs: 40g | sugars: 10g | fiber: 8g | sodium: 390mg

Creamy Garlic Chicken with Broccoli

Prep time: 5 minutes | Cook time: 15 minutes | Serves 4

½ cup uncooked brown rice or quinoa
4 (4 ounces) boneless, skinless chicken breasts
¼ teaspoon salt
¼ teaspoon freshly ground black pepper

1 teaspoon garlic powder, divided
Avocado oil cooking spray
3 cups fresh or frozen broccoli florets
1 cup half-and-half

1. Cook the rice according to the package instructions. 2. Meanwhile, season both sides of the chicken breasts with the salt, pepper, and ½ teaspoon of garlic powder. 3. Heat a large skillet over medium-low heat. When hot, coat the cooking surface with cooking spray and add the chicken and broccoli in a single layer. 4. Cook for 4 minutes, then flip the chicken breasts over and cover. Cook for 5 minutes more. 5. Add the half-and-half and remaining ½ teaspoon of garlic powder to the skillet and stir. Increase the heat to high and simmer for 2 minutes. 6. Divide the rice into four equal portions. Top each portion with 1 chicken breast and one-quarter of the broccoli and cream sauce.

Per Serving:

calorie: 274 | fat: 5g | protein: 31g | carbs: 27g | sugars: 3g | fiber: 1g | sodium: 271mg

Turkey Bolognese with Chickpea Pasta

Prep time: 5 minutes | Cook time: 25 minutes | Serves 4

1 onion, coarsely chopped	½ cup milk
1 large carrot, coarsely chopped	¾ cup red or white wine
2 celery stalks, coarsely chopped	1 (28 ounces) can diced tomatoes
1 tablespoon extra-virgin olive oil	10 ounces cooked chickpea pasta
1 pound ground turkey	

1. Place the onion, carrots, and celery in a food processor and pulse until finely chopped. 2. Heat the extra-virgin olive oil in a Dutch oven or medium skillet over medium-high heat. Sauté the chopped vegetables for 3 to 5 minutes, or until softened. Add the ground turkey, breaking the poultry into smaller pieces, and cook for 5 minutes. 3. Add the milk and wine and cook until the liquid is nearly evaporated (turn up the heat to high to quicken the process). 4. Add the tomatoes and bring the sauce to a simmer. Reduce the heat to low and simmer for 10 to 15 minutes. 5. Meanwhile, cook the pasta according to the package instructions and set aside. 6. Serve the sauce with the cooked chickpea pasta. 7. Store any leftovers in an airtight container in the refrigerator for 3 to 4 days.

Per Serving:
calorie: 419 | fat: 15g | protein: 31g | carbs: 34g | sugars: 8g | fiber: 11g | sodium: 150mg

BBQ Turkey Meat Loaf

Prep time: 5 minutes | Cook time: 40 minutes | Serves 6

1 pound 93 percent lean ground turkey	½ small yellow onion, finely diced
⅓ cup low-sugar or unsweetened barbecue sauce, plus 2 tablespoons	1 garlic clove, minced
	½ teaspoon fine sea salt
⅓ cup gluten-free panko (Japanese bread crumbs)	½ teaspoon freshly ground black pepper
1 large egg	Cooked cauliflower "rice" or brown rice for serving

1. Pour 1 cup water into the Instant Pot. Lightly grease a 7 by 3-inch round cake pan or a 5½ by 3-inch loaf pan with olive oil or coat with nonstick cooking spray. 2. In a medium bowl, combine the turkey, ⅓ cup barbecue sauce, panko, egg, onion, garlic, salt, and pepper and mix well with your hands until all of the ingredients are evenly distributed. Transfer the mixture to the prepared pan, pressing it into an even layer. Cover the pan tightly with aluminum foil. Place the pan on a long-handled silicone steam rack, then, holding the handles of the steam rack, lower it into the pot. (If you don't have the long-handled rack, use the wire metal steam rack and a homemade sling) 3. Secure the lid and set the Pressure Release to Sealing. Select the Pressure Cook or Manual setting and set the cooking time for 25 minutes at high pressure if using a 7-inch round cake pan, or for 35 minutes at high pressure if using a 5½ by 3-inch loaf pan. (The pot will take about 10 minutes to come up to pressure before the cooking program begins.) 4. Preheat a toaster oven or position an oven rack 4 to 6 inches below the heat source and preheat the broiler. 5. When the cooking program ends, perform a quick pressure release by moving the Pressure Release to Venting. Open the pot and, wearing heat-resistant mitts, grasp the handles of the steam rack and lift it out of the pot. Uncover the pan, taking care not to get burned by the steam or to drip condensation onto the meat loaf. Brush the remaining 2 tablespoons barbecue sauce on top of the meat loaf. 6. Broil the meat loaf for a few minutes, just until the glaze becomes bubbly and browned. Cut the meat loaf into slices and serve hot, with the cauliflower "rice" alongside.

Per Serving:
calories: 236 | fat: 11g | protein: 25g | carbs: 10g | sugars: 2g | fiber: 3g | sodium: 800mg

Grilled Lemon Mustard Chicken

Prep time: 5 minutes | Cook time: 15 minutes | Serves 6

Juice of 6 medium lemons	4 garlic cloves, minced
½ cup mustard seeds	2 tablespoons extra-virgin olive oil
1 tablespoon minced fresh tarragon	Three 8 ounces boneless, skinless chicken breasts, halved
2 tablespoons freshly ground black pepper	

1. In a small mixing bowl, combine the lemon juice, mustard seeds, tarragon, pepper, garlic, and oil; mix well. 2. Place the chicken in a baking dish, and pour the marinade on top. Cover, and refrigerate overnight. 3. Grill the chicken over medium heat for 10 to 15 minutes, basting with the marinade. Serve hot.

Per Serving:
calorie: 239 | fat: 11g | protein: 28g | carbs: 8g | sugars: 2g | fiber: 2g | sodium: 54mg

Cast Iron Hot Chicken

Prep time: 10 minutes | Cook time: 40 minutes | Serves 4

2 boneless, skinless chicken breasts	1 medium yellow onion, chopped
Juice of 2 limes	1½ teaspoons cayenne pepper
2 garlic cloves, minced	1 teaspoon smoked paprika

1. Preheat the oven to 375°F. 2. In a shallow bowl, massage the chicken all over with the lime juice, garlic, onion, cayenne, and paprika. 3. In a cast iron skillet, place the chicken in one even layer. 4. Transfer the skillet to the oven and cook for 35 to 40 minutes, or until cooked through. 5. Remove the chicken from the oven, and let rest for 5 minutes. 6. Divide each breast into two portions. Serve.

Per Serving:
calorie: 286 | fat: 4g | protein: 31g | carbs: 6g | sugars: 2g | fiber: 1g | sodium: 64mg

Peach-Glazed Chicken over Dandelion Greens

Prep time: 10 minutes | Cook time: 30 minutes | Serves 4

4 boneless, skinless chicken thighs	Pinch ground cloves
Juice of 1 lime	Pinch ground nutmeg
½ cup white vinegar	⅛ teaspoon vanilla extract
2 garlic cloves, smashed	½ cup store-bought low-sodium chicken broth
1 cup frozen peaches	1 bunch dandelion greens, cut into ribbons
½ cup water	
Pinch ground cinnamon	1 medium onion, thinly sliced

1. Set oven to broil. In a bowl, combine the chicken, lime juice, vinegar, and garlic, coating the chicken thoroughly. 2. Meanwhile, to make the peach glaze, in a small pot, combine the peaches, water, cinnamon, cloves, nutmeg, and vanilla. Cook over medium heat, stirring often, for 10 minutes, or until the peaches have softened. 3. In a large cast iron skillet, bring the broth to a simmer over medium heat. 4. Add the greens, and sauté for 5 minutes, or until the greens are wilted. 5. Add the onion and cook, stirring occasionally, for 3 minutes, or until slightly reduced. 6. Add the chicken and cover with the peach glaze. 7. Transfer the pan to the oven, and broil for 10 to 12 minutes, or until the chicken is golden brown.

Per Serving:

calorie: 317 | fat: 9g | protein: 42g | carbs: 16g | sugars: 5g | fiber: 5g | sodium: 281mg

Mexican Turkey Tenderloin

Prep time: 5 minutes | Cook time: 8 minutes | Serves 6

1 cup Low-Sodium Salsa or bottled salsa	tenderloin or boneless turkey breast, cut into 6 pieces
1 teaspoon chili powder	Freshly ground black pepper
½ teaspoon ground cumin	½ cup shredded Monterey Jack cheese or Mexican cheese blend
¼ teaspoon dried oregano	
1½ pounds unseasoned turkey	

1. In a small bowl or measuring cup, combine the salsa, chili powder, cumin, and oregano. Pour half of the mixture into the electric pressure cooker. 2. Nestle the turkey into the sauce. Grind some pepper onto each piece of turkey. Pour the remaining salsa mixture on top. 3. Close and lock the lid of the pressure cooker. Set the valve to sealing. 4. Cook on high pressure for 8 minutes. 5. When the cooking is complete, hit Cancel. Allow the pressure to release naturally for 10 minutes, then quick release any remaining pressure. 6. Once the pin drops, unlock and remove the lid. 7. Sprinkle the cheese on top, and put the lid back on for a few minutes to let the cheese melt. 8. Serve immediately.

Per Serving:

calorie: 156 | fat: 4g | protein: 28g | carbs: 4g | sugars: 2g | fiber: 1g | sodium: 525mg

Herbed Whole Turkey Breast

Prep time: 10 minutes | Cook time:30 minutes | Serves 12

3 tablespoons extra-virgin olive oil	1 tablespoon kosher salt
1½ tablespoons herbes de Provence or poultry seasoning	1½ teaspoons freshly ground black pepper
2 teaspoons minced garlic	1 (6 pounds) bone-in, skin-on whole turkey breast, rinsed and patted dry
1 teaspoon lemon zest (from 1 small lemon)	

1. In a small bowl, whisk together the olive oil, herbes de Provence, garlic, lemon zest, salt, and pepper. 2. Rub the outside of the turkey and under the skin with the olive oil mixture. 3. Pour 1 cup of water into the electric pressure cooker and insert a wire rack or trivet. 4. Place the turkey on the rack, skin-side up. 5. Close and lock the lid of the pressure cooker. Set the valve to sealing. 6. Cook on high pressure for 30 minutes. 7. When the cooking is complete, hit Cancel. Allow the pressure to release naturally for 20 minutes, then quick release any remaining pressure. 8. Once the pin drops, unlock and remove the lid. 9. Carefully transfer the turkey to a cutting board. Remove the skin, slice, and serve.

Per Serving:

calorie: 389 | fat: 19g | protein: 50g | carbs: 1g | sugars: 0g | fiber: 0g | sodium: 582mg

Chicken in Wine

Prep time: 10 minutes | Cook time: 12 minutes | Serves 6

2 pounds chicken breasts, trimmed of skin and fat	10¾ ounces can French onion soup
10¾ ounces can 98% fat-free, reduced-sodium cream of mushroom soup	1 cup dry white wine or chicken broth

1. Place the chicken into the Instant Pot. 2. Combine soups and wine. Pour over chicken. 3. Secure the lid and make sure vent is set to sealing. Cook on Manual mode for 12 minutes. 4. When cook time is up, let the pressure release naturally for 5 minutes and then release the rest manually.

Per Serving:

calories: 225 | fat: 5g | protein: 35g | carbs: 7g | sugars: 3g | fiber: 1g | sodium: 645mg

Chapter
8

Beef, Pork, and Lamb

Carnitas Burrito Bowls

Prep time: 10 minutes | Cook time: 1 hour | Serves 6

Carnitas
1 tablespoon chili powder
½ teaspoon garlic powder
1 teaspoon ground coriander
1 teaspoon fine sea salt
½ cup water
¼ cup fresh lime juice
One 2-pound boneless pork shoulder butt roast, cut into 2-inch cubes
Rice and Beans
1 cup Minute brand brown rice (see Note)
1½ cups drained cooked black beans, or one 15 ounces can black beans, rinsed and drained
Pico de Gallo
8 ounces tomatoes (see Note), diced
½ small yellow onion, diced
1 jalapeño chile, seeded and finely diced
1 tablespoon chopped fresh cilantro
1 teaspoon fresh lime juice
Pinch of fine sea salt
¼ cup sliced green onions, white and green parts
2 tablespoons chopped fresh cilantro
3 hearts romaine lettuce, cut into ¼-inch-wide ribbons
2 large avocados, pitted, peeled, and sliced
Hot sauce (such as Cholula or Tapatío) for serving

1. To make the carnitas: In a small bowl, combine the chili powder, garlic powder, coriander, and salt and mix well. 2. Pour the water and lime juice into the Instant Pot. Add the pork, arranging the pieces in a single layer. Sprinkle the chili powder mixture evenly over the pork. 3. Secure the lid and set the Pressure Release to Sealing. Select the Meat/Stew setting and set the cooking time for 30 minutes at high pressure. (The pot will take about 10 minutes to come up to pressure before the cooking program begins.) 4. When the cooking program ends, let the pressure release naturally for at least 15 minutes, then move the Pressure Release to Venting to release any remaining steam. Open the pot and, using tongs, transfer the pork to a plate or cutting board. 5. While the pressure is releasing, preheat the oven to 400°F. 6. Wearing heat-resistant mitts, lift out the inner pot and pour the cooking liquid into a fat separator. Pour the defatted cooking liquid into a liquid measuring cup and discard the fat. (Alternatively, use a ladle or large spoon to skim the fat off the surface of the liquid.) Add water as needed to the cooking liquid to total 1 cup (you may have enough without adding water). 7. To make the rice and beans: Pour the 1 cup cooking liquid into the Instant Pot and add the rice, making sure it is in an even layer. Place a tall steam rack into the pot. Add the black beans to a 1½-quart stainless-steel bowl and place the bowl on top of the rack. (The bowl should not touch the lid once the pot is closed.) 8. Secure the lid and set the Pressure Release to Sealing. Press the Cancel button to reset the cooking program, then select the Pressure Cook or Manual setting and set the cooking time for 15 minutes at high pressure. (The pot will take about 5 minutes to come to pressure before the cooking program begins.) 9. While the rice and beans are cooking, using two forks, shred the meat into bite-size pieces. Transfer the pork to a sheet pan, spreading it out in an even layer. Place in the oven for 20 minutes, until crispy and browned. 10. To make the pico de gallo: While the carnitas, rice, and beans are cooking, in a medium bowl, combine the tomatoes, onion, jalapeño, cilantro, lime juice, and salt and mix well. Set aside. 11.

When the cooking program ends, let the pressure release naturally for 5 minutes, then move the Pressure Release to Venting to release any remaining steam. Open the pot and, wearing heat-resistant mitts, remove the bowl of beans and then the steam rack from the pot. Then remove the inner pot. Add the green onions and cilantro to the rice and, using a fork, fluff the rice and mix in the green onions and cilantro. 12. Divide the rice, beans, carnitas, pico de gallo, lettuce, and avocados evenly among six bowls. Serve warm, with the hot sauce on the side.

Per Serving:
calories: 447 | fat: 20g | protein: 31g | carbs: 35g | sugars: 4g | fiber: 9g | sodium: 653mg

BBQ Ribs and Broccoli Slaw

Prep time: 10 minutes | Cook time: 50 minutes | Serves 6

BBQ Ribs
4 pounds baby back ribs
1 teaspoon fine sea salt
1 teaspoon freshly ground black pepper
Broccoli Slaw
½ cup plain 2 percent Greek yogurt
1 tablespoon olive oil
1 tablespoon fresh lemon juice
½ teaspoon fine sea salt
¼ teaspoon freshly ground black pepper
1 pound broccoli florets (or florets from 2 large crowns), chopped
10 radishes, halved and thinly sliced
1 red bell pepper, seeded and cut lengthwise into narrow strips
1 large apple (such as Fuji, Jonagold, or Gala), thinly sliced
½ red onion, thinly sliced
¾ cup low-sugar or unsweetened barbecue sauce

1. To make the ribs: Pat the ribs dry with paper towels, then cut the racks into six sections (three to five ribs per section, depending on how big the racks are). Season the ribs all over with the salt and pepper. 2. Pour 1 cup water into the Instant Pot and place the wire metal steam rack into the pot. Place the ribs on top of the wire rack (it's fine to stack them up). 3. Secure the lid and set the Pressure Release to Sealing. Select the Pressure Cook or Manual setting and set the cooking time for 20 minutes at high pressure. (The pot will take about 15 minutes to come up to pressure before the cooking program begins.) 4. To make the broccoli slaw: While the ribs are cooking, in a small bowl, stir together the yogurt, oil, lemon juice, salt, and pepper, mixing well. In a large bowl, combine the broccoli, radishes, bell pepper, apple, and onion. Drizzle with the yogurt mixture and toss until evenly coated. 5. When the ribs have about 10 minutes left in their cooking time, preheat the oven to 400°F. Line a sheet pan with aluminum foil. 6. When the cooking program ends, perform a quick pressure release by moving the Pressure Release to Venting. Open the pot and, using tongs, transfer the ribs in a single layer to the prepared sheet pan. Brush the barbecue sauce onto both sides of the ribs, using 2 tablespoons of sauce per section of ribs. Bake, meaty-side up, for 15 to 20 minutes, until lightly browned. 7. Serve the ribs warm, with the slaw on the side.

Per Serving:
calories: 392 | fat: 15g | protein: 45g | carbs: 19g | sugars: 9g | fiber: 4g | sodium: 961mg

Italian Sausages with Peppers and Onions

Prep time: 5 minutes | Cook time: 28 minutes | Serves 3

1 medium onion, thinly sliced
1 yellow or orange bell pepper, thinly sliced
1 red bell pepper, thinly sliced
¼ cup avocado oil or melted

coconut oil
1 teaspoon fine sea salt
6 Italian sausages
Dijon mustard, for serving (optional)

1. Preheat the air fryer to 400ºF (204ºC). 2. Place the onion and peppers in a large bowl. Drizzle with the oil and toss well to coat the veggies. Season with the salt. 3. Place the onion and peppers in a pie pan and cook in the air fryer for 8 minutes, stirring halfway through. Remove from the air fryer and set aside. 4. Spray the air fryer basket with avocado oil. Place the sausages in the air fryer basket and air fry for 20 minutes, or until crispy and golden brown. During the last minute or two of cooking, add the onion and peppers to the basket with the sausages to warm them through. 5. Place the onion and peppers on a serving platter and arrange the sausages on top. Serve Dijon mustard on the side, if desired. 6. Store leftovers in an airtight container in the fridge for up to 7 days or in the freezer for up to a month. Reheat in a preheated 390ºF (199ºC) air fryer for 3 minutes, or until heated through.

Per Serving:

calorie: 455 | fat: 33g | protein: 29g | carbs: 13g | sugars: 3g | fiber: 2g | sodium: 392mg

Beef and Pepper Fajita Bowls

Prep time: 10 minutes | Cook time: 15 minutes | Serves 4

4 tablespoons extra-virgin olive oil, divided
1 head cauliflower, riced
1 pound sirloin steak, cut into ¼-inch-thick strips
1 red bell pepper, seeded and

sliced
1 onion, thinly sliced
2 garlic cloves, minced
Juice of 2 limes
1 teaspoon chili powder

1. In a large skillet over medium-high heat, heat 2 tablespoons of olive oil until it shimmers. Add the cauliflower. Cook, stirring occasionally, until it softens, about 3 minutes. Set aside. 2. Wipe out the skillet with a paper towel. Add the remaining 2 tablespoons of oil to the skillet, and heat it on medium-high until it shimmers. Add the steak and cook, stirring occasionally, until it browns, about 3 minutes. Use a slotted spoon to remove the steak from the oil in the pan and set aside. 3. Add the bell pepper and onion to the pan. Cook, stirring occasionally, until they start to brown, about 5 minutes. 4. Add the garlic and cook, stirring constantly, for 30 seconds. 5. Return the beef along with any juices that have collected and the cauliflower to the pan. Add the lime juice and chili powder. Cook, stirring, until everything is warmed through, 2 to 3 minutes.

Per Serving:

calorie: 390 | fat: 27g | protein: 27g | carbs: 12g | sugars: 5g | fiber: 4g | sodium: 126mg

Grilled Steak and Vegetables

Prep time: 15 minutes | Cook time: 25 minutes | Serves 2

Extra-virgin olive oil cooking spray
2 (8 ounces) sirloin steaks
2 medium pear-shaped tomatoes, halved lengthwise
1 medium zucchini, cut into chunks
1 medium yellow squash, cut into chunks
1 bell pepper (any color), cut

into 1-inch pieces
2 tablespoons extra-virgin olive oil, divided
1 garlic clove, minced
¼ cup fresh basil, plus fresh sprigs, for garnish
Pinch salt
Freshly ground black pepper, to season

1. Preheat the grill (charcoal or gas). 2. Lightly coat a grill rack with cooking spray. 3. Place the steaks on the grill rack, about 4 to 6 inches above the heat—whether a solid bed of medium-hot coals or gas. Cook for about 15 minutes, turning as needed, until evenly browned on the outside and an instant-read thermometer inserted in the center registers 145°F for medium-rare. 4. While the steaks cook, place the tomatoes, zucchini, yellow squash, and bell pepper on the grill. Brush lightly with 1 tablespoon of olive oil. Grill for about 3 minutes, or until the vegetables are browned on the bottom. Turn them over. Continue to cook for about 3 minutes more, or until soft. 5. In a medium skillet with a heatproof handle set over medium-high heat, stir together the remaining 1 tablespoon of olive oil, garlic, and basil. 6. Transfer the grilled vegetables to the skillet. Stir to combine. Reduce the heat to low. 7. Serve each steak accompanied by half of the vegetables. Season with salt and pepper. Garnish with the basil sprigs.

Per Serving:

calorie: 631 | fat: 38g | protein: 52g | carbs: 18g | sugars: 8g | fiber: 5g | sodium: 239mg

Kielbasa and Cabbage

Prep time: 10 minutes | Cook time: 20 to 25 minutes | Serves 4

1 pound (454 g) smoked kielbasa sausage, sliced into ½-inch pieces
1 head cabbage, very coarsely chopped
½ yellow onion, chopped

2 cloves garlic, chopped
2 tablespoons olive oil
½ teaspoon salt
½ teaspoon freshly ground black pepper
¼ cup water

1. Preheat the air fryer to 400ºF (204ºC). 2. In a large bowl, combine the sausage, cabbage, onion, garlic, olive oil, salt, and black pepper. Toss until thoroughly combined. 3. Transfer the mixture to the basket of the air fryer and pour the water over the top. Pausing two or three times during the cooking time to shake the basket, air fry for 20 to 25 minutes, until the sausage is browned and the vegetables are tender.

Per Serving:

calorie: 446 | fat: 36g | protein: 19g | carbs: 14g | sugars: 7g | fiber: 6g | sodium: 1340mg

Mustard Herb Pork Tenderloin

Prep time: 5 minutes | Cook time: 20 minutes | Serves 6

¼ cup mayonnaise	1 (1 pound / 454 g) pork
2 tablespoons Dijon mustard	tenderloin
½ teaspoon dried thyme	½ teaspoon salt
¼ teaspoon dried rosemary	¼ teaspoon ground black pepper

1. In a small bowl, mix mayonnaise, mustard, thyme, and rosemary. Brush tenderloin with mixture on all sides, then sprinkle with salt and pepper on all sides. 2. Place tenderloin into ungreased air fryer basket. Adjust the temperature to 400ºF (204ºC) and air fry for 20 minutes, turning tenderloin halfway through cooking. Tenderloin will be golden and have an internal temperature of at least 145ºF (63ºC) when done. Serve warm.

Per Serving:

calorie: 118 | fat: 5g | protein: 17g | carbs: 1g | sugars: 0g | fiber: 0g | sodium: 368mg

Dry-Rubbed Sirloin

Prep time: 5 minutes | Cook time: 15 minutes | Serves 6

1⅛ pounds beef round sirloin tip   2 tablespoons Creole seasoning

1. Preheat the oven to 375°F. 2. Massage the beef all over with the Creole seasoning. 3. Put the beef in a Dutch oven, cover, and transfer to the oven. Cook for 15 minutes, or until the juices run clear when you pierce the beef. 4. Remove the beef from the oven, and let rest for 15 minutes. 5. Carve, and serve.

Per Serving:

calorie: 134 | fat: 4g | protein: 19g | carbs: 4g | sugars: 0g | fiber: 1g | sodium: 260mg

Jalapeño Popper Pork Chops

Prep time: 15 minutes | Cook time: 6 to 8 minutes | Serves 4

1¾ pounds (794 g) bone-in, center-cut loin pork chops	4 ounces (113 g) sliced bacon, cooked and crumbled
Sea salt and freshly ground black pepper, to taste	4 ounces (113 g) Cheddar cheese, shredded
6 ounces (170 g) cream cheese, at room temperature	1 jalapeño, seeded and diced
	1 teaspoon garlic powder

1. Cut a pocket into each pork chop, lengthwise along the side, making sure not to cut it all the way through. Season the outside of the chops with salt and pepper. 2. In a small bowl, combine the cream cheese, bacon, Cheddar cheese, jalapeño, and garlic powder. Divide this mixture among the pork chops, stuffing it into the pocket of each chop. 3. Set the air fryer to 400ºF (204ºC). Place the pork chops in the air fryer basket in a single layer, working in batches if necessary. Air fry for 3 minutes. Flip the chops and cook for 3 to 5 minutes more, until an instant-read thermometer reads 145ºF (63ºC). 4. Allow the chops to rest for 5 minutes, then serve warm.

Per Serving:

calorie: 469 | fat: 21g | protein: 60g | carbs: 5g | sugars: 3g | fiber: 0g | sodium: 576mg

"Smothered" Steak

Prep time: 20 minutes | Cook time: 15 minutes | Serves 6

1 tablespoon olive oil	14½ ounces can stewed
¼ teaspoon pepper	tomatoes
⅓ cup flour	4 ounces can mushrooms,
1½ pounds chuck, or round,	drained
steak, cut into strips, trimmed	2 tablespoons soy sauce
of fat	10 ounces package frozen
1 large onion, sliced	French-style green beans
1 green pepper, sliced	

1. Press Sauté and add the oil to the Instant Pot. 2. Mix together the flour and pepper in a small bowl. Place the steak pieces into the mixture in the bowl and coat each of them well. 3. Lightly brown each of the steak pieces in the Instant Pot, about 2 minutes on each side. Press Cancel when done. 4. Add the remaining ingredients to the Instant Pot and mix together gently. 5. Secure the lid and make sure vent is set to sealing. Press Manual and set for 15 minutes. 6. When cook time is up, let the pressure release naturally for 15 minutes, then perform a quick release.

Per Serving:

calories: 386 | fat: 24g | protein: 25g | carbs: 20g | sugars: 4g | fiber: 4g | sodium: 746mg

Pot Roast with Gravy and Vegetables

Prep time: 30 minutes | Cook time: 1 hour 15 minutes | Serves 6

1 tablespoon olive oil	1 teaspoon Kitchen Bouquet, or
3 to 4 pound bottom round,	gravy browning seasoning sauce
rump, or arm roast, trimmed	1 garlic clove, minced
of fat	2 medium onions, cut in wedges
¼ teaspoon salt	4 medium potatoes, cubed,
2 to 3 teaspoons pepper	unpeeled
2 tablespoons flour	2 carrots, quartered
1 cup cold water	1 green bell pepper, sliced

1. Press the Sauté button on the Instant Pot and pour the oil inside, letting it heat up. Sprinkle each side of the roast with salt and pepper, then brown it for 5 minutes on each side inside the pot. 2. Mix together the flour, water and Kitchen Bouquet and spread over roast. 3. Add garlic, onions, potatoes, carrots, and green pepper. 4. Secure the lid and make sure the vent is set to sealing. Press Manual and set the Instant Pot for 1 hour and 15 minutes. 5. When cook time is up, let the pressure release naturally.

Per Serving:

calories: 551 | fat: 30g | protein: 49g | carbs: 19g | sugars: 2g | fiber: 3g | sodium: 256mg

Roasted Beef with Peppercorn Sauce

Prep time: 10 minutes | Cook time:1hour | Serves 4

1½ pounds top rump beef roast
Sea salt
Freshly ground black pepper
3 teaspoons extra-virgin olive oil, divided
3 shallots, minced

2 teaspoons minced garlic
1 tablespoon green peppercorns
2 tablespoons dry sherry
2 tablespoons all-purpose flour
1 cup sodium-free beef broth

1. Heat the oven to 300°F. 2. Season the roast with salt and pepper. 3. Place a large skillet over medium-high heat and add 2 teaspoons of olive oil. 4. Brown the beef on all sides, about 10 minutes in total, and transfer the roast to a baking dish. 5. Roast until desired doneness, about 1½ hours for medium. When the roast has been in the oven for 1 hour, start the sauce. 6. In a medium saucepan over medium-high heat, sauté the shallots in the remaining 1 teaspoon of olive oil until translucent, about 4 minutes. 7. Stir in the garlic and peppercorns, and cook for another minute. Whisk in the sherry to deglaze the pan. 8. Whisk in the flour to form a thick paste, cooking for 1 minute and stirring constantly. 9. Pour in the beef broth and whisk until the sauce is thick and glossy, about 4 minutes. Season the sauce with salt and pepper. 10. Serve the beef with a generous spoonful of sauce.

Per Serving:

calorie: 272 | fat: 10g | protein: 40g | carbs: g | sugars: 0g | fiber: 0g | sodium: 331mg

Rosemary Lamb Chops

Prep time: 25 minutes | Cook time: 2 minutes | Serves 4

1½ pounds lamb chops (4 small chops)
1 teaspoon kosher salt
Leaves from 1 (6-inch) rosemary sprig

2 tablespoons avocado oil
1 shallot, peeled and cut in quarters
1 tablespoon tomato paste
1 cup beef broth

1. Place the lamb chops on a cutting board. Press the salt and rosemary leaves into both sides of the chops. Let rest at room temperature for 15 to 30 minutes. 2. Set the electric pressure cooker to Sauté/More setting. When hot, add the avocado oil. 3. Brown the lamb chops, about 2 minutes per side. (If they don't all fit in a single layer, brown them in batches.) 4. Transfer the chops to a plate. In the pot, combine the shallot, tomato paste, and broth. Cook for about a minute, scraping up the brown bits from the bottom. Hit Cancel. 5. Add the chops and any accumulated juices back to the pot. 6. Close and lock the lid of the pressure cooker. Set the valve to sealing. 7. Cook on high pressure for 2 minutes. 8. When the cooking is complete, hit Cancel and quick release the pressure. 9. Once the pin drops, unlock and remove the lid. 10. Place the lamb chops on plates and serve immediately.

Per Serving:

calorie: 352 | fat: 20g | protein: 37g | carbs: 7g | sugars: 1g | fiber: 0g | sodium: 440mg

Shepherd's Pie with Cauliflower-Carrot Mash

Prep time: 10 minutes | Cook time: 35 minutes | Serves 6

1 tablespoon coconut oil
2 garlic cloves, minced
1 large yellow onion, diced
1 pound ground lamb
1 pound 95 percent lean ground beef
½ cup low-sodium vegetable broth
1 teaspoons dried thyme
1 teaspoon dried sage
1 teaspoon freshly ground black pepper
1¾ teaspoons fine sea salt
2 tablespoons Worcestershire

sauce
One 12-ounce bag frozen baby lima beans, green peas, or shelled edamame
3 tablespoons tomato paste
1 pound cauliflower florets
1 pound carrots, halved lengthwise and then crosswise (or quartered if very large)
¼ cup coconut milk or other nondairy milk
½ cup sliced green onions, white and green parts

1. Select the Sauté setting on the Instant Pot and heat the oil and garlic for 2 minutes, until the garlic is bubbling but not browned. Add the onion and sauté for 3 minutes, until it begins to soften. Add the lamb and beef and sauté, using a wooden spoon or spatula to break up the meat as it cooks, for 6 minutes, until cooked through and no streaks of pink remain. 2. Stir in the broth, using the spoon or spatula to nudge any browned bits from the bottom of the pot. Add the thyme, sage, pepper, ¾ teaspoon of the salt, the Worcestershire sauce, and lima beans and stir to mix. Dollop the tomato paste on top. Do not stir it in. 3. Place a tall steam rack in the pot, then place the cauliflower and carrots on top of the rack. 4. Secure the lid and set the Pressure Release to Sealing. Press the Cancel button to reset the cooking program, then select the Pressure Cook or Manual setting and set the cooking time for 4 minutes at low pressure. (The pot will take about 15 minutes to come up to pressure before the cooking program begins.) 5. Position an oven rack 4 to 6 inches below the heat source and preheat the broiler. 6. When the cooking program ends, perform a quick pressure release by moving the Pressure Release to Venting. Open the pot and, using tongs, transfer the cauliflower and carrots to a bowl. Add the coconut milk and remaining 1 teaspoon salt to the bowl. Using an immersion blender, blend the vegetables until smooth. 7. Wearing heat-resistant mitts, remove the steam rack from the pot. Stir ½ cup of the mashed vegetables into the filling mixture in the pot, incorporating the tomato paste at the same time. Remove the inner pot from the housing. Transfer the mixture to a broiler-safe 9 by 13-inch baking dish, spreading it in an even layer. Dollop the mashed vegetables on top and spread them out evenly with a fork. Broil, checking often, for 5 to 8 minutes, until the mashed vegetables are lightly browned. 8. Spoon the shepherd's pie onto plates, sprinkle with the green onions, and serve hot.

Per Serving:

calories: 437 | fat: 18g | protein: 39g | carbs: 33g | sugars: 8g | fiber: 9g | sodium: 802mg

Bacon-Wrapped Vegetable Kebabs

Prep time: 10 minutes | Cook time: 10 to 12 minutes | Serves 4

4 ounces (113 g) mushrooms, sliced

1 small zucchini, sliced

12 grape tomatoes

4 ounces (113 g) sliced bacon,

halved

Avocado oil spray

Sea salt and freshly ground black pepper, to taste

1. Stack 3 mushroom slices, 1 zucchini slice, and 1 grape tomato. Wrap a bacon strip around the vegetables and thread them onto a skewer. Repeat with the remaining vegetables and bacon. Spray with oil and sprinkle with salt and pepper. 2. Set the air fryer to 400°F (204°C). Place the skewers in the air fryer basket in a single layer, working in batches if necessary, and air fry for 5 minutes. Flip the skewers and cook for 5 to 7 minutes more, until the bacon is crispy and the vegetables are tender. 3. Serve warm.

Per Serving:

calorie: 140 | fat: 11g | protein: 5g | carbs: 5g | sugars: 4g | fiber: 1g | sodium: 139mg

Spicy Beef Stew with Butternut Squash

Prep time: 15 minutes | Cook time: 30 minutes | Serves 8

1½ tablespoons smoked paprika

2 teaspoons ground cinnamon

1½ teaspoons kosher salt

1 teaspoon ground ginger

1 teaspoon red pepper flakes

½ teaspoon freshly ground black pepper

2 pounds beef shoulder roast, cut into 1-inch cubes

2 tablespoons avocado oil, divided

1 cup low-sodium beef or

vegetable broth

1 medium red onion, cut into wedges

8 garlic cloves, minced

1 (28 ounces) carton or can no-salt-added diced tomatoes

2 pounds butternut squash, peeled and cut into 1-inch pieces

Chopped fresh cilantro or parsley, for serving

1. In a zip-top bag or medium bowl, combine the paprika, cinnamon, salt, ginger, red pepper, and black pepper. Add the beef and toss to coat. 2. Set the electric pressure cooker to the Sauté setting. When the pot is hot, pour in 1 tablespoon of avocado oil. 3. Add half of the beef to the pot and cook, stirring occasionally, for 3 to 5 minutes or until the beef is no longer pink. Transfer it to a plate, then add the remaining 1 tablespoon of avocado oil and brown the remaining beef. Transfer to the plate. Hit Cancel. 4. Stir in the broth and scrape up any brown bits from the bottom of the pot. Return the beef to the pot and add the onion, garlic, tomatoes and their juices, and squash. Stir well. 5. Close and lock lid of pressure cooker. Set the valve to sealing. 6. Cook on high pressure for 30 minutes. 7. When cooking is complete, hit Cancel. Allow the pressure to release naturally for 10 minutes, then quick release any remaining pressure. 8. Unlock and remove lid. 9. Spoon into serving bowls, sprinkle with cilantro or parsley, and serve.

Per Serving:

calorie: 275 | fat: 9g | protein: 28g | carbs: 24g | sugars: 7g | fiber: 6g | sodium: 512mg

Orange-Marinated Pork Tenderloin

Prep time: 10 minutes | Cook time: 30 minutes | Serves 4

¼ cup freshly squeezed orange juice

2 teaspoons orange zest

2 teaspoons minced garlic

1 teaspoon low-sodium soy sauce

1 teaspoon grated fresh ginger

1 teaspoon honey

1½ pounds pork tenderloin roast, trimmed of fat

1 tablespoon extra-virgin olive oil

1. In a small bowl, whisk together the orange juice, zest, garlic, soy sauce, ginger, and honey. 2. Pour the marinade into a resealable plastic bag and add the pork tenderloin. 3. Remove as much air as possible and seal the bag. Marinate the pork in the refrigerator, turning the bag a few times, for 2 hours. 4. Preheat the oven to 400°F. 5. Remove the tenderloin from the marinade and discard the marinade. 6. Place a large ovenproof skillet over medium-high heat and add the oil. 7. Sear the pork tenderloin on all sides, about 5 minutes in total. 8. Transfer the skillet to the oven and roast the pork until just cooked through, about 25 minutes. 9. Let the meat stand for 10 minutes before serving.

Per Serving:

calorie: 232 | fat: 7g | protein: 36g | carbs: 4g | sugars: 3g | fiber: 0g | sodium: 131mg

Slow-Cooked Pork Burrito Bowls

Prep time: 15 minutes | Cook time: 8 to 10 hours | Serves 10

1 boneless pork shoulder (2 lb), trimmed of excess fat

1 can (15 to 16 ounces) pinto beans, drained, rinsed

1 package (1 ounce) 40% less-sodium taco seasoning mix

1 can (4.5 ounces) diced green chiles, undrained

2 packages (7.6 ounces each) Spanish rice mix

5 cups water

1½ cups shredded Mexican cheese blend (6 ounces)

3 cups shredded lettuce

¾ cup chunky-style salsa

1. Spray 3- to 4-quart slow cooker with cooking spray. If pork comes in netting or is tied, remove netting or strings. Place pork in slow cooker. Pour beans around pork. Sprinkle taco seasoning mix over pork. Pour chiles over beans. 2. Cover; cook on Low heat setting 8 to 10 hours. 3. About 45 minutes before serving, in 3-quart saucepan, make rice mixes as directed on package, using water and omitting butter. 4. Remove pork from slow cooker; place on cutting board. Use 2 forks to pull pork into shreds. Return pork to slow cooker; gently stir to mix with beans. 5. To serve, spoon rice into each of 10 serving bowls; top each with pork mixture, cheese, lettuce and salsa.

Per Serving:

calories: 460 | fat: 17g | protein: 30g | carbs: 48g | sugars: 4g | fiber: 5g | sodium: 1030mg

Steaks with Walnut-Blue Cheese Butter

Prep time: 30 minutes | Cook time: 10 minutes | Serves 6

½ cup unsalted butter, at room temperature

½ cup crumbled blue cheese

2 tablespoons finely chopped walnuts

1 tablespoon minced fresh rosemary

1 teaspoon minced garlic

¼ teaspoon cayenne pepper

Sea salt and freshly ground black pepper, to taste

1½ pounds (680 g) New York strip steaks, at room temperature

1. In a medium bowl, combine the butter, blue cheese, walnuts, rosemary, garlic, and cayenne pepper and salt and black pepper to taste. Use clean hands to ensure that everything is well combined. Place the mixture on a sheet of parchment paper and form it into a log. Wrap it tightly in plastic wrap. Refrigerate for at least 2 hours or freeze for 30 minutes. 2. Season the steaks generously with salt and pepper. 3. Place the air fryer basket or grill pan in the air fryer. Set the air fryer to 400ºF (204ºC) and let it preheat for 5 minutes. 4. Place the steaks in the basket in a single layer and air fry for 5 minutes. Flip the steaks, and cook for 5 minutes more, until an instant-read thermometer reads 120ºF (49ºC) for medium-rare (or as desired). 5. Transfer the steaks to a plate. Cut the butter into pieces and place the desired amount on top of the steaks. Tent a piece of aluminum foil over the steaks and allow to sit for 10 minutes before serving. 6. Store any remaining butter in a sealed container in the refrigerator for up to 2 weeks.

Per Serving:

calorie: 620 | fat: 56g | protein: 26g | carbs: 2g | sugars: 0g | fiber: 1g | sodium: 442mg

Pork Chops with Raspberry-Chipotle Sauce and Herbed Rice

Prep time: 25 minutes | Cook time: 10 minutes | Serves 4

Pork Chops

4 bone-in pork rib chops, about ¾ inch thick

½ teaspoon garlic-pepper blend

1 tablespoon canola oil

Raspberry-Chipotle Sauce

⅓ cup all-fruit raspberry spread

1 tablespoon water

1 tablespoon raspberry-flavored vinegar

1 large or 2 small chipotle chiles

in adobo sauce, finely chopped (from 7 ounce can)

Herbed Rice

1 package (8.8 ounces) quick-cooking (ready in 90 seconds) whole-grain brown rice

¼ teaspoon salt-free garlic-herb blend

½ teaspoon lemon peel

1 tablespoon chopped fresh cilantro

1 Sprinkle pork with garlic pepper. In 12-inch nonstick skillet, heat oil over medium-high heat. Add pork to oil. Cook 8 to 10 minutes, turning once, until pork is no longer pink and meat thermometer inserted in center reads 145°F. Remove from skillet to serving platter (reserve pork drippings); keep warm. 2 Meanwhile, in small bowl, stir raspberry spread, water, vinegar and chile; set aside. Make rice as directed on package. Stir in remaining rice ingredients; keep

warm. 3 In skillet with pork drippings, pour raspberry mixture. Cook and stir over low heat about 1 minute or until sauce is bubbly and slightly thickened. Serve pork chops with sauce and rice.

Per Serving:

calories: 370 | fat: 12g | protein: 31g | carbs: 34g | sugars: 12g | fiber: 0g | sodium: 140mg

Dutch Oven Apple Pork Chops

Prep time: 20 minutes | Cook time: 20 minutes | Serves 4

4 bone-in pork loin chops, trimmed

¼ cup apple cider vinegar

1 teaspoon freshly ground black pepper

1 teaspoon ground cinnamon

1 teaspoon ground nutmeg

½ cup store-bought low-sodium

chicken broth

3 celery stalks, cut into matchsticks

1 Candy Crisp apple, thinly sliced

1 small yellow onion, thinly sliced

1. Put the pork chops on a rimmed baking sheet. Season both sides with the vinegar, pepper, cinnamon, and nutmeg. 2. In a Dutch oven, bring the broth to a simmer over medium heat. 3. Add the pork chops and cook for 3 minutes, or until the exterior is browned. Transfer to a plate. 4. Add the celery, apple, and onion to the pot, making a bed. 5. Place the pork chops on top and cover. Cook for 10 to 15 minutes, taking care not to overcook. 6. Serve each pork chop with generous spoonfuls of apple, celery, and onion on the side.

Per Serving:

calorie: 298 | fat: 7g | protein: 40g | carbs: 18g | sugars: 12g | fiber: 2g | sodium: 122mg

Tenderloin with Crispy Shallots

Prep time: 30 minutes | Cook time: 18 to 20 minutes | Serves 6

1½ pounds (680 g) beef tenderloin steaks

Sea salt and freshly ground black pepper, to taste

4 medium shallots

1 teaspoon olive oil or avocado oil

1. Season both sides of the steaks with salt and pepper, and let them sit at room temperature for 45 minutes. 2. Set the air fryer to 400ºF (204ºC) and let it preheat for 5 minutes. 3. Working in batches if necessary, place the steaks in the air fryer basket in a single layer and air fry for 5 minutes. Flip and cook for 5 minutes longer, until an instant-read thermometer inserted in the center of the steaks registers 120ºF (49ºC) for medium-rare (or as desired). Remove the steaks and tent with aluminum foil to rest. 4. Set the air fryer to 300ºF (149ºC). In a medium bowl, toss the shallots with the oil. Place the shallots in the basket and air fry for 5 minutes, then give them a toss and cook for 3 to 5 minutes more, until crispy and golden brown. 5. Place the steaks on serving plates and arrange the shallots on top.

Per Serving:

calorie: 357 | fat: 20g | protein: 38g | carbs: 4g | sugars: 1g | fiber: 0g | sodium: 94mg

Steak Stroganoff

Prep time: 15 minutes | Cook time: 30 minutes | Serves 6

1 tablespoon olive oil
2 tablespoons flour
½ teaspoon garlic powder
½ teaspoon pepper
¼ teaspoon paprika
1¾ pounds boneless beef round steak, trimmed of fat, cut into 1½ × ½-inch strips.
10¾ ounces can reduced-sodium, 98% fat-free cream of

mushroom soup
½ cup water
1 envelope sodium-free dried onion soup mix
9 ounces jar sliced mushrooms, drained
½ cup fat-free sour cream
1 tablespoon minced fresh parsley

1. Place the oil in the Instant Pot and press Sauté. 2. Combine flour, garlic powder, pepper, and paprika in a small bowl. Stir the steak pieces through the flour mixture until they are evenly coated. 3. Lightly brown the steak pieces in the oil in the Instant Pot, about 2 minutes each side. Press Cancel when done. 4. Stir the mushroom soup, water, and onion soup mix then pour over the steak. 5. Secure the lid and set the vent to sealing. Press the Manual button and set for 15 minutes. 6. When cook time is up, let the pressure release naturally for 15 minutes, then release the rest manually. 7. Remove the lid and press Cancel then Sauté. Stir in mushrooms, sour cream, and parsley. Let the sauce come to a boil and cook for about 10 to 15 minutes.

Per Serving:

calories: 248 | fat: 6g | protein: 33g | carbs: 12g | sugars: 2g | fiber: 2g | sodium: 563mg

5-Ingredient Mexican Lasagna

Prep time: 15 minutes | Cook time: 15 minutes | Serves 4

Nonstick cooking spray
½ (15 ounces) can light red kidney beans, rinsed and drained
4 (6-inch) gluten-free corn tortillas

1½ cups cooked shredded beef, pork, or chicken
1⅓ cups salsa
1⅓ cups shredded Mexican cheese blend

1. Spray a 6-inch springform pan with nonstick spray. Wrap the bottom in foil. 2. In a medium bowl, mash the beans with a fork. 3. Place 1 tortilla in the bottom of the pan. Add about ⅓ of the beans, ½ cup of meat, ⅓ cup of salsa, and ⅓ cup of cheese. Press down. Repeat for 2 more layers. Add the remaining tortilla and press down. Top with the remaining salsa and cheese. There are no beans or meat on the top layer. 4. Tear off a piece of foil big enough to cover the pan, and spray it with nonstick spray. Line the pan with the foil, sprayed-side down. 5. Pour 1 cup of water into the electric pressure cooker. 6. Place the pan on the wire rack and carefully lower it into the pot. Close and lock the lid of the pressure cooker. Set the valve to sealing. 7. Cook on high pressure for 15 minutes. 8. When the cooking is complete, hit Cancel. Allow the pressure to release naturally for 10 minutes, then quick release any remaining pressure.

9. Once the pin drops, unlock and remove the lid. 10. Using the handles of the wire rack, carefully remove the pan from the pot. Let the lasagna sit for 5 minutes. Carefully remove the ring. 11. Slice into quarters and serve.

Per Serving:

calorie: 380 | fat: 18g | protein: 32g | carbs: 22g | sugars: 4g | fiber: 4g | sodium: 594mg

Marjoram-Pepper Steaks

Prep time: 5 minutes | Cook time: 8 minutes | Serves 2

1 tablespoon freshly ground black pepper
¼ teaspoon dried marjoram
2 (6 ounces, 1-inch-thick) beef tenderloins

1 tablespoon extra-virgin olive oil
¼ cup low-sodium beef broth
Fresh marjoram sprigs, for garnish

1. In a large bowl, mix together the pepper and marjoram. 2. Add the steaks. Coat both sides with the spice mixture. 3. In a skillet set over medium-high heat, heat the olive oil. 4. Add the steaks. Cook for 5 to 7 minutes, or until an instant-read thermometer inserted in the center registers 160°F (for medium). Remove from the skillet. Cover to keep warm. 5. Add the broth to the skillet. Increase the heat to high. Bring to a boil, scraping any browned bits from the bottom. Boil for about 1 minute, or until the liquid is reduced by half. 6. Spoon the broth sauce over the steaks. Garnish with marjoram sprigs and serve immediately.

Per Serving:

calorie: 339 | fat: 19g | protein: 38g | carbs: 2g | sugars: 0g | fiber: 1g | sodium: 209mg

Lamb Kofta Meatballs with Cucumber Quick-Pickled Salad

Prep time: 10 minutes | Cook time: 15 minutes | Serves 4

¼ cup red wine vinegar
Pinch red pepper flakes
1 teaspoon sea salt, divided
2 cucumbers, peeled and chopped
½ red onion, finely chopped

1 pound ground lamb
2 teaspoons ground coriander
1 teaspoon ground cumin
3 garlic cloves, minced
1 tablespoon fresh mint, chopped

1. Preheat the oven to 375°F. Line a rimmed baking sheet with parchment paper. 2. In a medium bowl, whisk together the vinegar, red pepper flakes, and ½ teaspoon of salt. Add the cucumbers and onion and toss to combine. Set aside. 3. In a large bowl, mix the lamb, coriander, cumin, garlic, mint, and remaining ½ teaspoon of salt. Form the mixture into 1-inch meatballs and place them on the prepared baking sheet. 4. Bake until the lamb reaches 140°F internally, about 15 minutes. 5. Serve with the salad on the side.

Per Serving:

calorie: 255 | fat: 14g | protein: 24g | carbs: 8g | sugars: 3g | fiber: 1g | sodium: 652mg

Open-Faced Philly Cheesesteak Sandwiches

Prep time: 5 minutes | Cook time: 25 minutes | Serves 4

Avocado oil cooking spray
1 cup chopped yellow onion
1 green bell pepper, chopped
12 ounces 93% lean ground beef
Pinch salt
¾ teaspoon freshly ground black

pepper
4 slices provolone or Swiss cheese
4 English muffins, 100% whole-wheat

1. Heat a large skillet over medium-low heat. When hot, coat the cooking surface with cooking spray, and arrange the onion and pepper in an even layer. Cook for 8 to 10 minutes, stirring every 3 to 4 minutes. 2. Push the vegetables to one side of the skillet and add the beef, breaking it into large chunks. Cook for 7 to 9 minutes, until a crisp crust forms on the bottom of the meat. 3. Season the beef with the salt and pepper, then flip the beef over and break it down into smaller chunks. 4. Stir the vegetables and the beef together, then top with the cheese and cook for 2 minutes. 5. Meanwhile, split each muffin in half, if necessary, then toast the muffins in a toaster. 6. Place one-eighth of the filling on each muffin half.

Per Serving:

calorie: 373 | fat: 13g | protein: 33g | carbs: 33g | sugars: 8g | fiber: 6g | sodium: 303mg

Loaded Cottage Pie

Prep time: 15 minutes | Cook time: 1 hour | Serves 6 to 8

4 large russet potatoes, peeled and halved
3 tablespoons extra-virgin olive oil, divided
1 small onion, chopped
1 bunch collard greens, stemmed and thinly sliced
2 carrots, peeled and chopped
2 medium tomatoes, chopped
1 garlic clove, minced

1 pound 90 percent lean ground beef
½ cup store-bought low-sodium chicken broth
1 teaspoon Worcestershire sauce
1 teaspoon celery seeds
1 teaspoon smoked paprika
½ teaspoon dried chives
½ teaspoon ground mustard
½ teaspoon cayenne pepper

1. Preheat the oven to 400°F. 2. Bring a large pot of water to a boil. 3. Add the potatoes, and boil for 15 to 20 minutes, or until fork-tender. 4. Transfer the potatoes to a large bowl and mash with 1 tablespoon of olive oil. 5. In a large cast iron skillet, heat the remaining 2 tablespoons of olive oil. 6. Add the onion, collard greens, carrots, tomatoes, and garlic and sauté, stirring often, for 7 to 10 minutes, or until the vegetables are softened. 7. Add the beef, broth, Worcestershire sauce, celery seeds, and smoked paprika. 8. Spread the meat and vegetable mixture evenly onto the bottom of a casserole dish. Sprinkle the chives, ground mustard, and cayenne on top of the mixture. Spread the mashed potatoes evenly over the top. 9. Transfer the casserole dish to the oven, and bake for 30 minutes, or until the top is light golden brown.

Per Serving:

calorie: 358 | fat: 10g | protein: 22g | carbs: 48g | sugars: 4g | fiber: 8g | sodium: 98mg

30-Minute Garlic Lamb Lollipops

Prep time: 10 minutes | Cook time: 10 minutes | Serves 4

2 tablespoon (18 g) minced garlic
¼ cup (60 ml) avocado or olive oil
2 tbsp (30 ml) red wine vinegar
1 tablespoon (3 g) Italian seasoning
½ teaspoon sea salt

¼ teaspoon black pepper
12 to 16 ounces (340 to 454 g) lamb rib chops
1 tablespoon (15 ml) avocado or grapeseed oil
Minced fresh rosemary, thyme, or basil, as needed

1. In a small bowl, combine the garlic, avocado oil, vinegar, Italian seasoning, salt, and black pepper. Whisk to mix the ingredients. 2. Place the lamb rib chops in an airtight container, like a plastic bag or glass storage container. Pour the marinade over the lamb rib chops and let them marinate at room temperature for 10 to 15 minutes. 3. Heat the avocado or grapeseed oil in a large cast-iron skillet over medium-high heat. Gently add the lamb rib chops to the skillet and cook them for 4 minutes. Flip the lamb and cook the meat for another 4 minutes, until it is brown on both sides. 4. Remove the lamb rib chops from the skillet, and let them rest for 10 minutes before serving. Garnish them with the herbs and serve.

Per Serving:

calorie: 568 | fat: 54.5g | protein: 19g | carbs: 2g | sugars: 0g | fiber: 0g | sodium: 361mg

Sirloin Steaks with Cilantro Chimichurri

Prep time: 25 minutes | Cook time: 7 to 10 minutes | Serves 4

1 cup loosely packed fresh cilantro
1 small onion, cut into quarters
2 cloves garlic, cut in half
1 jalapeño chile, cut in half, seeded
2 teaspoons lime juice

2 teaspoons canola oil
½ teaspoon salt
2 teaspoons ground cumin
½ teaspoon pepper
4 beef sirloin steaks, 1 inch thick (about 1½ lb)

1. Heat gas or charcoal grill. In food processor, place cilantro, onion, garlic, chile, lime juice, oil and ¼ teaspoon of the salt. Cover; process until finely chopped. Blend in 2 to 3 teaspoons water to make sauce thinner, if desired. Transfer to small bowl; set aside until serving time. 2. In small bowl, mix cumin, pepper and remaining ¼ teaspoon salt; rub evenly over steaks. Place steaks on grill over medium heat. Cover grill; cook 7 to 10 minutes for medium-rare (145°F), turning once halfway through cooking. 3. Serve 2 tablespoons chimichurri over each steak.

Per Serving:

calorie: 266 | fat: 10g | protein: 38g | carbs: 3g | sugars: 1g | fiber: 1g | sodium: 392mg

Autumn Pork Chops with Red Cabbage and Apples

Prep time: 15 minutes | Cook time: 30 minutes | Serves 4

¼ cup apple cider vinegar

2 tablespoons granulated sweetener

4 (4 ounces) pork chops, about 1 inch thick

Sea salt

Freshly ground black pepper

1 tablespoon extra-virgin olive oil

½ red cabbage, finely shredded

1 sweet onion, thinly sliced

1 apple, peeled, cored, and sliced

1 teaspoon chopped fresh thyme

1. In a small bowl, whisk together the vinegar and sweetener. Set it aside. 2. Season the pork with salt and pepper. 3. Place a large skillet over medium-high heat and add the olive oil. 4. Cook the pork chops until no longer pink, turning once, about 8 minutes per side. 5. Transfer the chops to a plate and set aside. 6. Add the cabbage and onion to the skillet and sauté until the vegetables have softened, about 5 minutes. 7. Add the vinegar mixture and the apple slices to the skillet and bring the mixture to a boil. 8. Reduce the heat to low and simmer, covered, for 5 additional minutes. 9. Return the pork chops to the skillet, along with any accumulated juices and thyme, cover, and cook for 5 more minutes.

Per Serving:

calorie: 251 | fat: 8g | protein: 26g | carbs: 19g | sugars: 13g | fiber: 2g | sodium: 76mg

Grilled Pork Loin Chops

Prep time: 15 minutes | Cook time: 30 minutes | Serves 2

2 garlic cloves, minced

3 tablespoons Worcestershire sauce

2 tablespoons water

1 tablespoon low-sodium soy sauce

2 teaspoons tomato paste

1 teaspoon granulated stevia

½ teaspoon ground ginger

½ teaspoon onion powder

¼ teaspoon cinnamon

⅛ teaspoon cayenne pepper

2 (6 ounces) thick-cut boneless pork loin chops

Olive oil, for greasing the grill

1. In a small bowl, mix together the garlic, Worcestershire sauce, water, soy sauce, tomato paste, stevia, ginger, onion powder, cinnamon, and cayenne pepper. Pour half of the marinade into a large plastic sealable bag. Cover and refrigerate the remaining marinade. 2. Add the pork chops to the bag and seal. Refrigerate for 4 to 8 hours, turning occasionally. 3. Preheat the grill to medium. 4. With the olive oil, lightly oil the grill grate. 5. Remove the pork chops from the bag. Discard the marinade in the bag. 6. Place the chops on the preheated grill, basting with the remaining reserved half of the marinade. Grill for 8 to 12 minutes per side, or until the meat is browned, no longer pink inside, and an instant-read thermometer inserted into the thickest part of the chop reads at least 145°F. 7. In a saucepan set over medium heat, pour any remaining reserved marinade. Bring to a boil. Reduce the heat to low. Simmer for about 5 minutes, stirring constantly, until slightly thickened. 8. To serve, plate the chops and spoon the sauce over.

Per Serving:

calorie: 254 | fat: 6g | protein: 39g | carbs: 9g | sugars: 3g | fiber: 1g | sodium: 593mg

Mediterranean Steak Sandwiches

Prep time: 10 minutes | Cook time: 10 minutes | Serves 4

2 tablespoons extra-virgin olive oil

2 tablespoons balsamic vinegar

2 teaspoons minced garlic

2 teaspoons freshly squeezed lemon juice

2 teaspoons chopped fresh oregano

1 teaspoon chopped fresh

parsley

1 pound flank steak, trimmed of fat

4 whole-wheat pitas

2 cups shredded lettuce

1 red onion, thinly sliced

1 tomato, chopped

1 ounce low-sodium feta cheese

1. In a large bowl, whisk together the olive oil, balsamic vinegar, garlic, lemon juice, oregano, and parsley. 2. Add the steak to the bowl, turning to coat it completely. 3. Marinate the steak for 1 hour in the refrigerator, turning it over several times. 4. Preheat the broiler. Line a baking sheet with aluminum foil. 5. Take the steak out of the bowl and discard the marinade. 6. Place the steak on the baking sheet and broil until it is done to your liking, about 5 minutes per side for medium. 7. Let the steak rest for 10 minutes before slicing it thinly on a bias. 8. Stuff the pitas with the sliced steak, lettuce, onion, tomato, and feta.

Per Serving:

calorie: 331 | fat: 15g | protein: 30g | carbs: 20g | sugars: 3g | fiber: 3g | sodium: 191mg

Zesty Swiss Steak

Prep time: 35 minutes | Cook time: 35 minutes | Serves 6

3 to 4 tablespoons flour

½ teaspoon salt

¼ teaspoon pepper

1½ teaspoons dry mustard

1½ to 2 pounds round steak, trimmed of fat

1 tablespoon canola oil

1 cup sliced onions

1 pound carrots, sliced

14½ ounces can whole tomatoes

⅓ cup water

1 tablespoon brown sugar

1½ tablespoons Worcestershire sauce

1. Combine flour, salt, pepper, and dry mustard. 2. Cut steak in serving pieces. Dredge in flour mixture. 3. Set the Instant Pot to Sauté and add in the oil. Brown the steak pieces on both sides in the oil. Press Cancel. 4. Add onions and carrots into the Instant Pot. 5. Combine the tomatoes, water, brown sugar, and Worcestershire sauce. Pour into the Instant Pot. 6. Secure the lid and make sure the vent is set to sealing. Press Manual and set the time for 35 minutes. 7. When cook time is up, let the pressure release naturally for 15 minutes, then perform a quick release.

Per Serving:

calories: 236 | fat: 8g | protein: 23g | carbs: 18g | sugars: 9g | fiber: 3g | sodium: 426mg

Pork Chop Diane

Prep time: 10 minutes | Cook time: 20 minutes | Serves 4

¼ cup low-sodium chicken broth	loin chops, about 1 inch thick
1 tablespoon freshly squeezed lemon juice	Sea salt
	Freshly ground black pepper
2 teaspoons Worcestershire sauce	1 teaspoon extra-virgin olive oil
	1 teaspoon lemon zest
2 teaspoons Dijon mustard	1 teaspoon butter
4 (5 ounces) boneless pork top	2 teaspoons chopped fresh chives

1. In a small bowl, stir together the chicken broth, lemon juice, Worcestershire sauce, and Dijon mustard and set it aside. 2. Season the pork chops lightly with salt and pepper. 3. Place a large skillet over medium-high heat and add the olive oil. 4. Cook the pork chops, turning once, until they are no longer pink, about 8 minutes per side. 5. Transfer the chops to a plate and set it aside. 6. Pour the broth mixture into the skillet and cook until warmed through and thickened, about 2 minutes. 7. Whisk in the lemon zest, butter, and chives. 8. Serve the chops with a generous spoonful of sauce.

Per Serving:
calorie: 203 | fat: 7g | protein: 32g | carbs: 1g | sugars: 0g | fiber: 0g | sodium: 130mg

Mustard-Glazed Pork Chops

Prep time: 5 minutes | Cook time: 25 minutes | Serves 4

¼ cup Dijon mustard	2 tablespoons rice vinegar
1 tablespoon pure maple syrup	4 bone-in, thin-cut pork chops

1. Preheat the oven to 400°F. 2. In a small saucepan, combine the mustard, maple syrup, and rice vinegar. Stir to mix and bring to a simmer over medium heat. Cook for about 2 minutes until just slightly thickened. 3. In a baking dish, place the pork chops and spoon the sauce over them, flipping to coat. 4. Bake, uncovered, for 18 to 22 minutes until the juices run clear.

Per Serving:
calories: 257 | fat: 7g | protein: 39g | carbs: 7g | sugars: 4g | fiber: 0g | sodium: 466mg

Spice-Infused Roast Beef

Prep time: 5 minutes | Cook time: 1 hour 30 minutes | Serves 8

¾ cup grated onion, divided	1 tablespoon extra-virgin olive oil
1 tablespoon caraway seeds	
1 teaspoon ground coriander	⅓ cup red wine vinegar
1 teaspoon ground ginger	1 cup unsweetened apple juice
2-pound lean boneless chuck roast	1 bunch fresh parsley, minced

1. Preheat the oven to 325 degrees. 2. In a small bowl, combine ¼ cup of the onion, caraway seeds, coriander, and ginger, and rub into the roast. 3. In a medium saucepan over medium heat, sauté the remaining ½ cup of onion in olive oil. Place the roast in a roasting pan, and add the sautéed onion. 4. Add the vinegar, apple juice, parsley, and ½ cup water to the roasting pan. Bake the roast uncovered at 325 degrees for 1 to 1½ hours, basting frequently. Transfer the roast to a platter, and slice.

Per Serving:
calorie: 194 | fat: 8g | protein: 24g | carbs: 6g | sugars: 4g | fiber: 1g | sodium: 105mg

Pork Tenderloin Stir-Fry

Prep time: 5 minutes | Cook time: 20 minutes | Serves 6

1 tablespoon sesame oil	broth
1-pound pork tenderloin, cut into thin strips	1 tablespoon light soy sauce
	1 cup fresh snow peas, trimmed
1 tablespoon oyster sauce (found in the Asian food section of the grocery store)	1 cup broccoli florets
	½ cup sliced water chestnuts, drained
1 tablespoon cornstarch	1 cup diced red pepper
½ cup low-sodium chicken	¼ cup sliced scallions

1. In a large skillet or wok, heat the oil. Stir-fry the pork until the strips are no longer pink. 2. In a measuring cup, combine the oyster sauce, cornstarch, chicken broth, and soy sauce. Add the sauce to the pork, and cook until the sauce thickens. 3. Add the vegetables, cover, and steam for 5 minutes. Serve.

Per Serving:
calorie: 149 | fat: 5g | protein: 18g | carbs: 8g | sugars: 3g | fiber: g | sodium: 174mg

Broccoli Beef Stir-Fry

Prep time: 10 minutes | Cook time: 15 minutes | Serves 4

2 tablespoons extra-virgin olive oil	fresh ginger
	2 tablespoons reduced-sodium soy sauce
1 pound sirloin steak, cut into ¼-inch-thick strips	¼ cup beef broth
2 cups broccoli florets	½ teaspoon Chinese hot mustard
1 garlic clove, minced	Pinch red pepper flakes
1 teaspoon peeled and grated	

1. In a large skillet over medium-high heat, heat the olive oil until it shimmers. Add the beef. Cook, stirring, until it browns, 3 to 5 minutes. With a slotted spoon, remove the beef from the oil and set it aside on a plate. 2. Add the broccoli to the oil. Cook, stirring, until it is crisp-tender, about 4 minutes. 3. Add the garlic and ginger and cook, stirring constantly, for 30 seconds. 4. Return the beef to the pan, along with any juices that have collected. 5. In a small bowl, whisk together the soy sauce, broth, mustard, and red pepper flakes. 6. Add the soy sauce mixture to the skillet and cook, stirring, until everything warms through, about 3 minutes.

Per Serving:
calorie: 305 | fat: 21g | protein: 25g | carbs: 3g | sugars: 2g | fiber: 1g | sodium: 234mg

Easy Tuna Patties

Prep time: 5 minutes | Cook time: 10 minutes | Serves 4

1 pound canned tuna, drained
1 cup whole-wheat bread crumbs
2 large eggs, beaten
½ onion, grated
1 tablespoon chopped fresh dill
Juice and zest of 1 lemon
3 tablespoons extra-virgin olive oil
½ cup tartar sauce, for serving

1. In a large bowl, combine the tuna, bread crumbs, eggs, onion, dill, and lemon juice and zest. Form the mixture into 4 patties and chill for 10 minutes. 2. In a large nonstick skillet over medium-high heat, heat the olive oil until it shimmers. Add the patties and cook until browned on both sides, 4 to 5 minutes per side. 3. Serve topped with the tartar sauce.

Per Serving:
calories: 473 | fat: 25g | protein: 34g | carbs: 27g | sugars: 4g | fiber: 2g | sodium: 479mg

Asian Cod with Brown Rice, Asparagus, and Mushrooms

Prep time: 5 minutes | Cook time: 25 minutes | Serves 2

¾ cup Minute brand brown rice
½ cup water
Two 5 ounces skinless cod fillets
1 tablespoon soy sauce or tamari
1 tablespoon fresh lemon juice
½ teaspoon peeled and grated fresh ginger
1 tablespoon extra-virgin olive oil or 1 tablespoon unsalted
butter, cut into 8 pieces
2 green onions, white and green parts, thinly sliced
12 ounces asparagus, trimmed
4 ounces shiitake mushrooms, stems removed and sliced
⅛ teaspoon fine sea salt
⅛ teaspoon freshly ground black pepper
Lemon wedges for serving

1. Pour 1 cup water into the Instant Pot. Have ready two-tier stackable stainless-steel containers. 2. In one of the containers, combine the rice and ½ cup water, then gently shake the container to spread the rice into an even layer, making sure all of the grains are submerged. Place the fish fillets on top of the rice. In a small bowl, stir together the soy sauce, lemon juice, and ginger. Pour the soy sauce mixture over the fillets. Drizzle 1 teaspoon olive oil on each fillet (or top with two pieces of the butter), and sprinkle the green onions on and around the fish. 3. In the second container, arrange the asparagus in the center in as even a layer as possible. Place the mushrooms on either side of the asparagus. Drizzle with the remaining 2 teaspoons olive oil (or put the remaining six pieces butter on top of the asparagus, spacing them evenly). Sprinkle the salt and pepper evenly over the vegetables. 4. Place the container with the rice and fish on the bottom and the vegetable container on top. Cover the top container with its lid and then latch the containers together. Grasping the handle, lower the containers into the Instant Pot. 5. Secure the lid and set the Pressure Release to Sealing. Select the Pressure Cook or Manual setting and set the cooking time for 15 minutes at high pressure. (The pot will take about 10 minutes to come up to pressure before the cooking program begins.) 6. When the cooking program ends, let the pressure release naturally for 5 minutes, then move the Pressure Release to Venting to release any remaining steam. Open the pot and, wearing heat-resistant mitts, lift out the stacked containers. Unlatch, unstack, and open the containers, taking care not to get burned by the steam. 7. Transfer the vegetables, rice, and fish to plates and serve right away, with the lemon wedges on the side.

Per Serving:
calories: 344 | fat: 11g | protein: 27g | carbs: 46g | sugars: 6g | fiber: 7g | sodium: 637mg

Peppercorn-Crusted Baked Salmon

Prep time: 5 minutes | Cook time: 20 minutes | Serves 4

Nonstick cooking spray
½ teaspoon freshly ground black pepper
¼ teaspoon salt
Zest and juice of ½ lemon
¼ teaspoon dried thyme
1 pound salmon fillet

1. Preheat the oven to 425°F. Spray a baking sheet with nonstick cooking spray. 2. In a small bowl, combine the pepper, salt, lemon zest and juice, and thyme. Stir to combine. 3. Place the salmon on the prepared baking sheet, skin-side down. Spread the seasoning mixture evenly over the fillet. 4. Bake for 15 to 20 minutes, depending on the thickness of the fillet, until the flesh flakes easily.

Per Serving:
calories: 163 | fat: 7g | protein: 23g | carbs: 1g | sugars: 0g | fiber: 0g | sodium: 167mg

Grilled Scallop Kabobs

Prep time: 15 minutes | Cook time: 20 minutes | Serves 6

15 ounces pineapple chunks, packed in their own juice, undrained
¼ cup dry white wine
¼ cup light soy sauce
2 tablespoons minced fresh parsley
4 garlic cloves, minced
⅛ teaspoon freshly ground black pepper
1 pound scallops
18 large cherry tomatoes
1 large green bell pepper, cut into 1-inch squares
18 medium mushroom caps

1. Drain the pineapple, reserving the juice. In a shallow baking dish, combine the pineapple juice, wine, soy sauce, parsley, garlic, and pepper. Mix well. 2. Add the pineapple, scallops, tomatoes, green pepper, and mushrooms to the marinade. Marinate 30 minutes at room temperature, stirring occasionally. 3. Alternate pineapple, scallops, and vegetables on metal or wooden skewers (remember to soak wooden skewers in water before using). 4. Grill the kabobs over medium-hot coals about 4 to 5 inches from the heat, turning frequently, for 5 to 7 minutes.

Per Serving:
calories: 132 | fat: 1g | protein: 13g | carbs: 18g | sugars: 10g | fiber: 3g | sodium: 587mg

Whole Veggie-Stuffed Trout

Prep time: 10 minutes | Cook time: 25 minutes | Serves 2

Nonstick cooking spray

2 (8 ounces) whole trout fillets, dressed (cleaned but with bones and skin intact)

1 tablespoon extra-virgin olive oil

¼ teaspoon salt

⅛ teaspoon freshly ground black pepper

½ red bell pepper, seeded and thinly sliced

1 small onion, thinly sliced

2 or 3 shiitake mushrooms, sliced

1 poblano pepper, seeded and thinly sliced

1 lemon, sliced

1. Preheat the oven to 425°F. Spray a baking sheet with nonstick cooking spray. 2. Rub both trout, inside and out, with the olive oil, then season with the salt and pepper. 3. In a large bowl, combine the bell pepper, onion, mushrooms, and poblano pepper. Stuff half of this mixture into the cavity of each fish. Top the mixture with 2 or 3 lemon slices inside each fish. 4. Arrange the fish on the prepared baking sheet side by side and roast for 25 minutes until the fish is cooked through and the vegetables are tender.

Per Serving:

calories: 452 | fat: 22g | protein: 49g | carbs: 14g | sugars: 2g | fiber: 3g | sodium: 357mg

Walnut-Crusted Halibut with Pear Salad

Prep time: 10 minutes | Cook time: 10 minutes | Serves 4

For the halibut

¾ cup finely chopped toasted walnuts

2 tablespoons bread crumbs

¼ cup chopped fresh parsley

2 tablespoons chopped fresh chives

4 (6 to 8 ounces) halibut fillets

Kosher salt

Freshly ground black pepper

1 tablespoon extra-virgin olive

oil

For the salad

6 cups packed mixed greens

1 pear, thinly sliced

¼ cup chopped fresh parsley

¼ cup chopped fresh chives

Zest and juice of 1 lemon

Extra-virgin olive oil, for the dressing

Kosher salt

Freshly ground black pepper

To make the halibut 1. Preheat the broiler. Line a baking sheet with parchment paper. 2. In a small bowl, combine the walnuts, bread crumbs, parsley, and chives. 3. Pat the halibut fillets dry, season them with salt and pepper and rub ½ tablespoon of extra-virgin olive oil on each fillet. Place the fillets on the prepared baking sheet. Sprinkle the walnut mixture evenly on top of each fillet and press slightly, so the topping will stick. 4. Broil the fish until the crust is golden and the fish is fully cooked, 5 to 8 minutes. To make the salad 5. Meanwhile, in a large bowl, toss the greens, pear, parsley, chives, and zest until well combined. Drizzle the salad with the lemon juice and a bit of extra-virgin olive oil to taste. Season with salt and pepper to taste. 6. Evenly divide the salad among four plates and top with the fish. Serve. 7. Store any leftovers in an airtight container in the refrigerator for up to 2 days.

Per Serving:

calories: 551 | fat: 43g | protein: 31g | carbs: 13g | sugars: 4g | fiber: 5g | sodium: 196mg

Shrimp with Tomatoes and Feta

Prep time: 10 minutes | Cook time: 30 minutes | Serves 4

3 tomatoes, coarsely chopped

½ cup chopped sun-dried tomatoes

2 teaspoons minced garlic

2 teaspoons extra-virgin olive oil

1 teaspoon chopped fresh oregano

Freshly ground black pepper

1½ pounds (16–20 count) shrimp, peeled, deveined, tails removed

4 teaspoons freshly squeezed lemon juice

½ cup low-sodium feta cheese, crumbled

1. Heat the oven to 450°F. 2. In a medium bowl, toss the tomatoes, sun-dried tomatoes, garlic, oil, and oregano until well combined. 3. Season the mixture lightly with pepper. 4. Transfer the tomato mixture to a 9-by-13-inch glass baking dish. 5. Bake until softened, about 15 minutes. 6. Stir the shrimp and lemon juice into the hot tomato mixture and top evenly with the feta. 7. Bake until the shrimp are cooked through, about 15 minutes more.

Per Serving:

calories: 252 | fat: 8g | protein: 39g | carbs: 9g | sugars: 6g | fiber: 2g | sodium: 396mg

Roasted Halibut with Red Peppers, Green Beans, and Onions

Prep time: 10 minutes | Cook time: 15 minutes | Serves 4

1 pound green beans, trimmed

2 red bell peppers, seeded and cut into strips

1 onion, sliced

Zest and juice of 2 lemons

3 garlic cloves, minced

2 tablespoons extra-virgin olive

oil

1 teaspoon dried dill

1 teaspoon dried oregano

4 (4 ounces) halibut fillets

½ teaspoon salt

¼ teaspoon freshly ground black pepper

1. Preheat the oven to 400°F. Line a baking sheet with parchment paper. 2. In a large bowl, toss the green beans, bell peppers, onion, lemon zest and juice, garlic, olive oil, dill, and oregano. 3. Use a slotted spoon to transfer the vegetables to the prepared baking sheet in a single layer, leaving the juice behind in the bowl. 4. Gently place the halibut fillets in the bowl, and coat in the juice. Transfer the fillets to the baking sheet, nestled between the vegetables, and drizzle them with any juice left in the bowl. Sprinkle the vegetables and halibut with the salt and pepper. 5. Bake for 15 to 20 minutes until the vegetables are just tender and the fish flakes apart easily.

Per Serving:

calories: 234 | fat: 9g | protein: 24g | carbs: 16g | sugars: 8g | fiber: 5g | sodium: 349mg

Savory Shrimp

Prep time: 5 minutes | Cook time: 8 to 10 minutes | Serves 4

1 pound (454 g) fresh large shrimp, peeled and deveined

1 tablespoon avocado oil

2 teaspoons minced garlic, divided

½ teaspoon red pepper flakes

Sea salt and freshly ground black pepper, to taste

2 tablespoons unsalted butter, melted

2 tablespoons chopped fresh parsley

1. Place the shrimp in a large bowl and toss with the avocado oil, 1 teaspoon of minced garlic, and red pepper flakes. Season with salt and pepper. 2. Set the air fryer to 350ºF (177ºC). Arrange the shrimp in a single layer in the air fryer basket, working in batches if necessary. Cook for 6 minutes. Flip the shrimp and cook for 2 to 4 minutes more, until the internal temperature of the shrimp reaches 120ºF (49ºC). (The time it takes to cook will depend on the size of the shrimp.) 3. While the shrimp are cooking, melt the butter in a small saucepan over medium heat and stir in the remaining 1 teaspoon of garlic. 4. Transfer the cooked shrimp to a large bowl, add the garlic butter, and toss well. Top with the parsley and serve warm.

Per Serving:

calories: 182 | fat: 10g | protein: 23g | carbs: 1g | sugars: 0g | fiber: 0g | sodium: 127mg

Avo-Tuna with Croutons

Prep time: 10 minutes | Cook time: 0 minutes | Serves 3

2 (5 ounces) cans chunk-light tuna, drained

2 tablespoons low-fat mayonnaise

½ teaspoon freshly ground black

pepper

3 avocados, halved and pitted

6 tablespoons packaged croutons

1. In a medium bowl, combine the tuna, mayonnaise, and pepper, and mix well. 2. Top the avocados with the tuna mixture and croutons.

Per Serving:

calories: 441 | fat: 32g | protein: 23g | carbs: 22g | sugars: 2g | fiber: 14g | sodium: 284mg

Sole Piccata

Prep time: 10 minutes | Cook time: 20 minutes | Serves 4

1 teaspoon extra-virgin olive oil

4 (5 ounces) sole fillets, patted dry

3 tablespoons butter

2 teaspoons minced garlic

2 tablespoons all-purpose flour

2 cups low-sodium chicken broth

Juice and zest of ½ lemon

2 tablespoons capers

1. Place a large skillet over medium-high heat and add the olive oil. 2. Pat the sole fillets dry with paper towels then pan-sear them until the fish flakes easily when tested with a fork, about 4 minutes on each side. Transfer the fish to a plate and set it aside. 3. Return the skillet to the stove and add the butter. 4. Sauté the garlic until translucent, about 3 minutes. 5. Whisk in the flour to make a thick paste and cook, stirring constantly, until the mixture is golden brown, about 2 minutes. 6. Whisk in the chicken broth, lemon juice, and lemon zest. 7. Cook until the sauce has thickened, about 4 minutes. 8. Stir in the capers and serve the sauce over the fish.

Per Serving:

calories: 224 | fat: 13g | protein: 21g | carbs: 6g | sugars: 0g | fiber: 1g | sodium: 558mg

Creamy Cod with Asparagus

Prep time: 5 minutes | Cook time: 15 minutes | Serves 4

½ cup uncooked brown rice or quinoa

4 (4 ounces) cod fillets

¼ teaspoon salt

¼ teaspoon freshly ground black pepper

½ teaspoon garlic powder, divided

24 asparagus spears

Avocado oil cooking spray

1 cup half-and-half

1. Cook the rice according to the package instructions. 2. Meanwhile, season both sides of the cod fillets with the salt, pepper, and ¼ teaspoon of garlic powder. 3. Cut the bottom 1½ inches from the asparagus. 4. Heat a large pan over medium-low heat. When hot, coat the cooking surface with cooking spray, and arrange the cod and asparagus in a single layer. 5. Cover and cook for 8 minutes. 6. Add the half-and-half and the remaining ¼ teaspoon of garlic powder and stir. Increase the heat to high and simmer for 2 minutes. 7. Divide the rice, cod, and asparagus into four equal portions.

Per Serving:

calories: 219 | fat: 2g | protein: 24g | carbs: 24g | sugars: 4g | fiber: 1g | sodium: 267mg

Salmon with Brussels Sprouts

Prep time: 5 minutes | Cook time: 20 minutes | Serves 4

2 tablespoons unsalted butter, divided

20 Brussels sprouts, halved lengthwise

4 (4 ounces) skinless salmon fillets

½ teaspoon salt

¼ teaspoon garlic powder

1. Heat a medium skillet over medium-low heat. When hot, melt 1 tablespoon of butter in the skillet, then add the Brussels sprouts cut-side down. Cook for 10 minutes. 2. Season both sides of the salmon fillets with the salt and garlic powder. 3. Heat another medium skillet over medium-low heat. When hot, melt the remaining 1 tablespoon of butter in the skillet, then add the salmon. Cover and cook for 6 to 8 minutes, or until the salmon is opaque and flakes easily with a fork. 4. Meanwhile, flip the Brussels sprouts and cover. Cook for 10 minutes or until tender. 5. Divide the Brussels sprouts into four equal portions and add 1 salmon fillet to each portion.

Per Serving:

calories: 236 | fat: 11g | protein: 27g | carbs: 9g | sugars: 2g | fiber: 4g | sodium: 400mg

Shrimp Creole

Prep time: 5 minutes | Cook time: 20 minutes | Serves 3

One 8 ounces can no-salt-added fire-roasted tomatoes

½ cup sliced mushrooms

¼ cup dry white wine

½ cup chopped onion

2 garlic cloves, minced

1 cup chopped green bell pepper

1 cup chopped celery

2 bay leaves

¼ teaspoon cayenne pepper

1 pound shrimp, shelled and deveined

1. In a large skillet, combine the tomatoes, mushrooms, wine, onion, garlic, green pepper, celery, bay leaves, and cayenne pepper. Bring to a boil; cover, reduce the heat, and let simmer for 10 to 15 minutes. 2. Add the shrimp to the tomato sauce, and cook uncovered for 3 to 5 minutes until the shrimp are bright pink. 3. Discard the bay leaves, and serve on a platter.

Per Serving:

calories: 199 | fat: 3g | protein: 34g | carbs: 10g | sugars: 5g | fiber: 4g | sodium: 364mg

Blackened Pollock

Prep time: 15 minutes | Cook time: 10 minutes | Serves 2

8 ounces pollock (or other white fish) fillet, skinned and halved

3 teaspoons extra-virgin olive oil, divided

1 teaspoon blackening seasoning, or Cajun seasoning, divided

¼ cup thinly sliced onion

4 cups baby spinach, divided

½ small grapefruit, peeled and segmented

2 tablespoons shaved fennel

2 tablespoons pepitas

½ small avocado, peeled, pitted, and sliced, divided

1. Brush both sides of each pollock half with 1½ teaspoons of olive oil. 2. Rub each half all over with ½ teaspoon of blackening seasoning. 3. In a large heavy skillet set over high heat, cook the pollock and onions for 2 to 3 minutes, until blackened. Turn the fillets. Cook for 2 to 3 minutes more, or until blackened and the fish flakes easily with a fork. 4. Put 2 cups of arugula on each serving plate. Top each with 1 pollock half. 5. Top each serving with half of the grapefruit, fennel, pepitas, and avocado.

Per Serving:

calories: 302 | fat: 19g | protein: 20g | carbs: 16g | sugars: 5g | fiber: 8g | sodium: 436mg

Charcuterie Dinner For One

Prep time: 5 minutes | Cook time: 10 to 12 minutes | Serves 1

1 (6 ounces [170 g]) salmon fillet

Cooking oil spray, as needed

1 ounce (28 g) fresh mozzarella cheese slices or balls

½ cup (60 g) thinly sliced

cucumbers

¼ cup (50 g) plain nonfat Greek yogurt

1 ounce (28 g) grain-free or whole-grain crackers

1. Preheat the oven to 400°F (204°C). Line a medium baking sheet with parchment paper. 2. Lightly spray the salmon fillet with the cooking oil spray and place the salmon on the prepared baking sheet. Bake the salmon for 10 to 12 minutes, or until it has browned slightly on top. 3. Meanwhile, assemble the mozzarella cheese, cucumbers, yogurt, and crackers on a plate. 4. Transfer the salmon to the plate and serve.

Per Serving:

calorie: 517 | fat: 29g | protein: 47g | carbs: 16g | sugars: 5g | fiber: 1g | sodium: 418mg

Grilled Salmon with Dill Sauce

Prep time: 10 minutes | Cook time: 15 minutes | Serves 8

1 cup plain fat-free Greek yogurt

2 teaspoons minced fresh dill

¼ cup chopped scallions or onion

1 teaspoon capers

2 teaspoons minced fresh

parsley

1 teaspoon minced fresh chives

Nonstick cooking spray

2 pounds salmon steaks

1 tablespoon extra-virgin olive oil

1. In a small bowl, combine the yogurt, dill, scallions or onion, capers, parsley, and chives; set aside. 2. Spray the racks of your grill with nonstick cooking spray. 3. Brush the salmon steaks with olive oil, and grill them over medium-hot coals for 4 minutes per side, or just until the salmon flakes with a fork. 4. Transfer the salmon to a platter, and serve with the dill sauce on the side.

Per Serving:

calories: 181 | fat: 7g | protein: 25g | carbs: 3g | sugars: 2g | fiber: 0g | sodium: 116mg

Faux Conch Fritters

Prep time: 15 minutes | Cook time: 20 minutes | Serves 4

4 medium egg whites

½ cup fat-free milk

1 cup chickpea crumbs

¼ teaspoon freshly ground black pepper

½ teaspoon ground cumin

3 cups frozen chopped scallops,

thawed

1 small onion, finely chopped

1 small green bell pepper, finely chopped

2 celery stalks, finely chopped

2 garlic cloves, minced

Juice of 2 limes

1. Preheat the oven to 350°F. 2. In a large bowl, combine the egg whites, milk, and chickpea crumbs. 3. Add the black pepper and cumin and mix well. 4. Add the scallops, onion, bell pepper, celery, and garlic. 5. Form golf ball–size patties and place on a rimmed baking sheet 1 inch apart. 6. Transfer the baking sheet to the oven and cook for 5 to 7 minutes, or until golden brown. 7. Flip the patties, return to the oven, and bake for 5 to 7 minutes, or until golden brown. 8. Top with the lime juice, and serve.

Per Serving:

calories: 280 | fat: 4g | protein: 23g | carbs: 40g | sugars: 9g | fiber: 7g | sodium: 327mg

Sesame-Crusted Halibut

Prep time: 5 minutes | Cook time: 15 minutes | Serves 2

1 tablespoon freshly squeezed lemon juice

1 tablespoon extra-virgin olive oil

1 garlic clove, minced

Freshly ground black pepper, to season

1 (8 ounces) halibut fillet, halved

2 tablespoons sesame seeds, toasted

1 teaspoon dried basil

1 teaspoon dried marjoram

½ cup minced chives

⅛ teaspoon salt

2 lemon wedges

1. Preheat the oven to 450°F. 2. Line a baking sheet with aluminum foil. 3. In a shallow glass dish, mix together the lemon juice, olive oil, and garlic. Season with pepper. 4. Add the halibut and turn to coat. Cover and refrigerate for 15 minutes. 5. In a small bowl, combine the sesame seeds, basil, marjoram, and chives. 6. Remove the fish from the refrigerator. Sprinkle with the salt. Coat evenly with the sesame seed mixture, covering the sides as well as the top. 7. Transfer the fish to the prepared baking sheet. Place the sheet in the preheated oven. Roast for 10 to 14 minutes, or until just cooked through. 8. Garnish each serving with 1 lemon wedge.

Per Serving:

calories: 331 | fat: 27g | protein: 18g | carbs: 3g | sugars: 0g | fiber: 2g | sodium: 251mg

Citrus-Glazed Salmon

Prep time: 10 minutes | Cook time: 13 to 17 minutes | Serves 4

2 medium limes

1 small orange

⅓ cup agave syrup

1 teaspoon salt

1 teaspoon pepper

4 cloves garlic, finely chopped

1¼ pounds salmon fillet, cut

into 4 pieces

2 tablespoons sliced green onions

1 lime slice, cut into 4 wedges

1 orange slice, cut into 4 wedges

Hot cooked orzo pasta or rice, if desired

1. Heat oven to 400°F. Line 15x10x1-inch pan with cooking parchment paper or foil. In small bowl, grate lime peel from limes. Squeeze enough lime juice to equal 2 tablespoons; add to peel in bowl. Grate orange peel from oranges into bowl. Squeeze enough orange juice to equal 2 tablespoons; add to peel mixture. Stir in agave syrup, salt, pepper and garlic. In small cup, measure ¼ cup citrus mixture for salmon (reserve remaining citrus mixture). 2. Place salmon fillets in pan, skin side down. Using ¼ cup citrus mixture, brush tops and sides of salmon. Bake 13 to 17 minutes or until fish flakes easily with fork. Lift salmon pieces from skin with metal spatula onto serving plate. Sprinkle with green onions. Top each fish fillet with lime and orange wedges. Serve each fillet with 3 tablespoons reserved sauce and rice.

Per Serving:

calories: 320 | fat: 8g | protein: 31g | carbs: 30g | sugars: 23g | fiber: 3g | sodium: 680mg

Salmon Florentine

Prep time: 10 minutes | Cook time: 30 minutes | Serves 4

1 teaspoon extra-virgin olive oil

½ sweet onion, finely chopped

1 teaspoon minced garlic

3 cups baby spinach

1 cup kale, tough stems removed, torn into 3-inch pieces

Sea salt

Freshly ground black pepper

4 (5 ounces) salmon fillets

Lemon wedges, for serving

1. Preheat the oven to 350°F. 2. Place a large skillet over medium-high heat and add the oil. 3. Sauté the onion and garlic until softened and translucent, about 3 minutes. 4. Add the spinach and kale and sauté until the greens wilt, about 5 minutes. 5. Remove the skillet from the heat and season the greens with salt and pepper. 6. Place the salmon fillets so they are nestled in the greens and partially covered by them. Bake the salmon until it is opaque, about 20 minutes. 7. Serve immediately with a squeeze of fresh lemon.

Per Serving:

calories: 211 | fat: 8g | protein: 30g | carbs: 5g | sugars: 2g | fiber: 1g | sodium: 129mg

Roasted Red Snapper and Shrimp in Parchment

Prep time: 10 minutes | Cook time:45 minutes | Serves 8

One 3-pound whole red snapper or bass, cleaned

1 medium garlic clove, minced

¼ cup extra-virgin olive oil

⅛ teaspoon freshly ground black pepper

½ teaspoon finely chopped fresh thyme

1 teaspoon flour

½ pound large shrimp, shelled and deveined

½ pound sliced mushrooms

3 tablespoons lemon juice, divided

½ cup dry white wine, divided

¼ cup minced fresh parsley

Zest of 1 lemon

1. Preheat oven to 375 degrees. Wash the fish, inside and out, under cold running water, and pat dry with paper towels. 2. In a small bowl, combine the garlic, olive oil, pepper, thyme, and flour. Mix well. 3. Place the fish on a double thickness of parchment paper. In the cavity of the fish, place 1 tablespoon of the garlic mixture, 4. shrimp, and ½ cup sliced mushrooms. Sprinkle with 1 tablespoon of the lemon juice and 2 tablespoons of the wine. 4 Dot the top of the fish with the remaining garlic mixture, and arrange the remaining shrimp and mushrooms on top. Sprinkle with the remaining lemon juice and wine, and the parsley. 5. Bring the long sides of the parchment together over the fish, and secure with a double fold. Fold both ends of the parchment upward several times. 6. Place the fish on a baking sheet; bake for 30–35 minutes at 375 degrees. Transfer to a serving platter, garnish with lemon zest, and serve.

Per Serving:

calories: 272 | fat: 9g | protein: 40g | carbs: 3g | sugars: 1g | fiber: 1g | sodium: 273mg

Caribbean Haddock in a Packet

Prep time: 10 minutes | Cook time: 20 minutes | Serves 2

1 tablespoon extra-virgin olive oil, divided
1 cup angel hair coleslaw, divided
1 (8 ounces) haddock fillet, halved and rinsed
1 small tomato, thinly sliced
1 small red bell pepper, thinly sliced
½ cup chopped fresh chives
2 tablespoons chopped fresh cilantro
Juice of 1 lime
4 dashes hot pepper sauce
Dash salt
Dash freshly ground black pepper

1. Preheat the oven to 450°F. 2. Fold 2 (12-by-24-inch) aluminum foil sheets in half widthwise into 2 (12-by-12-inch) squares. 3. In the center of each foil square, brush ½ teaspoon of olive oil. 4. Place ½ cup of coleslaw in each square. 5. Top each with 1 piece of haddock. 6. Add half of the tomato slices and half of the red bell pepper slices atop each fillet. 7. Sprinkle each with 1 of the remaining 2 teaspoons of olive oil, ¼ cup of chives, 1 tablespoon of cilantro, half of the lime juice, and 2 dashes of hot pepper sauce. Season with salt and pepper. 8. Fold and seal the foil into airtight packets. Place the packets in a baking dish and into the preheated oven. Bake for 20 minutes. 9. Carefully avoiding the steam that will be released, open a packet and check that the fish is cooked. It should be opaque and flake easily. To test for doneness, poke the tines of a fork into the thickest portion of the fish at a 45-degree angle. Gently twist the fork and pull up some of the fish. If the fish resists flaking, return it to the oven for another 2 minutes then test again. Fish cooks very quickly, so be careful not to overcook it. 10. Divide the fish, vegetables, and juices between 2 serving plates.

Per Serving:

calories: 310 | fat: 16g | protein: 21g | carbs: 21g | sugars: 16g | fiber: 4g | sodium: 536mg

Roasted Salmon with Salsa Verde

Prep time: 5 minutes | Cook time: 25 minutes | Serves 4

Nonstick cooking spray
8 ounces tomatillos, husks removed
½ onion, quartered
1 jalapeño or serrano pepper, seeded
1 garlic clove, unpeeled
1 teaspoon extra-virgin olive oil
½ teaspoon salt, divided
4 (4 ounces) wild-caught salmon fillets
¼ teaspoon freshly ground black pepper
¼ cup chopped fresh cilantro
Juice of 1 lime

1. Preheat the oven to 425°F. Spray a baking sheet with nonstick cooking spray. 2. In a large bowl, toss the tomatillos, onion, jalapeño, garlic, olive oil, and ¼ teaspoon of salt to coat. Arrange in a single layer on the prepared baking sheet, and roast for about 10 minutes until just softened. Transfer to a dish or plate and set aside. 3. Arrange the salmon fillets skin-side down on the same baking sheet, and season with the remaining ¼ teaspoon of salt and the pepper. Bake for 12 to 15 minutes until the fish is firm and flakes easily. 4. Meanwhile, peel the roasted garlic and place it and the roasted vegetables in a blender or food processor. Add a scant ¼ cup of water to the jar, and process until smooth. 5. Add the cilantro and lime juice and process until smooth. Serve the salmon topped with the salsa verde.

Per Serving:

calories: 199 | fat: 9g | protein: 23g | carbs: 6g | sugars: 3g | fiber: 2g | sodium: 295mg

Teriyaki Salmon

Prep time: 30 minutes | Cook time: 12 minutes | Serves 4

4 (6 ounces / 170 g) salmon fillets
½ cup soy sauce
¼ cup packed light brown sugar
2 teaspoons rice vinegar
1 teaspoon minced garlic
¼ teaspoon ground ginger
2 teaspoons olive oil
½ teaspoon salt
¼ teaspoon freshly ground black pepper
Oil, for spraying

1. Place the salmon in a small pan, skin-side up. 2. In a small bowl, whisk together the soy sauce, brown sugar, rice vinegar, garlic, ginger, olive oil, salt, and black pepper. 3. Pour the mixture over the salmon and marinate for about 30 minutes. 4. Line the air fryer basket with parchment and spray lightly with oil. Place the salmon in the prepared basket, skin-side down. You may need to work in batches, depending on the size of your air fryer. 5. Air fry at 400°F (204°C) for 6 minutes, brush the salmon with more marinade, and cook for another 6 minutes, or until the internal temperature reaches 145°F (63°C). Serve immediately.

Per Serving:

calories: 319 | fat: 14g | protein: 37g | carbs: 8g | sugars: 6g | fiber: 1g | sodium: 762mg

Haddock with Creamy Cucumber Sauce

Prep time: 10 minutes | Cook time: 10 minutes | Serves 4

¼ cup 2 percent plain Greek yogurt
½ English cucumber, grated, liquid squeezed out
½ scallion, white and green parts, finely chopped
2 teaspoons chopped fresh mint
1 teaspoon honey
Sea salt
4 (5 ounces) haddock fillets
Freshly ground black pepper
Nonstick cooking spray

1. In a small bowl, stir together the yogurt, cucumber, scallion, mint, honey, and a pinch of salt. Set it aside. 2. Pat the fish fillets dry with paper towels and season them lightly with salt and pepper. 3. Place a large skillet over medium-high heat and spray lightly with cooking spray. 4. Cook the haddock, turning once, until it is just cooked through, about 5 minutes per side. 5. Remove the fish from the heat and transfer to plates. 6. Serve topped with the cucumber sauce.

Per Serving:

calories: 123 | fat: 1g | protein: 24g | carbs: 3g | sugars: 3g | fiber: 0g | sodium: 310mg

Salmon en Papillote

Prep time: 15 minutes | Cook time: 15 minutes | Serves 2

For the roasted vegetables
½ pound fresh green beans, trimmed
½ onion, cut into ¼-inch-thick slices
1 tablespoon extra-virgin olive oil
1 teaspoon capers (optional)
For the salmon
2 teaspoons extra-virgin olive oil, divided
2 medium parsnips, cut into

¼-inch-thick rounds, divided
2 (4 ounces) salmon fillets
2 garlic cloves, thinly sliced, divided
1 lemon, divided (½ cut into slices, the other ½ cut into 2 wedges)
1 tablespoon chopped fresh thyme, divided
Kosher salt
Freshly ground black pepper

To make the roasted vegetables 1. Preheat the oven to 400°F. Line a baking sheet with parchment paper. 2. In a medium bowl, toss the green beans, onion, extra-virgin olive oil, and capers (if using) until well coated. 3. Spread the vegetables on half of the baking sheet and set aside until the salmon is ready to bake. To make the salmon 4. Cut two pieces of parchment paper, fold them in half, and cut each into a heart shape (about 10 to 12 inches in circumference). Lightly brush the parchment with ½ teaspoon of extra-virgin olive oil. 5. Open one of the hearts and place half the parsnips on the right half in the center, fanning them out. Place one piece of salmon on the fanned parsnips. Add half the garlic, half the lemon slices, half the thyme, ½ teaspoon of extra-virgin olive oil, and a pinch each of kosher salt and pepper. 6. Seal the packet by folding the left half of the heart over the right side. Fold along the edge of the heart and create a seal. Repeat with the other piece of parchment. 7. Place the packets on the empty side of the baking sheet and bake until the salmon is cooked through, 10 to 15 minutes. Allow the fish to rest a few minutes before serving with the roasted green beans and remaining lemon wedges. 8. Store any leftovers in an airtight container in the refrigerator for 1 to 2 days.

Per Serving:
calories: 389 | fat: 17g | protein: 28g | carbs: 35g | sugars: 11g | fiber: 10g | sodium: 261mg

Baked Oysters

Prep time: 30 minutes | Cook time: 15 minutes | Serves 2

2 cups coarse salt, for holding the oysters
1 dozen fresh oysters, scrubbed
1 tablespoon butter
½ cup finely chopped artichoke hearts
¼ cup finely chopped scallions, both white and green parts

¼ cup finely chopped red bell pepper
1 garlic clove, minced
1 tablespoon finely chopped fresh parsley
Zest and juice of ½ lemon
Pinch salt
Freshly ground black pepper

1. Pour the coarse salt into an 8-by-8-inch baking dish and spread to evenly fill the bottom of the dish. 2. Prepare a clean surface to shuck the oysters. Using a shucking knife, insert the blade at the joint of the shell, where it hinges open and shut. Firmly apply pressure to pop the blade in, and work the knife around the shell to open. Discard the empty half of the shell. Use the knife to gently loosen the oyster, and remove any shell particles. Set the oysters in their shells on the salt, being careful not to spill the juices. 3. Preheat the oven to 425°F. 4. In a large skillet, melt the butter over medium heat. Add the artichoke hearts, scallions, and bell pepper, and cook for 5 to 7 minutes. Add the garlic and cook an additional minute. Remove from the heat and mix in the parsley, lemon zest and juice, and season with salt and pepper. 5. Divide the vegetable mixture evenly among the oysters and bake for 10 to 12 minutes until the vegetables are lightly browned.

Per Serving:
calories: 134 | fat: 7g | protein: 6g | carbs: 11g | sugars: 7g | fiber: 2g | sodium: 281mg

Tomato Tuna Melts

Prep time: 5 minutes | Cook time: 5 minutes | Serves 2

1 (5 ounces) can chunk light tuna packed in water, drained
2 tablespoons plain nonfat Greek yogurt
2 teaspoons freshly squeezed lemon juice
2 tablespoons finely chopped

celery
1 tablespoon finely chopped red onion
Pinch cayenne pepper
1 large tomato, cut into ¾-inch-thick rounds
½ cup shredded cheddar cheese

1. Preheat the broiler to high. 2. In a medium bowl, combine the tuna, yogurt, lemon juice, celery, red onion, and cayenne pepper. Stir well. 3. Arrange the tomato slices on a baking sheet. Top each with some tuna salad and cheddar cheese. 4. Broil for 3 to 4 minutes until the cheese is melted and bubbly. Serve.

Per Serving:
calories: 243 | fat: 10g | protein: 30g | carbs: 7g | sugars: 2g | fiber: 1g | sodium: 444mg

Broiled Sole with Mustard Sauce

Prep time: 5 minutes | Cook time: 20 minutes | Serves 6

Nonstick cooking spray
1½ pound fresh sole filets
3 tablespoons low-fat mayonnaise
2 tablespoons Dijon mustard

2 tablespoons chopped parsley
⅛ teaspoon freshly ground black pepper
1 large lemon, cut into wedges

1. Preheat broiler. Coat a baking sheet with nonstick cooking spray. Arrange the filets so they don't overlap. 2. In a small bowl, combine the mayonnaise, mustard, parsley, and pepper, and mix thoroughly. Spread the mixture evenly over the filets. Broil 3–4 inches from the heat for 4 minutes until the fish flakes easily with a fork. 3. Arrange the filets on a serving platter, garnish with lemon wedges, and serve.

Per Serving:
calories: 104 | fat: 4g | protein: 14g | carbs: 3g | sugars: 1g | fiber: 1g | sodium: 402mg

Catfish with Corn and Pepper Relish

Prep time: 10 minutes | Cook time: 10 minutes | Serves 4

3 tablespoons extra-virgin olive oil, divided

4 (5 ounces) catfish fillets

¼ teaspoon salt

¼ teaspoon freshly ground black pepper

1 (15 ounces) can low-sodium black beans, drained and rinsed

1 cup frozen corn

1 medium red bell pepper, diced

1 tablespoon apple cider vinegar

3 tablespoons chopped scallions

1. Use 1½ tablespoons of oil to coat both sides of the catfish fillets, then season the fillets with the salt and pepper. 2. Heat a small saucepan over medium-high heat. Put the remaining 1½ tablespoons of oil, beans, corn, bell pepper, and vinegar in the pan and stir. Cover and cook for 5 minutes. 3. Place the catfish fillets on top of the relish mixture and cover. Cook for 5 to 7 minutes. 4. Serve each catfish fillet with one-quarter of the relish and top with the scallions.

Per Serving:

calories: 379 | fat: 15g | protein: 32g | carbs: 31g | sugars: 2g | fiber: 10g | sodium: 366mg

Quinoa Pilaf with Salmon and Asparagus

Prep time: 30 minutes | Cook time: 15 minutes | Serves 4

1 cup uncooked quinoa

6 cups water

1 vegetable bouillon cube

1 pound salmon fillets

2 teaspoons butter or margarine

20 stalks fresh asparagus, cut diagonally into 2-inch pieces (2 cups)

4 medium green onions, sliced (¼ cup)

1 cup frozen sweet peas (from 1 pound bag), thawed

½ cup halved grape tomatoes

½ cup vegetable or chicken broth

1 teaspoon lemon-pepper seasoning

2 teaspoons chopped fresh or ½ teaspoon dried dill weed

1. Rinse quinoa thoroughly by placing in a fine-mesh strainer and holding under cold running water until water runs clear; drain well. 2. In 2-quart saucepan, heat 2 cups of the water to boiling over high heat. Add quinoa; reduce heat to low. Cover; simmer 10 to 12 minutes or until water is absorbed. 3. Meanwhile, in 12-inch skillet, heat remaining 4 cups water and the bouillon cube to boiling over high heat. Add salmon, skin side up; reduce heat to low. Cover; simmer 10 to 12 minutes or until fish flakes easily with fork. Transfer with slotted spoon to plate; let cool. Discard water. Remove skin from salmon; break into large pieces. 4. Meanwhile, rinse and dry skillet. Melt butter in skillet over medium heat. Add asparagus; cook 5 minutes, stirring frequently. Stir in onions; cook 1 minute, stirring frequently. Stir in peas, tomatoes and broth; cook 1 minute. 5. Gently stir quinoa, salmon, lemon-pepper seasoning and dill weed into asparagus mixture. Cover; cook about 2 minutes or until hot.

Per Serving:

calories: 380 | fat: 12g | protein: 32g | carbs: 37g | sugars: 7g | fiber: 6g | sodium: 600mg

Lobster Fricassee

Prep time: 5 minutes | Cook time: 20 minutes | Serves 4

2 cups shelled lobster meat

1 tablespoon extra-virgin olive oil

¾ pound mushrooms, sliced

1 small onion, minced

½ cup fat-free milk

¼ cup flour

¼ teaspoon paprika

¼ teaspoon salt

⅛ teaspoon freshly ground black pepper

2 cups cooked whole-wheat pasta

¼ cup finely chopped parsley

1. Cut the lobster meat into bite-size pieces. In a saucepan, heat the oil; add the mushrooms and onion, and sauté for 5 to 6 minutes. 2. In a small bowl, whisk the milk and flour, whisking quickly to eliminate any lumps. Pour the milk mixture into the mushroom mixture; mix thoroughly, and continue cooking for 3 to 5 minutes. 3. Add the lobster, paprika, salt, and pepper; continue cooking for 5 to 10 minutes until the lobster is heated through. 4. Spread the pasta onto a serving platter, spoon the lobster and sauce over the top, and garnish with parsley to serve.

Per Serving:

calories: 248 | fat: 5g | protein: 22g | carbs: 31g | sugars: 5g | fiber: 5g | sodium: 523mg

Tuna Poke with Riced Broccoli

Prep time: 15 minutes | Cook time: 5 minutes | Serves 2

For the tuna poke

½ pound sushi-grade tuna (see tip), cut into ½-inch cubes

2 tablespoons soy sauce or tamari

1 tablespoon rice vinegar

1 teaspoon sesame oil

For the bowl

½ tablespoon extra-virgin olive oil

1 small head broccoli, grated

1 cup thawed (if frozen) edamame

1 medium carrot, julienned

1 cucumber, diced

2 scallions, both white and green parts, thinly sliced

Optional toppings

Avocado slices

Shaved radish

Toasted sesame seeds

Pickled ginger

To make the tuna poke 1. In a medium bowl, toss together the tuna, soy sauce, rice vinegar, and sesame oil. 2. Set aside. To make the bowl 3. Heat the oil in a large skillet over medium heat and sauté the broccoli until tender, 2 to 3 minutes. Remove the skillet from the heat and allow the broccoli to cool. 4. Assemble two bowls by placing riced broccoli as the base. Top each bowl with the tuna poke, edamame, carrot, and cucumber. Drizzle the remaining juices from the tuna marinade over the bowls and garnish with sliced scallions. 5. Store any leftovers in an airtight container in the refrigerator for up to 2 days.

Per Serving:

calories: 454 | fat: 18g | protein: 43g | carbs: 34g | sugars: 13g | fiber: 13g | sodium: 412mg

Scallops and Asparagus Skillet

Prep time: 10 minutes | Cook time: 15 minutes | Serves 4

3 teaspoons extra-virgin olive oil, divided

1 pound asparagus, trimmed and cut into 2-inch segments

1 tablespoon butter

1 pound sea scallops

¼ cup dry white wine

Juice of 1 lemon

2 garlic cloves, minced

¼ teaspoon freshly ground black pepper

1. In a large skillet, heat 1½ teaspoons of oil over medium heat. 2. Add the asparagus and sauté for 5 to 6 minutes until just tender, stirring regularly. Remove from the skillet and cover with aluminum foil to keep warm. 3. Add the remaining 1½ teaspoons of oil and the butter to the skillet. When the butter is melted and sizzling, place the scallops in a single layer in the skillet. Cook for about 3 minutes on one side until nicely browned. Use tongs to gently loosen and flip the scallops, and cook on the other side for another 3 minutes until browned and cooked through. Remove and cover with foil to keep warm. 4. In the same skillet, combine the wine, lemon juice, garlic, and pepper. Bring to a simmer for 1 to 2 minutes, stirring to mix in any browned pieces left in the pan. 5. Return the asparagus and the cooked scallops to the skillet to coat with the sauce. Serve warm.

Per Serving:

calories: 252 | fat: 7g | protein: 26g | carbs: 15g | sugars: 3g | fiber: 2g | sodium: 493mg

Fish Tacos

Prep time: 5 minutes | Cook time: 10 minutes | Serves 4

For the Tacos

2 tablespoons extra-virgin olive oil

4 (6 ounces) cod fillets

8 (10-inch) yellow corn tortillas

2 cups packaged shredded cabbage

¼ cup chopped fresh cilantro

4 lime wedges

For the Sauce

½ cup plain low-fat Greek yogurt

⅓ cup low-fat mayonnaise

½ teaspoon garlic powder

½ teaspoon ground cumin

To Make the Tacos 1. Heat a medium skillet over medium-low heat. When hot, pour the oil into the skillet, then add the fish and cover. Cook for 4 minutes, then flip and cook for 4 minutes more. 2. Top each tortilla with one-eighth of the cabbage, sauce, cilantro, and fish. Finish each taco with a squeeze of lime. To Make the Sauce 3. In a small bowl, whisk together the yogurt, mayonnaise, garlic powder, and cumin.

Per Serving:

calories: 373 | fat: 13g | protein: 36g | carbs: 30g | sugars: 4g | fiber: 4g | sodium: 342mg

Stuffed Flounder Florentine

Prep time: 10 minutes | Cook time: 25 minutes | Serves 4

¼ cup pine nuts

2 tablespoons olive oil

½ cup chopped tomatoes

1 (6 ounces / 170 g) bag spinach, coarsely chopped

2 cloves garlic, chopped

Salt and freshly ground black

pepper, to taste

2 tablespoons unsalted butter, divided

4 flounder fillets (about 1½ pounds / 680 g)

Dash of paprika

½ lemon, sliced into 4 wedges

1. Place the pine nuts in a baking dish that fits in your air fryer. Set the air fryer to 400°F (204°C) and air fry for 4 minutes until the nuts are lightly browned and fragrant. Remove the baking dish from the air fryer, tip the nuts onto a plate to cool, and continue preheating the air fryer. When the nuts are cool enough to handle, chop them into fine pieces. 2. In the baking dish, combine the oil, tomatoes, spinach, and garlic. Use tongs to toss until thoroughly combined. Air fry for 5 minutes until the tomatoes are softened and the spinach is wilted. 3. Transfer the vegetables to a bowl and stir in the toasted pine nuts. Season to taste with salt and freshly ground black pepper. 4. Place 1 tablespoon of the butter in the bottom of the baking dish. Lower the heat on the air fryer to 350°F (177°C). 5. Place the flounder on a clean work surface. Sprinkle both sides with salt and black pepper. Divide the vegetable mixture among the flounder fillets and carefully roll up, securing with toothpicks. 6. Working in batches if necessary, arrange the fillets seam-side down in the baking dish along with 1 tablespoon of water. Top the fillets with remaining 1 tablespoon butter and sprinkle with a dash of paprika. 7.Cover loosely with foil and air fry for 10 to 15 minutes until the fish is opaque and flakes easily with a fork. Remove the toothpicks before serving with the lemon wedges.

Per Serving:

calories: 287 | fat: 21g | protein: 21g | carbs: 5g | sugars: 1g | fiber: 2g | sodium: 692mg

Chapter 10

Vegetables and Sides

Roasted Lemon and Garlic Broccoli

Prep time: 10 minutes | Cook time: 25 minutes | Serves 8

2 large broccoli heads, cut into florets
3 garlic cloves, minced
2 tablespoons extra-virgin olive oil
¼ teaspoon salt
¼ teaspoon freshly ground black pepper
2 tablespoons freshly squeezed lemon juice

1. Preheat the oven to 425°F. 2. On a rimmed baking sheet, toss the broccoli, garlic, and olive oil. Season with the salt and pepper. 3. Roast, tossing occasionally, for 25 to 30 minutes until tender and browned. Season with the lemon juice and serve.

Per Serving:
calories: 30 | fat: 2g | protein: 1g | carbs: 3g | sugars: 1g | fiber: 1g | sodium: 84mg

Blooming Onion

Prep time: 10 minutes | Cook time: 10 minutes | Serves 8

2 Vidalia onions, peeled
1 cup whole-wheat flour
1 cup chickpea flour
2 tablespoons paprika
1 teaspoon ground cumin
1 teaspoon Creole seasoning
1 cup low-fat buttermilk
2 medium egg whites

1. Cut off the top of each onion, then cut each onion vertically until you almost reach the base, taking care not to cut all the way through. Rotate each onion, and make 4 to 6 more vertical cuts to create blooming flowers. 2. In a mixing bowl, use a fork to combine the whole-wheat flour, chickpea flour, paprika, cumin, and Creole seasoning. 3. In another bowl, whisk the buttermilk and egg whites together. 4. Soak the onions in the buttermilk-egg mixture for 60 to 90 seconds, then dredge in the flour mixture. Dunk again in the buttermilk-egg mixture, and place the coated onion in the basket of an air fryer. 5. Set the air fryer to 390°F, close, and cook for 10 minutes. 6. Serve with a plate of greens.

Per Serving:
calories: 135 | fat: 2g | protein: 7g | carbs: 23g | sugars: 4g | fiber: 4g | sodium: 82mg

Peas with Mushrooms and Thyme

Prep time: 10 minutes | Cook time: 10 minutes | Serves 6

2 teaspoons olive, canola or soybean oil
1 medium onion, diced (½ cup)
1 cup sliced fresh mushrooms
1 bag (16 ounces) frozen sweet peas
¼ teaspoon coarse (kosher or sea) salt
⅛ teaspoon white pepper
1 teaspoon chopped fresh or ¼ teaspoon dried thyme leaves

1. In 10-inch skillet, heat oil over medium heat. Add onion and mushrooms; cook 3 minutes, stirring occasionally. Stir in peas. Cook 3 to 5 minutes, stirring occasionally, until vegetables are tender. 2.

Sprinkle with salt, pepper and thyme. Serve immediately.

Per Serving:
calorie: 80 | fat: 1g | protein: 4g | carbs: 11g | sugars: 4g | fiber: 2g | sodium: 150mg

Lean Green Avocado Mashed Potatoes

Prep time: 15 minutes | Cook time: 30 minutes | Serves 4

2 large russet potatoes, chopped
1 large head cauliflower, cut into 1-inch (2.5 cm) florets
2 medium leeks, washed and coarsely chopped
2 teaspoons (10 ml) olive oil
1 tablespoon (3 g) dried
rosemary
1 tablespoon (3 g) dried thyme
2 cloves garlic
1 medium avocado, peeled and pitted
2 tablespoons (8 g) finely chopped fresh chives

1. Preheat the oven to 400°F (204°C). 2. Spread out the potatoes, cauliflower, and leeks on a large baking sheet. Drizzle the vegetables with the oil, then sprinkle them with the rosemary and thyme. Add the garlic to the baking sheet. Bake the vegetables for about 30 minutes, until the potatoes are fork-tender. 3. Transfer the vegetables to a food processor and add the avocado. Process the mixture to the desired consistency. 4. Top the mashed potatoes with the chives and serve.

Per Serving:
calorie: 248 | fat: 10g | protein: 7g | carbs: 37g | sugars: 6g | fiber: 9g | sodium: 69mg

Ribboned Squash with Bacon

Prep time: 15 minutes | Cook time: 10 minutes | Serves 4

¼ cup dried currants or golden raisins
¼ cup red wine vinegar
1 pound butternut squash, seeded and skin removed
4 bacon slices
2 tablespoons extra-virgin olive oil (optional)
½ cup chopped, toasted walnuts
4 cups arugula
Freshly ground black pepper
½ cup chopped fresh parsley

1. In a small bowl, combine the currants and vinegar and allow to soak until tender, about 10 minutes. 2. Using a vegetable peeler, peel the squash into long ribbons into a large bowl. Set aside. 3. Place the bacon slices in a medium skillet over medium heat, cover, and fry for 8 to 10 minutes until cooked through and crispy. Remove the bacon from the heat and drain it on a paper towel. Chop the bacon into bite-size pieces when it's cool enough to handle. 4. Return the pan to medium heat with the bacon fat (or wipe it out and then add the extra-virgin olive oil). Add the walnuts. Heat the walnuts for 2 minutes, then transfer the mixture from the skillet to the squash noodles and toss well. Add the currants with their soaking liquid, along with the arugula and reserved bacon. 5. Season with pepper and serve topped with parsley. 6. Store any leftovers in an airtight container in the refrigerator for up to 4 days.

Per Serving:
calories: 294 | fat: 24g | protein: 7g | carbs: 16g | sugars: 3g | fiber: 4g | sodium: 138mg

Spicy Roasted Cauliflower with Lime

Prep time: 5 minutes | Cook time: 10 minutes | Serves 4

1 cauliflower head, broken into small florets	½ teaspoon ground chipotle chili powder
2 tablespoons extra-virgin olive oil	½ teaspoon salt
	Juice of 1 lime

1. Preheat the oven to 450°F. Line a rimmed baking sheet with parchment paper. 2. In a large mixing bowl, toss the cauliflower with the olive oil, chipotle chili powder, and salt. Arrange in a single layer on the prepared baking sheet. 3. Roast for 15 minutes, flip, and continue to roast for 15 more minutes until well-browned and tender. 4. Sprinkle with the lime juice, adjust the salt as needed, and serve.

Per Serving:

calories: 99 | fat: 7 | protein: 3g | carbs: 8g | sugars: 3g | fiber: 3g | sodium: 284mg

Sweet-and-Sour Cabbage Slaw

Prep time: 10 minutes | Cook time: 0 minutes | Serves 2

2 tablespoons apple cider vinegar	1 tart apple, cored and diced
1 tablespoon granulated stevia	½ cup shredded carrot
2 cups angel hair cabbage	2 medium scallions, sliced
	2 tablespoons sliced almonds

1. In a medium bowl, stir together the vinegar and stevia. 2. In a large bowl, mix together the cabbage, apple, carrot, and scallions. 3. Pour the sweetened vinegar over the vegetable mixture. Toss to combine. 4. Garnish with the sliced almonds and serve.

Per Serving:

calories: 125 | fat: 1g | protein: 2g | carbs: 30g | sugars: 21g | fiber: 5g | sodium: 47mg

Smashed Cucumber Salad

Prep time: 10 minutes | Cook time: 0 minutes | Serves 4 to 6

2 pounds mini cucumbers (English or Persian), unpeeled	¾ teaspoon ground cumin
½ teaspoon kosher salt	¼ teaspoon turmeric
1 tablespoon extra-virgin olive oil	Juice of 1 lime
	½ cup cilantro leaves

1. Cut the cucumbers crosswise into 4-inch pieces and again in half lengthwise. 2. On a work surface, place one cucumber, flesh-side down. Place the side of the knife blade on the cucumber and carefully smash down lightly with your hand. Alternatively, put in a plastic bag, seal, and smash with a rolling pin or similar tool. Be careful not to break the bag. The skin of the cucumber should crack and flesh will break away. Repeat with all the cucumbers and cut the smashed pieces on a bias into bite-size pieces. 3. Transfer the cucumber pieces to a strainer and toss them with the salt. Allow the cucumbers to rest for at least 15 minutes. 4. Meanwhile, prepare the dressing by whisking together the extra-virgin olive oil, cumin, turmeric, and lime juice in a small bowl. 5. When the cucumbers are ready, shake them to remove any excess liquid. Transfer the cucumbers to a large bowl with the dressing and cilantro and toss to combine. Serve. 6. Store any leftovers in an airtight container in the refrigerator for up to 2 days.

Per Serving:

calories: 55 | fat: 3g | protein: 1g | carbs: 8g | sugars: 3g | fiber: 1g | sodium: 238mg

Squash and Tomato Cassoulet

Prep time: 5 minutes | Cook time: 30 minutes | Serves 6

1 tablespoon extra-virgin olive oil	¼ teaspoon salt
6 small yellow squash, sliced	⅛ teaspoon freshly ground black pepper
1 medium onion, minced	2 medium tomatoes, sliced
2 garlic cloves, minced	3 egg whites
2 tablespoons chopped fresh parsley	1 cup fat-free milk

1. Preheat the oven to 350 degrees. 2. In a large skillet over medium heat, heat the oil. Add the squash, onion, and garlic, and sauté for 5 minutes. Add the parsley, salt, and pepper. 3. Layer the squash mixture and tomatoes in a casserole dish. 4. In a bowl, combine the egg whites and milk, blending well. Pour over the vegetables. 5. Bake at 350 degrees for 20–25 minutes or until the custard is set. Remove from the oven, and let cool slightly before serving.

Per Serving:

calories: 55 | fat: 2g | protein: 4g | carbs: 5g | sugars: 3g | fiber: 1g | sodium: 148mg

Italian Wild Mushrooms

Prep time: 30 minutes | Cook time: 3 minutes | Serves 10

2 tablespoons canola oil	mushrooms, cleaned and chopped
2 large onions, chopped	3 fresh bay leaves
4 garlic cloves, minced	10 fresh basil leaves, chopped
3 large red bell peppers, chopped	1 teaspoon salt
3 large green bell peppers, chopped	1½ teaspoons pepper
12 ounces package oyster	28 ounces can Italian plum tomatoes, crushed or chopped

1. Press Sauté on the Instant Pot and add in the oil. Once the oil is heated, add the onions, garlic, peppers, and mushroom to the oil. Sauté just until mushrooms begin to turn brown. 2. Add remaining ingredients. Stir well. 3. Secure the lid and make sure vent is set to sealing. Press Manual and set time for 3 minutes. 4. When cook time is up, release the pressure manually. Discard bay leaves.

Per Serving:

calories: 82 | fat: 3g | protein: 3g | carbs: 13g | sugars: 8g | fiber: 4g | sodium: 356mg

Snow Peas with Sesame Seeds

Prep time: 5 minutes | Cook time: 5 minutes | Serves 6

2 cups water	¼ teaspoon salt
1 pound trimmed fresh snow peas	⅛ teaspoon freshly ground black pepper
3 tablespoons sesame seeds	1 teaspoon ground ginger
1 tablespoon chopped shallots	

1. In a saucepan over high heat, boil the water. Add the snow peas, and then turn off the heat. After 1 minute, rinse the snow peas under cold running water to stop the cooking process; drain. (This method of blanching helps the snow peas to retain their bright green color and crispness.) 2. In a skillet, toast the sesame seeds for 1 minute over medium heat. Add the snow peas, shallots, salt, pepper, and ginger. Continue sautéing for 1–2 minutes until the snow peas are coated with sesame seeds. Serve.

Per Serving:

calories: 59 | fat: 3g | protein: 3g | carbs: 7g | sugars: 3g | fiber: 3g | sodium: 104mg

Garlic Roasted Radishes

Prep time: 5 minutes | Cook time: 15 minutes | Serves 2 to 4

1 pound radishes, halved	4 garlic cloves, thinly sliced
1 tablespoon canola oil	¼ cup chopped fresh dill
Pinch kosher salt	

1. Preheat the oven to 425°F. Line a baking sheet with parchment paper. 2. In a medium bowl, toss the radishes with the canola oil and salt. Spread the vegetables on the prepared baking sheet and roast for 10 minutes. Remove the sheet from the oven, add the garlic, mix well, and return to the oven for 5 minutes. 3. Remove the radishes from the oven, adjust the seasoning as desired, and serve topped with dill on a serving plate or as a side dish. 4. Store any leftovers in an airtight container in the refrigerator for 3 to 4 days.

Per Serving:

calories: 75 | fat: 5g | protein: 1g | carbs: 8g | sugars: 4g | fiber: 3g | sodium: 420mg

Artichokes Parmesan

Prep time: 5 minutes | Cook time: 20 minutes | Serves 6

½ cup dried whole-wheat bread crumbs	9 ounces frozen artichoke hearts, thawed
2 tablespoons grated Parmigiano-Reggiano cheese	2 tablespoons extra-virgin olive oil, divided
⅛ teaspoon freshly ground black pepper	2 medium tomatoes, diced

1. Preheat the oven to 425 degrees. 2. In a small bowl, combine the bread crumbs, cheese, and black pepper, and stir to combine. 3. Arrange the artichoke hearts in a 1-quart casserole dish. Sprinkle the tomatoes over the top. Season with salt, if desired. 4. Sprinkle the bread crumb mixture over the vegetables, and bake for 15–20 minutes or until the topping is light brown.

Per Serving:

calories: 78 | fat: 5g | protein: 2g | carbs:7 g | sugars: 1g | fiber: 2g | sodium: 67mg

Sautéed Spinach with Parmesan and Almonds

Prep time: 5 minutes | Cook time: 5 minutes | Serves 2

2 teaspoons extra-virgin olive oil	2 teaspoons balsamic vinegar
2 tablespoons sliced almonds	⅛ teaspoon salt
2 garlic cloves, minced	2 tablespoons soy Parmesan cheese
2 (5 ounces) bags prewashed spinach	Freshly ground black pepper, to season

1. In a large nonstick skillet or Dutch oven set over medium-high heat, heat the olive oil. 2. Add the almonds and garlic. Cook for 30 seconds, stirring, or until fragrant. 3. Add the spinach. Cook for about 2 minutes, stirring, until just wilted. Remove the pan from the heat. 4. Stir in the balsamic vinegar and salt. 5. Sprinkle with the soy Parmesan cheese. Season with pepper and serve immediately.

Per Serving:

calories: 84 | fat: 7g | protein: 3g | carbs: 4g | sugars: 1g | fiber: 1g | sodium: 262mg

Callaloo Redux

Prep time: 15 minutes | Cook time: 25 minutes | Serves 6

3 cups store-bought low-sodium vegetable broth	1 small onion, chopped
1 (13½ ounces) can light coconut milk	½ butternut squash, peeled, seeded, and cut into 4-inch chunks
¼ cup coconut cream	1 bunch collard greens, stemmed and chopped
1 tablespoon unsalted non-hydrogenated plant-based butter	1 hot pepper (Scotch bonnet or habanero)
12 ounces okra, cut into 1-inch chunks	

1. In an electric pressure cooker, combine the vegetable broth, coconut milk, coconut cream, and butter. 2. Layer the okra, onion, squash, collard greens, and whole hot pepper on top. 3. Close and lock the lid, and set the pressure valve to sealing. 4. Select the Manual/Pressure Cook setting, and cook for 20 minutes. 5. Once cooking is complete, quick-release the pressure. Carefully remove the lid. 6. Remove and discard the hot pepper. Carefully transfer the callaloo to a blender, and blend until smooth. Serve spooned over grits.

Per Serving:

calories: 258 | fat: 21g | protein: 5g | carbs: 17g | sugars: 8g | fiber: 5g | sodium: 88mg

Sautéed Sweet Peppers

Prep time: 5 minutes | Cook time: 10 minutes | Serves 6

1 tablespoon extra-virgin olive oil

2 medium green bell peppers, cut into 1-inch squares

2 medium red bell peppers, cut into 1-inch squares

2 tablespoons water

¼ teaspoon salt

⅛ teaspoon freshly ground black pepper

2 tablespoons finely chopped fresh basil or oregano

2 cups precooked brown rice, hot

1. In a large skillet over medium heat, heat the oil. Add the peppers, and sauté for 3–5 minutes, stirring frequently. 2. Add the water, salt, and pepper; continue sautéing for 4–5 minutes or until the peppers are just tender. Stir in the basil, and remove from the heat. 3. Spread the rice over a serving platter, spoon the peppers and liquid on top, and serve.

Per Serving:

calories: 111 | fat: 3g | protein: 2g | carbs: 19g | sugars: 3g | fiber: 2g | sodium: 103mg

Lemony Brussels Sprouts with Poppy Seeds

Prep time: 10 minutes | Cook time: 2 minutes | Serves 4

1 pound (454 g) Brussels sprouts

2 tablespoons avocado oil, divided

1 cup vegetable broth or chicken bone broth

1 tablespoon minced garlic

½ teaspoon kosher salt

Freshly ground black pepper, to taste

½ medium lemon

½ tablespoon poppy seeds

1. Trim the Brussels sprouts by cutting off the stem ends and removing any loose outer leaves. Cut each in half lengthwise (through the stem). 2. Set the electric pressure cooker to the Sauté/More setting. When the pot is hot, pour in 1 tablespoon of the avocado oil. 3. Add half of the Brussels sprouts to the pot, cut-side down, and let them brown for 3 to 5 minutes without disturbing. Transfer to a bowl and add the remaining tablespoon of avocado oil and the remaining Brussels sprouts to the pot. Hit Cancel and return all of the Brussels sprouts to the pot. 4. Add the broth, garlic, salt, and a few grinds of pepper. Stir to distribute the seasonings. 5. Close and lock the lid of the pressure cooker. Set the valve to sealing. 6. Cook on high pressure for 2 minutes. 7. While the Brussels sprouts are cooking, zest the lemon, then cut it into quarters. 8. When the cooking is complete, hit Cancel and quick release the pressure. 9. Once the pin drops, unlock and remove the lid. 10. Using a slotted spoon, transfer the Brussels sprouts to a serving bowl. Toss with the lemon zest, a squeeze of lemon juice, and the poppy seeds. Serve immediately.

Per Serving:

calories: 125 | fat: 8g | protein: 4g | carbs: 13g | sugars: 3g | fiber: 5g | sodium: 504mg

Roasted Eggplant

Prep time: 15 minutes | Cook time: 15 minutes | Serves 4

1 large eggplant

2 tablespoons olive oil

¼ teaspoon salt

½ teaspoon garlic powder

1. Remove top and bottom from eggplant. Slice eggplant into ¼-inch-thick round slices. 2. Brush slices with olive oil. Sprinkle with salt and garlic powder. Place eggplant slices into the air fryer basket. 3. Adjust the temperature to 390ºF (199ºC) and set the timer for 15 minutes. 4. Serve immediately.

Per Serving:

calories: 98 | fat: 7g | protein: 2g | carbs: 8g | sugars: 3g | fiber: 3g | sodium: 200mg

Balsamic Green Beans and Fennel

Prep time: 20 minutes | Cook time: 18 minutes | Serves 4

2 teaspoons olive or canola oil

1 medium bulb fennel, cut into thin wedges

1 small onion, cut into thin wedges

2 cups frozen whole green beans

¼ cup water

2 teaspoons packed brown sugar

¼ teaspoon salt

¼ teaspoon freshly ground pepper

1 tablespoon balsamic vinegar

1. In 12-inch nonstick skillet, heat oil over medium heat. Add fennel and onion; cook 7 to 8 minutes, stirring frequently, until fennel is light golden brown. 2. Add beans and water; heat to boiling. Stir; reduce heat to low. Cover; simmer 6 to 8 minutes or until beans are crisp-tender. 3. Stir in remaining ingredients; cook and stir 15 to 30 seconds longer or until vegetables are coated.

Per Serving:

calorie: 80 | fat: 3g | protein: 1g | carbs: 13g | sugars: 6g | fiber: 4g | sodium: 180mg

Dandelion Greens with Sweet Onion

Prep time: 15 minutes | Cook time: 15 minutes | Serves 4

1 tablespoon extra-virgin olive oil

1 Vidalia onion, thinly sliced

2 garlic cloves, minced

½ cup store-bought low-sodium

vegetable broth

2 bunches dandelion greens, roughly chopped

Freshly ground black pepper

1. In a large skillet, heat the olive oil over low heat. 2. Add the onion and garlic and cook, stirring to prevent the garlic from scorching, for 2 to 3 minutes, or until the onion is translucent. 3. Add the broth and greens and cook, stirring often, for 5 to 7 minutes, or until the greens are wilted. 4. Season with pepper, and serve warm.

Per Serving:

calories: 53 | fat: 4g | protein: 1g | carbs: 5g | sugars: 1g | fiber: 1g | sodium: 39mg

Cheesy Broiled Tomatoes

Prep time: 5 minutes | Cook time: 10 minutes | Serves 2

2 large ripe tomatoes, halved widthwise

¼ cup nonfat ricotta cheese, divided

½ teaspoon dried basil, divided

Salt, to season

Freshly ground black pepper, to season

1. Preheat the broiler. 2. Top each tomato half with 1 tablespoon of ricotta cheese. Sprinkle with ⅛ teaspoon of basil. Season with salt and pepper. 3. On a broiler rack, place the tomatoes cut-side up. Place the rack into the preheated oven. Broil for 7 to 10 minutes. 4. Enjoy!

Per Serving:

calories: 49 | fat: 0g | protein: 4g | carbs: 9g | sugars: 5g | fiber: 3g | sodium: 658mg

Summer Squash Casserole

Prep time: 15 minutes | Cook time: 30 minutes | Serves 8

1 tablespoon extra-virgin olive oil

6 yellow summer squash, thinly sliced

1 large portobello mushroom, thinly sliced

1 Vidalia onion, thinly sliced

1 cup shredded Parmesan

cheese, divided

1 cup shredded reduced-fat extra-sharp Cheddar cheese

½ cup whole-wheat bread crumbs

½ cup tri-color quinoa

1 tablespoon Creole seasoning

1. Preheat the oven to 350°F. 2. In a large cast iron pan, heat the oil over medium heat. 3. Add the squash, mushroom, and onion, and sauté for 7 to 10 minutes, or until softened. 4. Remove from the heat. Add ½ cup of Parmesan cheese and the Cheddar cheese and mix well. 5. In a small bowl, whisk the bread crumbs, quinoa, the remaining ½ cup of Parmesan, and the Creole seasoning together. Evenly distribute over the casserole. 6. Transfer the pan to the oven, and bake for 20 minutes, or until browned. Serve warm and enjoy.

Per Serving:

calories: 163 | fat: 7g | protein: 10g | carbs: 14g | sugars: 1g | fiber: 2g | sodium: 484mg

Cauliflower Rice

Prep time: 5 minutes | Cook time: 5 minutes | Makes 2½ cups

1½ pounds cauliflower, coarsely chopped

½ tablespoon extra-virgin olive

oil

Kosher salt

Freshly ground black pepper

1. Pulse the cauliflower in a food processor until it has a crumbly texture, almost like rice. Be careful not to over-pulse and make it too fine. It's okay to have some larger chunks. Another option is to use a box grater if you don't have a food processor. Put the crumbled cauliflower in a bowl and set aside. 2. Heat the oil in a large skillet over medium-high heat. Add the cauliflower, coat it with hot oil, and sauté 3 to 5 minutes. Season with salt and pepper and serve. 3. Store any leftovers in an airtight container in the refrigerator for 3 to 4 days.

Per Serving:

calories: 118 | fat: 4g | protein: 7g | carbs: 18g | sugars: 7g | fiber: 7g | sodium: 684mg

Simple Bibimbap

Prep time: 15 minutes | Cook time: 15 minutes | Serves 2

4 teaspoons canola oil, divided

2½ cups cauliflower rice

2 cups fresh baby spinach

3 teaspoons low-sodium soy sauce or tamari, divided

8 ounces mushrooms, thinly

sliced

2 large eggs

1 cup bean sprouts, rinsed

1 cup kimchi

½ cup shredded carrots

1. Heat 1 teaspoon of canola oil in a medium skillet and sauté the cauliflower rice, spinach, and 2 teaspoons of soy sauce until the greens are wilted, about 5 minutes. Put the vegetables in a small bowl and set aside. 2. Return the skillet to medium heat, add 2 teaspoons of vegetable oil and, when it's hot, add the mushrooms in a single layer and cook for 3 to 5 minutes, then stir and cook another 3 minutes or until mostly golden-brown in color. Put the mushrooms in a small bowl and toss them with the remaining 1 teaspoon of soy sauce. 3. Wipe out the skillet and heat the remaining 1 teaspoon of vegetable oil over low heat. Crack in the eggs and cook until the whites are set and the yolks begin to thicken but not harden, 4 to 5 minutes. 4. Assemble two bowls with cauliflower rice and spinach at the bottom. Then arrange each ingredient separately around the rim of the bowl: bean sprouts, mushrooms, kimchi, and shredded carrots, with the egg placed in the center, and serve.

Per Serving:

calories: 275 | fat: 16g | protein: 20g | carbs: 20g | sugars: 8g | fiber: 8g | sodium: 518mg

Sautéed Garlicky Mushrooms

Prep time: 10 minutes | Cook time: 12 minutes | Serves 4

1 tablespoon butter

2 teaspoons extra-virgin olive oil

2 pounds button mushrooms, halved

2 teaspoons minced fresh garlic

1 teaspoon chopped fresh thyme

Sea salt

Freshly ground black pepper

1. Place a large skillet over medium-high heat and add the butter and olive oil. 2. Sauté the mushrooms, stirring occasionally, until they are lightly caramelized and tender, about 10 minutes. 3. Add the garlic and thyme and sauté for 2 more minutes. 4. Season the mushrooms with salt and pepper before serving.

Per Serving:

calories: 88 | fat: 5g | protein: 5g | carbs: 10g | sugars: 6g | fiber: 3g | sodium: 189mg

Mushroom "Bacon" Topper

Prep time: 10 minutes | Cook time: 16 to 17 minutes | Serves 4

½ pound shiitake mushrooms, stems removed	½ teaspoon smoked paprika
2½ teaspoons balsamic vinegar	½ teaspoon Dijon mustard
2½ teaspoons tamari	¼ teaspoon liquid smoke
1 tablespoon pure maple syrup	Freshly ground pepper or lemon pepper to taste

1. Preheat the oven to 400°F. Line a baking sheet with parchment paper. 2. Use a damp paper towel to clean the mushrooms. Slice the mushrooms thinly. In a large bowl, combine the vinegar, tamari, syrup, paprika, mustard, liquid smoke, and pepper. Whisk thoroughly. Add the mushrooms and stir to coat with the marinade. Transfer the mushrooms to the prepared baking sheet. Bake for 16 to 17 minutes, tossing once. Turn off the heat and let the mushrooms sit in the warm oven for 10 minutes, tossing once during this time. Remove and let cool. Serve on salads, soups, pizzas, and more.

Per Serving:

calorie: 45 | fat: 0.4g | protein: 2g | carbs: 9g | sugars: 6g | fiber: 2g | sodium: 233mg

Asparagus with Cashews

Prep time: 10 minutes | Cook time: 20 minutes | Serves 4

1 tablespoon extra-virgin olive oil	Freshly ground black pepper
Sea salt	½ cup chopped cashews
	Zest and juice of 1 lime

1. Preheat the oven to 400°F and line a baking sheet with aluminum foil. 2. In a large bowl, toss the asparagus with the oil and lightly season with salt and pepper. 3. Transfer the asparagus to the baking sheet and bake until tender and lightly browned, 15 to 20 minutes. 4. Transfer the asparagus to a serving bowl and toss them with the chopped cashews, lime zest, and lime juice.

Per Serving:

calories: 123 | fat: 11g | protein: 3g | carbs: 6g | sugars: 1g | fiber: 1g | sodium: 148mg

Zucchini on the Half Shell

Prep time: 15 minutes | Cook time: 30 minutes | Serves 4 to 8

4 zucchini, cut lengthwise, seeded, pulp removed	1 cup coarsely chopped tomatoes
1 (13.4 ounces) box borlotti beans, rinsed	2 teaspoons Creole seasoning
½ onion, finely chopped	½ cup grated reduced-fat Cheddar cheese
1 garlic clove, minced	

1. Preheat the oven to 350°F. 2. Arrange the zucchini on a rimmed baking sheet in a single layer, cavity-side up. 3. Transfer the baking sheet to the oven, and bake for 10 minutes, or until the exterior of the zucchini is soft. 4. Meanwhile, in a small pan, combine the beans, onion, garlic, tomatoes, and Creole seasoning. Cook over medium heat, stirring often, for 3 to 5 minutes, or until the onion and garlic are translucent. Remove from the heat. 5. Remove the zucchini from the oven, and spoon the tomato and bean mixture into the cavities. 6. Sprinkle 1 tablespoon of cheese on top of each stuffed zucchini. 7. Return the baking sheet to the oven and cook for 10 to 15 minutes, or until the cheese is melted and golden brown. Serve warm and enjoy.

Per Serving:

calories: 63 | fat: 1g | protein: 5g | carbs: 9g | sugars: 5g | fiber: 3g | sodium: 177mg

Mashed Sweet Potatoes

Prep time: 10 minutes | Cook time: 20 minutes | Serves 6 to 8

2 medium sweet potatoes, cut into 1- to 2-inch cubes	¼ teaspoon kosher salt
4 medium carrots, cut into 1-inch cubes	2 tablespoons unsalted butter
6 garlic cloves, halved	⅓ cup unsweetened almond milk
	Freshly ground black pepper

1. Place the potatoes, carrots, garlic, and salt in a large stockpot and cover them with water by 1½ inches. Bring to a boil over high heat, reduce the heat to medium-high, and simmer for 10 to 15 minutes, until the vegetables become tender. 2. Drain the vegetables and return them to the pot. Add the butter and almond milk and mash until smooth with a potato masher. Season with pepper. Thin out with water or more milk to reach the desired consistency. Serve. 3. Store any leftovers in an airtight container in the refrigerator for up to 4 days.

Per Serving:

calories: 90 | fat: 3g | protein: 2g | carbs: 15g | sugars: 6g | fiber: 3g | sodium: 150mg

Braised Kale with Ginger and Sesame Seeds

Prep time: 5 minutes | Cook time: 25 minutes | Serves 2

¼ cup balsamic vinegar	kale, thoroughly washed and stemmed
1 garlic clove, minced	¼ cup water, plus additional as needed
2 teaspoons chopped fresh ginger	1 tablespoon sesame seeds
6 cups (2 bunches) chopped	

1. In a saucepan set over medium heat, whisk together the balsamic vinegar, garlic, and ginger. Cook for 5 minutes. 2. Add the kale. Stir to combine. Cook for 10 to 15 minutes, or until wilted. 3. Add the water. Cover and simmer for 2 minutes, adding more water as needed to keep the kale from sticking. Uncover and cook for 1 to 2 minutes more, or until any remaining liquid evaporates. 4. Sprinkle with the sesame seeds and serve.

Per Serving:

calories: 81 | fat: 3g | protein: 3g | carbs: 11g | sugars: 6g | fiber: 2g | sodium: 29mg

Spaghetti Squash

Prep time: 5 minutes | Cook time: 7 minutes | Serves 4

1 spaghetti squash (about 2 pounds)

1. Cut the spaghetti squash in half crosswise and use a large spoon to remove the seeds. 2. Pour 1 cup of water into the electric pressure cooker and insert a wire rack or trivet. 3. Place the squash halves on the rack, cut-side up. 4. Close and lock the lid of the pressure cooker. Set the valve to sealing. 5. Cook on high pressure for 7 minutes. 6. When the cooking is complete, hit Cancel and quick release the pressure. 7. Once the pin drops, unlock and remove the lid. 8. With tongs, remove the squash from the pot and transfer it to a plate. When it is cool enough to handle, scrape the squash with the tines of a fork to remove the strands. Discard the skin.

Per Serving:

calories: 121 | fat: 2g | protein: 2g | carbs: 28g | sugars: 11g | fiber: 6g | sodium: 68mg

Zucchini Sauté

Prep time: 5 minutes | Cook time: 10 minutes | Serves 4

1 tablespoon olive oil	thick rounds
1 medium red onion, finely chopped	¼ teaspoon dried oregano
	⅛ teaspoon salt
3 medium zucchini (about 5 to 6 ounces each), cut into ¼-inch	⅛ teaspoon freshly ground black pepper

1. In a large skillet over medium heat, heat the oil. Add the onion, and sauté until the onion is translucent but not browned. 2. Add the zucchini, cover, and simmer 3 to 4 minutes. Sprinkle with the oregano, salt, and pepper, and serve hot.

Per Serving:

calories: 43 | fat: 3g | protein: 1g | carbs: 3g | sugars: 1g | fiber: 1g | sodium: 79mg

Garlic Herb Radishes

Prep time: 10 minutes | Cook time: 10 minutes | Serves 4

1 pound (454 g) radishes	½ teaspoon dried parsley
2 tablespoons unsalted butter, melted	¼ teaspoon dried oregano
	¼ teaspoon ground black pepper
½ teaspoon garlic powder	

1. Remove roots from radishes and cut into quarters. 2. In a small bowl, add butter and seasonings. Toss the radishes in the herb butter and place into the air fryer basket. 3. Adjust the temperature to 350°F (177°C) and set the timer for 10 minutes. 4. Halfway through the cooking time, toss the radishes in the air fryer basket. Continue cooking until edges begin to turn brown. 5. Serve warm.

Per Serving:

calories: 57 | fat: 4g | protein: 1g | carbs: 5g | sugars: 3g | fiber: 2g | sodium: 27mg

Sesame Bok Choy with Almonds

Prep time: 15 minutes | Cook time: 7 minutes | Serves 4

2 teaspoons sesame oil	sauce
2 pounds bok choy, cleaned and quartered	Pinch red pepper flakes
	½ cup toasted sliced almonds
2 teaspoons low-sodium soy	

1. Place a large skillet over medium heat and add the oil. 2. When the oil is hot, sauté the bok choy until tender-crisp, about 5 minutes. 3. Stir in the soy sauce and red pepper flakes and sauté 2 minutes more. 4. Remove the bok choy to a serving bowl and top with the sliced almonds.

Per Serving:

calories: 56 | fat: 3g | protein: 4g | carbs: 6g | sugars: 3g | fiber: 3g | sodium: 229mg

Fennel and Chickpeas

Prep time: 10 minutes | Cook time: 20 minutes | Serves 6

1 tablespoon extra-virgin olive oil	1 cup low-sodium chicken broth
	2 teaspoons chopped fresh thyme
1 small fennel bulb, trimmed and cut into ¼-inch-thick slices	¼ teaspoon sea salt
1 sweet onion, thinly sliced	¼ teaspoon freshly ground black pepper
1 (15½ ounces) can sodium-free chickpeas, rinsed and drained	1 tablespoon butter

1. Place a large saucepan over medium-high heat and add the oil. 2. Sauté the fennel and onion until tender and lightly browned, about 10 minutes. 3. Add the chickpeas, broth, thyme, salt, and pepper. 4. Cover and cook, stirring occasionally, for 10 minutes, until the liquid has reduced by about half. 5. Remove the pan from the heat and stir in the butter. 6. Serve hot.

Per Serving:

calories: 132 | fat: 6g | protein:5 g | carbs: 17g | sugars: 6g | fiber: 4g | sodium: 239mg

Sherried Peppers with Bean Sprouts

Prep time: 5 minutes | Cook time: 8 minutes | Serves 4

1 green bell pepper, julienned	2 teaspoons light soy sauce
1 red bell pepper, julienned	1 tablespoon dry sherry
2 cups canned, drained bean sprouts	1 teaspoon red wine vinegar

1. In a large skillet over medium heat, combine the peppers, bean sprouts, soy sauce, and sherry, mixing well. Cover, and cook 5–7 minutes, until the vegetables are just tender. 2. Stir in the vinegar, and remove from the heat. Serve hot.

Per Serving:

calories: 34 | fat: 1g | protein: 2g | carbs: 6g | sugars: 4g | fiber: 2g | sodium: 131mg

Perfect Sweet Potatoes

Prep time: 5 minutes | Cook time: 15 minutes | Serves 4 to 6

4 to 6 medium sweet potatoes

1 cup of water

1. Scrub skin of sweet potatoes with a brush until clean. Pour water into inner pot of the Instant Pot. Place steamer basket in the bottom of the inner pot. Place sweet potatoes on top of steamer basket. 2. Secure the lid and turn valve to seal. 3. Select the Manual mode and set to pressure cook on high for 15 minutes. 4. Allow pressure to release naturally (about 10 minutes). 5. Once the pressure valve lowers, remove lid and serve immediately.

Per Serving:

calories: 112 | fat: 0g | protein: 2g | carbs: 26g | sugars: 5g | fiber: 4g | sodium: 72mg

Radish Chips

Prep time: 10 minutes | Cook time: 5 minutes | Serves 4

2 cups water

1 pound (454 g) radishes

¼ teaspoon onion powder

¼ teaspoon paprika

½ teaspoon garlic powder

2 tablespoons coconut oil, melted

1. Place water in a medium saucepan and bring to a boil on stovetop. 2. Remove the top and bottom from each radish, then use a mandoline to slice each radish thin and uniformly. You may also use the slicing blade in the food processor for this step. 3. Place the radish slices into the boiling water for 5 minutes or until translucent. Remove them from the water and place them into a clean kitchen towel to absorb excess moisture. 4. Toss the radish chips in a large bowl with remaining ingredients until fully coated in oil and seasoning. Place radish chips into the air fryer basket. 5. Adjust the temperature to 320ºF (160ºC) and air fry for 5 minutes. 6. Shake the basket two or three times during the cooking time. Serve warm.

Per Serving:

calories: 83 | fat: 7g | protein: 1g | carbs: 5g | sugars: 3g | fiber: 2g | sodium: 28mg

Wilted Kale and Chard

Prep time: 10 minutes | Cook time: 10 minutes | Serves 4

2 tablespoons extra-virgin olive oil

1 pound kale, coarse stems removed and leaves chopped

1 pound Swiss chard, coarse stems removed and leaves chopped

1 tablespoon freshly squeezed lemon juice

½ teaspoon ground cardamom

Sea salt

Freshly ground black pepper

1. Place a large skillet over medium-high heat and add the olive oil. 2. Add the kale, chard, lemon juice, and cardamom to the skillet. Use tongs to toss the greens continuously until they are wilted, about 10 minutes or less. 3. Season the greens with salt and pepper. 4. Serve immediately.

Per Serving:

calories: 139 | fat: 8g | protein: 7g | carbs: 15g | sugars: 4g | fiber: 6g | sodium: 430mg

Chapter 11

Vegetarian Mains

Cashew-Kale and Chickpeas

Prep time: 15 minutes | Cook time: 15 minutes | Serves 2

For the cashew sauce
½ cup unsalted cashews soaked in ½ cup hot water for at least 20 minutes
1 cup reduced-sodium vegetable broth
1 garlic clove, minced
For the kale
1 medium red bell pepper, diced
1 medium carrot, julienned
½ cup sliced fresh mushrooms
1 cup canned chickpeas, drained

and rinsed
1 bunch kale, thoroughly washed, central stems removed, leaves thinly sliced (about 2½ cups)
2 to 3 tablespoons water
1 teaspoon red pepper flakes
½ teaspoon salt
Freshly ground black pepper, to season
¼ cup minced fresh cilantro

To make the cashew sauce 1. Drain the cashews. 2. In a blender or food processor, blend together the cashews, vegetable broth, and garlic until completely smooth. Set aside. To make the kale 1. In a large nonstick skillet or Dutch oven set over medium-low heat, stir together the red bell pepper, carrot, and mushrooms. Cook for 5 to 7 minutes, or until softened. 2. Stir in the chickpeas. Increase the heat to high. 3. Add the kale and the water. Stir to combine. Cover and cook for 5 minutes, or until the kale is tender. 4. Stir in the cashew sauce, red pepper flakes, and salt. Season with pepper. Cook for 2 to 3 minutes more, uncovered, or until the sauce thickens. 5. Garnish with the cilantro before serving. 6. Enjoy!

Per Serving:

calories: 480 | fat: 20g | protein: 20g | carbs: 62g | sugars: 17g | fiber: 15g | sodium: 843mg

Tofu and Bean Chili

Prep time: 10 minutes | Cook time 30 minutes | Serves 4

1 (15 ounces) can low-sodium dark red kidney beans, drained and rinsed, divided
2 (15 ounces) cans no-salt-added diced tomatoes
1½ cups low-sodium vegetable broth

½ teaspoon chili powder
½ teaspoon ground cumin
½ teaspoon garlic powder
½ teaspoon dried oregano
¼ teaspoon onion powder
¼ teaspoon salt
8 ounces extra-firm tofu

1. In a small bowl, mash ⅓ of the beans with a fork. 2. Put the mashed beans, the remaining whole beans, and the diced tomatoes with their juices in a large stockpot. 3. Add the broth, chili powder, cumin, garlic powder, dried oregano, onion powder, and salt. Simmer over medium-high heat for 15 minutes. 4. Press the tofu between 3 or 4 layers of paper towels to squeeze out any excess moisture. 5. Crumble the tofu into the stockpot and stir. Simmer for another 10 to 15 minutes.

Per Serving:

calories: 207 | fat: 5g | protein: 15g | carbs: 31g | sugars: 11g | fiber: 12g | sodium: 376mg

Pra Ram Vegetables and Peanut Sauce with Seared Tofu

Prep time: 5 minutes | Cook time: 20 minutes | Serves 4

Peanut Sauce
2 tablespoons cold-pressed avocado oil
2 garlic cloves, minced
½ cup creamy natural peanut butter
½ cup coconut milk
2 tablespoons brown rice syrup
1 tablespoon plus 1 teaspoon soy sauce, tamari, or coconut aminos
¼ cup water
Vegetables
2 carrots, sliced on the diagonal ¼ inch thick

8 ounces zucchini, julienned ¼ inch thick
1 pound broccoli florets
½ small head green cabbage, cut into 1-inch-thick wedges (with core intact so wedges hold together)
Tofu
One 14 ounces package extra-firm tofu, drained
¼ teaspoon fine sea salt
¼ teaspoon freshly ground black pepper
1 tablespoon cornstarch
2 tablespoons coconut oil

1. To make the peanut sauce: In a small saucepan over medium heat, warm the oil and garlic for about 2 minutes, until the garlic is bubbling but not browned. Add the peanut butter, coconut milk, brown rice syrup, soy sauce, and water; stir to combine; and bring to a simmer (this will take about 3 minutes). As soon as the mixture is fully combined and at a simmer, remove from the heat and keep warm. The peanut sauce will keep in an airtight container in the refrigerator for up to 5 days. 2. To make the vegetables: Pour 1 cup water into the Instant Pot and place a steamer basket into the pot. In order, layer the carrots, zucchini, broccoli, and cabbage in the steamer basket, finishing with the cabbage. 3. Secure the lid and set the Pressure Release to Sealing. Select the Steam setting and set the cooking time for 0 (zero) minutes at low pressure. (The pot will take about 15 minutes to come up to pressure before the cooking program begins.) 4. To prepare the tofu: While the vegetables are steaming, cut the tofu crosswise into eight ½-inch-thick slices. Cut each of the slices in half crosswise, creating squares. Sandwich the squares between double layers of paper towels or a folded kitchen towel and press firmly to wick away as much moisture as possible. Sprinkle the tofu squares on both sides with the salt and pepper, then sprinkle them on both sides with the cornstarch. Using your fingers, spread the cornstarch on the top and bottom of each square to coat evenly. 5. In a large nonstick skillet over medium-high heat, warm the oil for about 3 minutes, until shimmering. Add the tofu and sear, turning once, for about 6 minutes per side, until crispy and golden. Divide the tofu evenly among four plates. 6. When the cooking program ends, perform a quick pressure release by moving the Pressure Release to Venting. Open the pot and, wearing heat-resistant mitts, grasp the handles of the steamer basket and lift it out of the pot. 7. Divide the vegetables among the plates, arranging them around the tofu. Spoon the peanut sauce over the tofu and serve.

Per Serving:

calories: 380 | fat: 22g | protein: 18g | carbs: 30g | sugars: 9g | fiber: 10g | sodium: 381mg

Instant Pot Hoppin' John with Skillet Cauli "Rice"

Prep time: 0 minutes | Cook time: 30 minutes | Serves 6

Hoppin' John
1 pound dried black-eyed peas (about 2¼ cups)
8⅔ cups water
1½ teaspoons fine sea salt
2 tablespoons extra-virgin olive oil
2 garlic cloves, minced
8 ounces shiitake mushrooms, stemmed and chopped, or cremini mushrooms, chopped
1 small yellow onion, diced
1 green bell pepper, seeded and diced
2 celery stalks, diced
2 jalapeño chiles, seeded and

diced
½ teaspoon smoked paprika
½ teaspoon dried thyme
½ teaspoon dried sage
¼ teaspoon cayenne pepper
2 cups low-sodium vegetable broth
Cauli "Rice"
1 tablespoon vegan buttery spread or unsalted butter
1 pound riced cauliflower
½ teaspoon fine sea salt
2 green onions, white and green parts, sliced
Hot sauce (such as Tabasco or Crystal) for serving

1. To make the Hoppin' John: In a large bowl, combine the black-eyed peas, 8 cups of the water, and 1 teaspoon of the salt and stir to dissolve the salt. Let soak for at least 8 hours or up to overnight. 2. Select the Sauté setting on the Instant Pot and heat the oil and garlic for 3 minutes, until the garlic is bubbling but not browned. Add the mushrooms and the remaining ½ teaspoon salt and sauté for 5 minutes, until the mushrooms have wilted and begun to give up their liquid. Add the onion, bell pepper, celery, and jalapeños and sauté for 4 minutes, until the onion is softened. Add the paprika, thyme, sage, and cayenne and sauté for 1 minute. 3. Drain the black-eyed peas and add them to the pot along with the broth and remaining ⅔ cup water. The liquid should just barely cover the beans. (Add an additional splash of water if needed.) 4. Secure the lid and set the Pressure Release to Sealing. Press the Cancel button to reset the cooking program, then select the Bean/Chili, Pressure Cook, or Manual setting and set the cooking time for 5 minutes at high pressure. (The pot will take about 10 minutes to come up to pressure before the cooking program begins.) 5. When the cooking program ends, let the pressure release naturally for 10 minutes, then move the Pressure Release to Venting to release any remaining steam. 6. To make the cauli "rice": While the pressure is releasing, in a large skillet over medium heat, melt the buttery spread. Add the cauliflower and salt and sauté for 3 to 5 minutes, until cooked through and piping hot. (If using frozen riced cauliflower, this may take another 2 minutes or so.) 7. Spoon the cauli "rice" onto individual plates. Open the pot and spoon the black-eyed peas on top of the cauli "rice". Sprinkle with the green onions and serve right away, with the hot sauce on the side.

Per Serving:
calories: 287 | fat: 7g | protein: 23g | carbs: 56g | sugars: 8g | fiber: 24g | sodium: 894mg

Chickpea and Tofu Bolognese

Prep time: 5 minutes | Cook time: 25 minutes | Serves 4

1 (3 to 4 pounds) spaghetti squash
½ teaspoon ground cumin
1 cup no-sugar-added spaghetti

sauce
1 (15 ounces) can low-sodium chickpeas, drained and rinsed
6 ounces extra-firm tofu

1. Preheat the oven to 400°F. 2. Cut the squash in half lengthwise. Scoop out the seeds and discard. 3. Season both halves of the squash with the cumin, and place them on a baking sheet cut-side down. Roast for 25 minutes. 4. Meanwhile, heat a medium saucepan over low heat, and pour in the spaghetti sauce and chickpeas. 5. Press the tofu between two layers of paper towels, and gently squeeze out any excess water. 6. Crumble the tofu into the sauce and cook for 15 minutes. 7. Remove the squash from the oven, and comb through the flesh of each half with a fork to make thin strands. 8. Divide the "spaghetti" into four portions, and top each portion with one-quarter of the sauce.

Per Serving:
calories: 221 | fat: 6g | protein: 12g | carbs: 32g | sugars: 6g | fiber: 8g | sodium: 405mg

Sautéed Spinach and Lima Beans

Prep time: 5 minutes | Cook time: 40 minutes | Serves 2

Extra-virgin olive oil cooking spray
¼ cup chopped onion
½ cup low-sodium vegetable broth
1 cup frozen lima beans, thawed
2 teaspoons extra-virgin olive oil

2 garlic cloves, chopped
4 cups chopped fresh spinach
Pinch cayenne pepper
2 teaspoons balsamic vinegar
Salt, to season
Freshly ground black pepper, to season

1. Heat a large saucepan over medium heat. Spray with cooking spray. 2. Add the onion. Sauté for about 4 minutes, or until soft and translucent. 3. Add the vegetable broth. Bring to a boil. 4. Add the lima beans and just enough water to cover. Bring to a boil. Reduce the heat to low. Cover and simmer for 30 minutes, or until the beans are tender. Set aside. 5. Heat a large skillet over medium-high heat for 30 seconds. 6. Add the olive oil and garlic. Sauté for 1 to 2 minutes, or until golden. Remove the garlic and reserve. 7. To the skillet, add the spinach and cayenne. Cover and cook for about 1 minute, or until the leaves wilt. Drain to remove any excess water. 8. Stir in the balsamic vinegar. Season with salt and pepper. 9. To serve, mound half of the spinach on a plate, top with half of the lima beans, and sprinkle with the reserved garlic.

Per Serving:
calories: 201 | fat: 7g | protein: 9g | carbs: 29g | sugars: 3g | fiber: 7g | sodium: 418mg

Veggie Fajitas

Prep time: 10 minutes | Cook time: 15 minutes | Serves 4

For The Guacamole
2 small avocados pitted and peeled
1 teaspoon freshly squeezed lime juice
¼ teaspoon salt
9 cherry tomatoes, halved
For The Fajitas
1 red bell pepper

1 green bell pepper
1 small white onion
Avocado oil cooking spray
1 cup canned low-sodium black beans, drained and rinsed
½ teaspoon ground cumin
¼ teaspoon chili powder
¼ teaspoon garlic powder
4 (6-inch) yellow corn tortillas

Make The Guacamole 1. In a medium bowl, use a fork to mash the avocados with the lime juice and salt. 2. Gently stir in the cherry tomatoes. Make The Fajitas 1. Cut the red bell pepper, green bell pepper, and onion into ½-inch slices. 2. Heat a large skillet over medium heat. When hot, coat the cooking surface with cooking spray. Put the peppers, onion, and beans into the skillet. 3. Add the cumin, chili powder, and garlic powder, and stir. 4. Cover and cook for 15 minutes, stirring halfway through. 5. Divide the fajita mixture equally between the tortillas, and top with guacamole and any preferred garnishes.

Per Serving:
calories: 269 | fat: 15g | protein: 8g | carbs: 30g | sugars: 5g | fiber: 11g | sodium: 175mg

Quinoa–White Bean Loaf

Prep time: 15 minutes | Cook time: 1 hour | Serves 2

Extra-virgin olive oil cooking spray
2 teaspoons extra-virgin olive oil
2 garlic cloves, minced
½ cup sliced fresh button mushrooms
6 ounces extra-firm tofu, crumbled
Salt, to season

Freshly ground black pepper, to season
1 (8 ounces) can cannellini beans, drained and rinsed
2 tablespoons coconut flour
1 tablespoon chia seeds
⅓ cup water
½ cup cooked quinoa
¼ cup chopped red onion
¼ cup chopped fresh parsley

1. Preheat the oven to 350°F. 2. Lightly coat 2 mini loaf pans with cooking spray. Set aside. 3. In a large skillet set over medium-high heat, heat the olive oil. 4. Add the garlic, mushrooms, and tofu. Season with salt and pepper. 5. Cook for 6 to 8 minutes, stirring occasionally, until the mushrooms and tofu are golden brown. 6. In a food processor, combine the cannellini beans, coconut flour, chia seeds, and water. Pulse until almost smooth. 7. In a large bowl, mix together the mushroom and tofu mixture, cannellini bean mixture, quinoa, red onion, and parsley. Season with salt and pepper. 8. Evenly divide the mixture between the 2 prepared loaf pans, gently pressing down and mounding the mixture in the middle. 9. Place the pans in the preheated oven. Bake for about 1 hour, or until firm and golden brown. Remove from the oven. Let rest for 10 minutes. 10.

Slice and serve.

Per Serving:
calories: 193 | fat: 8g | protein: 12g | carbs: 20g | sugars: 4g | fiber: 4g | sodium: 366mg

Asparagus, Sun-Dried Tomato, and Green Pea Sauté

Prep time: 10 minutes | Cook time: 10 minutes | Serves 2

6 packaged sun-dried tomatoes (not packed in oil)
½ cup boiling water
1 tablespoon extra-virgin olive oil
2 garlic cloves, minced
¾ pound fresh asparagus, trimmed and cut into 2-inch pieces
¼ cup chopped red bell pepper
½ cup sliced fresh button

mushrooms
¼ cup reduced-sodium vegetable broth
2 tablespoons sliced almonds
1 large tomato, diced (about 1 cup)
1½ teaspoons dried tarragon
½ cup frozen peas
Freshly ground black pepper, to season

1. In a small heatproof bowl, place the sun-dried tomatoes. Cover with the boiling water. Set aside. 2. In a large skillet or wok set over high heat, heat the olive oil. 3. Add the garlic. Swirl in the oil for a few seconds. 4. Toss in the asparagus, red bell pepper, and mushrooms. Stir-fry for 30 seconds. 5. Add the vegetable broth and almonds. Cover and steam for about 2 minutes. Uncover the skillet. 6. Add the tomato and tarragon. Cook for 2 to 3 minutes to reduce the liquid. 7. Drain and chop the sun-dried tomatoes. Add them and the peas to the skillet. Stir-fry for 3 to 4 minutes, or until the vegetables are crisp-tender and the liquid is reduced to a sauce. 8. Season with pepper and serve immediately.

Per Serving:
calories: 165 | fat: 8g | protein: 8g | carbs: 20g | sugars: 9g | fiber: 7g | sodium: 46mg

Chickpea Coconut Curry

Prep time: 5 minutes | Cook time: 15 minutes | Serves 4

3 cups fresh or frozen cauliflower florets
2 cups unsweetened almond milk
1 (15 ounces) can coconut milk
1 (15 ounces) can low-sodium

chickpeas, drained and rinsed
1 tablespoon curry powder
¼ teaspoon ground ginger
¼ teaspoon garlic powder
⅛ teaspoon onion powder
¼ teaspoon salt

1. In a large stockpot, combine the cauliflower, almond milk, coconut milk, chickpeas, curry, ginger, garlic powder, and onion powder. Stir and cover. 2. Cook over medium-high heat for 10 minutes. 3. Reduce the heat to low, stir, and cook for 5 minutes more, uncovered. Season with up to ¼ teaspoon salt.

Per Serving:
calories: 225 | fat: 7g | protein: 12g | carbs: 31g | sugars: 14g | fiber: 9g | sodium: 489mg

No-Tuna Lettuce Wraps

Prep time: 10 minutes | Cook time: 0 minutes | Serves 4

1 (15 ounces) can low-sodium chickpeas, drained and rinsed	red onion
	2 tablespoons unsalted tahini
1 celery stalk, thinly sliced	1 tablespoon capers, undrained
3 tablespoons honey mustard	12 butter lettuce leaves
2 tablespoons finely chopped	

1. In a large bowl, mash the chickpeas. 2. Add the celery, honey mustard, onion, tahini, and capers, and mix well. 3. For each serving, place three lettuce leaves on a plate so they overlap, top with one-fourth of the chickpea filling, and roll up into a wrap. Repeat with the remaining lettuce leaves and filling.

Per Serving:

calories: 163 | fat: 8g | protein: 6g | carbs: 17g | sugars: 4g | fiber: 6g | sodium: 333mg

Italian Zucchini Boats

Prep time: 5 minutes | Cook time: 15 minutes | Serves 4

1 cup canned low-sodium chickpeas, drained and rinsed	2 zucchini
	¼ cup shredded Parmesan cheese
1 cup no-sugar-added spaghetti sauce	

1. Preheat the oven to 425°F. 2. In a medium bowl, mix the chickpeas and spaghetti sauce together. 3. Cut the zucchini in half lengthwise, and scrape a spoon gently down the length of each half to remove the seeds. 4. Fill each zucchini half with the chickpea sauce, and top with one-quarter of the Parmesan cheese. 5. Place the zucchini halves on a baking sheet and roast in the oven for 15 minutes.

Per Serving:

calories: 120 | fat: 4g | protein: 7g | carbs: 14g | sugars: 5g | fiber: 4g | sodium: 441mg

Stuffed Acorn Squash

Prep time: 10 minutes | Cook time: 1 hour | Serves 2

1 acorn squash, halved and seeded	1 garlic clove, chopped
	½ cup broccoli florets
½ cup water, plus more as needed	½ cup frozen peas
	Salt, to season
¼ cup uncooked quinoa, thoroughly rinsed	Freshly ground black pepper, to season
1 tablespoon extra-virgin olive oil	4 tablespoons chopped pistachios, divided
¼ cup diced onion	

1. Preheat the oven to 425°F. 2. In a large baking dish, place the acorn squash halves cut-side down. Add 1 inch of water to the dish. Place the dish in the preheated oven. Bake for 45 minutes, or until tender. 3. In a small pot set over high heat, bring the water to a boil. 4. Add the quinoa. Reduce the heat to low. Simmer for about 15 minutes, covered, or until tender and all the water is absorbed. Let cool. Fluff with a fork. 5. In a medium saucepan set over medium heat, add the olive oil, onion, and garlic. Sauté for 3 to 4 minutes. 6. Add the broccoli and peas. Cook for about 4 minutes, or until the vegetables are tender. 7. Add the cooked quinoa to the sautéed vegetables. Season with salt and pepper. 8. Spoon half of the mixture into each acorn half. 9. Garnish each half with about 2 tablespoons of pistachios. 10. Serve hot and enjoy!

Per Serving:

calories: 306 | fat: 12g | protein: 10g | carbs: 46g | sugars: 2g | fiber: 8g | sodium: 656mg

Vegetable Burgers

Prep time: 10 minutes | Cook time: 12 minutes | Serves 4

8 ounces (227 g) cremini mushrooms	yellow onion
	1 clove garlic, peeled and finely minced
2 large egg yolks	
½ medium zucchini, trimmed and chopped	½ teaspoon salt
	¼ teaspoon ground black pepper
¼ cup peeled and chopped	

1. Place all ingredients into a food processor and pulse twenty times until finely chopped and combined. 2. Separate mixture into four equal sections and press each into a burger shape. Place burgers into ungreased air fryer basket. Adjust the temperature to 375°F (191°C) and air fry for 12 minutes, turning burgers halfway through cooking. Burgers will be browned and firm when done. 3. Place burgers on a large plate and let cool 5 minutes before serving.

Per Serving:

calories: 77 | fat: 5g | protein: 3g | carbs: 6g | sugars: 2g | fiber: 1g | sodium: 309mg

Chickpea-Spinach Curry

Prep time: 5 minutes | Cook time: 10 minutes | Serves 2

1 cup frozen chopped spinach, thawed	chopped tomatoes, undrained
	1 tablespoon curry powder
1 cup canned chickpeas, drained and rinsed	1 tablespoon granulated garlic
	Salt, to season
½ cup frozen green beans	Freshly ground black pepper, to season
½ cup frozen broccoli florets	
½ cup no-salt-added canned	½ cup chopped fresh parsley

1. In a medium saucepan set over high heat, stir together the spinach, chickpeas, green beans, broccoli, tomatoes and their juice, curry powder, and garlic. Season with salt and pepper. Bring to a fast boil. Reduce the heat to low. Cover and simmer for 10 minutes, or until heated through. 2. Top with the parsley, serve, and enjoy!

Per Serving:

calories: 203 | fat: 3g | protein: 13g | carbs: 35g | sugars: 7g | fiber: 13g | sodium: 375mg

Stuffed Portobellos

Prep time: 10 minutes | Cook time: 8 minutes | Serves 4

3 ounces (85 g) cream cheese, softened
½ medium zucchini, trimmed and chopped
¼ cup seeded and chopped red bell pepper
1½ cups chopped fresh spinach

leaves
4 large portobello mushrooms, stems removed
2 tablespoons coconut oil, melted
½ teaspoon salt

1. In a medium bowl, mix cream cheese, zucchini, pepper, and spinach. 2. Drizzle mushrooms with coconut oil and sprinkle with salt. Scoop ¼ zucchini mixture into each mushroom. 3. Place mushrooms into ungreased air fryer basket. Adjust the temperature to 400ºF (204ºC) and air fry for 8 minutes. Portobellos will be tender and tops will be browned when done. Serve warm.

Per Serving:

calories: 154 | fat: 13g | protein: 4g | carbs: 6g | sugars: 3g | fiber: 2g | sodium: 355mg

Vegan Dal Makhani

Prep time: 0 minutes | Cook time: 55 minutes | Serves 6

1 cup dried kidney beans
⅓ cup urad dal or beluga or Puy lentils
4 cups water
1 teaspoon fine sea salt
1 tablespoon cold-pressed avocado oil
1 tablespoon cumin seeds
1-inch piece fresh ginger, peeled and minced
4 garlic cloves, minced
1 large yellow onion, diced
2 jalapeño chiles, seeded and diced
1 green bell pepper, seeded and

diced
1 tablespoon garam masala
1 teaspoon ground turmeric
¼ teaspoon cayenne pepper (optional)
One 15 ounces can fire-roasted diced tomatoes and liquid
2 tablespoons vegan buttery spread
Cooked cauliflower "rice" for serving
2 tablespoons chopped fresh cilantro
6 tablespoons plain coconut yogurt

1. In a medium bowl, combine the kidney beans, urad dal, water, and salt and stir to dissolve the salt. Let soak for 12 hours. 2. Select the Sauté setting on the Instant Pot and heat the oil and cumin seeds for 3 minutes, until the seeds are bubbling, lightly toasted, and aromatic. Add the ginger and garlic and sauté for 1 minute, until bubbling and fragrant. Add the onion, jalapeños, and bell pepper and sauté for 5 minutes, until the onion begins to soften. 3. Add the garam masala, turmeric, cayenne (if using), and the soaked beans and their liquid and stir to mix. Pour the tomatoes and their liquid on top. Do not stir them in. 4. Secure the lid and set the Pressure Release to Sealing. Press the Cancel button to reset the cooking program, then select the Pressure Cook or Manual setting and set the cooking time for 30 minutes at high pressure. (The pot will take about 15 minutes to come up to pressure before the cooking program begins.) 5. When the cooking program ends, let the pressure release naturally for 30 minutes, then move the Pressure Release to Venting to release any remaining steam. Open the pot and stir to combine, then stir in the buttery spread. If you prefer a smoother texture, ladle 1½ cups of the dal into a blender and blend until smooth, about 30 seconds, then stir the blended mixture into the rest of the dal in the pot. 6. Spoon the cauliflower "rice" into bowls and ladle the dal on top. Sprinkle with the cilantro, top with a dollop of coconut yogurt, and serve.

Per Serving:

calorie: 245 | fat: 7g | protein: 11g | carbs: 37g | sugars: 4g | fiber: 10g | sodium: 518mg

Orange Tofu

Prep time: 10 minutes | Cook time: 20 minutes | Serves 4

⅓ cup freshly squeezed orange juice (zest orange first; see orange zest ingredient below)
1 tablespoon tamari
1 tablespoon tahini
½ tablespoon coconut nectar or pure maple syrup
2 tablespoons apple cider vinegar
½ tablespoon freshly grated

ginger
1 large clove garlic, grated
½ to 1 teaspoon orange zest
¼ teaspoon sea salt
Few pinches of crushed red-pepper flakes (optional)
1 package (12 ounces) extra-firm tofu, sliced into ¼"–½" thick squares and patted to remove excess moisture

1. Preheat the oven to 400°F. 2. In a small bowl, combine the orange juice, tamari, tahini, nectar or syrup, vinegar, ginger, garlic, orange zest, salt, and red-pepper flakes (if using). Whisk until well combined. Pour the sauce into an 8" x 12" baking dish. Add the tofu and turn to coat both sides. Bake for 20 minutes. Add salt to taste.

Per Serving:

calorie: 122 | fat: 7g | protein: 10g | carbs: 7g | sugars: 4g | fiber: 1g | sodium: 410mg

Crispy Eggplant Rounds

Prep time: 15 minutes | Cook time: 10 minutes | Serves 4

1 large eggplant, ends trimmed, cut into ½-inch slices
½ teaspoon salt
2 ounces (57 g) Parmesan 100%

cheese crisps, finely ground
½ teaspoon paprika
¼ teaspoon garlic powder
1 large egg

1. Sprinkle eggplant rounds with salt. Place rounds on a kitchen towel for 30 minutes to draw out excess water. Pat rounds dry. 2. In a medium bowl, mix cheese crisps, paprika, and garlic powder. In a separate medium bowl, whisk egg. Dip each eggplant round in egg, then gently press into cheese crisps to coat both sides. 3. Place eggplant rounds into ungreased air fryer basket. Adjust the temperature to 400ºF (204ºC) and air fry for 10 minutes, turning rounds halfway through cooking. Eggplant will be golden and crispy when done. Serve warm.

Per Serving:

calorie: 109 | fat: 6g | protein: 8g | carbs: 7g | sugars: 3g | fiber: 4g | sodium: 545mg

Caprese Eggplant Stacks

Prep time: 5 minutes | Cook time: 12 minutes | Serves 4

1 medium eggplant, cut into ¼-inch slices

2 large tomatoes, cut into ¼-inch slices

4 ounces (113 g) fresh

Mozzarella, cut into ½-ounce / 14-g slices

2 tablespoons olive oil

¼ cup fresh basil, sliced

1. In a baking dish, place four slices of eggplant on the bottom. Place a slice of tomato on top of each eggplant round, then Mozzarella, then eggplant. Repeat as necessary. 2. Drizzle with olive oil. Cover dish with foil and place dish into the air fryer basket. 3. Adjust the temperature to 350ºF (177ºC) and bake for 12 minutes. 4. When done, eggplant will be tender. Garnish with fresh basil to serve.

Per Serving:

calories: 216 | fat: 16g | protein: 9g | carbs: 11g | sugars: 6g | fiber: 5g | sodium: 231mg

Spinach Salad with Eggs, Tempeh Bacon, and Strawberries

Prep time: 10 minutes | Cook time: 15 minutes | Serves 4

2 tablespoons soy sauce, tamari, or coconut aminos

1 tablespoon raw apple cider vinegar

1 tablespoon pure maple syrup

½ teaspoon smoked paprika

Freshly ground black pepper

One 8 ounces package tempeh, cut crosswise into ⅛-inch-thick slices

8 large eggs

3 tablespoons extra-virgin olive oil

1 shallot, minced

1 tablespoon red wine vinegar

1 tablespoon balsamic vinegar

1 teaspoon Dijon mustard

¼ teaspoon fine sea salt

One 6 ounces bag baby spinach

2 hearts romaine lettuce, torn into bite-size pieces

12 fresh strawberries, sliced

1. In a 1-quart ziplock plastic bag, combine the soy sauce, cider vinegar, maple syrup, paprika, and ½ teaspoon pepper and carefully agitate the bag to mix the ingredients to make a marinade. Add the tempeh, seal the bag, and turn the bag back and forth several times to coat the tempeh evenly with the marinade. Marinate in the refrigerator for at least 2 hours or up to 24 hours. 2. Pour 1 cup water into the Instant Pot and place the wire metal steam rack, an egg rack, or a steamer basket into the pot. Gently place the eggs on top of the rack or in the basket, taking care not to crack them. 3. Secure the lid and set the Pressure Release to Sealing. Select the Steam setting and set the cooking time for 3 minutes at high pressure. (The pot will take about 5 minutes to come up to pressure before the cooking program begins.) 4. While the eggs are cooking, prepare an ice bath. 5. When the cooking program ends, perform a quick pressure release by moving the Pressure Release to Venting. Open the pot and, using tongs, transfer the eggs to the ice bath to cool. 6. Remove the tempeh from the marinade and blot dry between layers of paper towels. Discard the marinade. In a large nonstick skillet over medium-high heat, warm 1 tablespoon of the oil for 2 minutes. Add the tempeh in a single layer and fry, turning once, for 2 to 3 minutes per side, until well browned. Transfer the tempeh to a plate and set aside. 7. Wipe out the skillet and set it over medium heat. Add the remaining 2 tablespoons oil and the shallot and sauté for about 2 minutes, until the shallot is golden brown. Turn off the heat and stir in the red wine vinegar, balsamic vinegar, mustard, salt, and ¼ teaspoon pepper to make a vinaigrette. 8. In a large bowl, combine the spinach and romaine. Pour in the vinaigrette and toss until all of the leaves are lightly coated. Divide the dressed greens evenly among four large serving plates or shallow bowls and arrange the strawberries and fried tempeh on top. Peel the eggs, cut them in half lengthwise, and place them on top of the salads. Top with a couple grinds of pepper and serve right away.

Per Serving:

calorie: 435 | fat: 25g | protein: 29g | carbs: 25g | sugars: 10g | fiber: 5g | sodium: 332mg

Stuffed Portobello Mushrooms

Prep time: 5 minutes | Cook time: 20 minutes | Serves 4

8 large portobello mushrooms

3 teaspoons extra-virgin olive oil, divided

4 cups fresh spinach

1 medium red bell pepper, diced

¼ cup crumbled feta

1. Preheat the oven to 450ºF. 2. Remove the stems from the mushrooms, and gently scoop out the gills and discard. Coat the mushrooms with 2 teaspoons of olive oil. 3. On a baking sheet, place the mushrooms cap-side down, and roast for 20 minutes. 4. Meanwhile, heat the remaining 1 teaspoon of olive oil in a medium skillet over medium heat. When hot, sauté the spinach and red bell pepper for 8 to 10 minutes, stirring occasionally. 5. Remove the mushrooms from the oven. Drain, if necessary. Spoon the spinach and pepper mix into the mushrooms, and top with feta.

Per Serving:

calories: 91 | fat: 4g | protein: 6g | carbs: 10g | sugars: g | fiber: 4g | sodium: 155mg

Roasted Veggie Bowl

Prep time: 10 minutes | Cook time: 15 minutes | Serves 2

1 cup broccoli florets

1 cup quartered Brussels sprouts

½ cup cauliflower florets

¼ medium white onion, peeled and sliced ¼ inch thick

½ medium green bell pepper,

seeded and sliced ¼ inch thick

1 tablespoon coconut oil

2 teaspoons chili powder

½ teaspoon garlic powder

½ teaspoon cumin

1. Toss all ingredients together in a large bowl until vegetables are fully coated with oil and seasoning. 2. Pour vegetables into the air fryer basket. 3. Adjust the temperature to 360ºF (182ºC) and roast for 15 minutes. 4. Shake two or three times during cooking. Serve warm.

Per Serving:

calories: 112 | fat: 8g | protein: 4g | carbs: 11g | sugars: 3g | fiber: 5g | sodium: 106mg

Italian Tofu with Mushrooms and Peppers

Prep time: 5 minutes | Cook time: 10 minutes | Serves 2

1 teaspoon extra-virgin olive oil
¼ cup chopped bell pepper, any color
¼ cup chopped onions
1 garlic clove, minced
8 ounces firm tofu, drained and rinsed
½ cup sliced fresh button mushrooms
1 portobello mushroom cap, chopped
1 tablespoon balsamic vinegar
1 teaspoon dried basil
Salt, to season
Freshly ground black pepper, to season

1. In a medium skillet set over medium heat, heat the olive oil. 2. Add the bell pepper, onions, and garlic. Sauté for 5 minutes, or until soft. 3. Add the tofu, button mushrooms, and portobello mushrooms, tossing and stirring. Reduce the heat to low. 4. Stir in the balsamic vinegar and basil. Season with salt and pepper. Simmer for 2 minutes. 5. Enjoy!

Per Serving:
calories: 142 | fat: 8g | protein: 13g | carbs: 9g | sugars: 4g | fiber: 2g | sodium: 326mg

Palak Tofu

Prep time: 5 minutes | Cook time: 40 minutes | Serves 4

One 14 ounces package extra-firm tofu, drained
5 tablespoons cold-pressed avocado oil
1 yellow onion, diced
1-inch piece fresh ginger, peeled and minced
3 garlic cloves, minced
1 teaspoon fine sea salt
½ teaspoon freshly ground black pepper
¼ teaspoon cayenne pepper
One 16 ounces bag frozen chopped spinach
⅓ cup water
One 14½-ounce can fire-roasted diced tomatoes and their liquid
¼ cup coconut milk
2 teaspoons garam masala
Cooked brown rice or cauliflower "rice" or whole-grain flatbread for serving

1. Cut the tofu crosswise into eight ½-inch-thick slices. Sandwich the slices between double layers of paper towels or a folded kitchen towel and press firmly to wick away as much moisture as possible. Cut the slices into ½-inch cubes. 2. Select the Sauté setting on the Instant Pot and and heat 4 tablespoons of the oil for 2 minutes. Add the onion and sauté for about 10 minutes, until it begins to brown. 3. While the onion is cooking in the Instant Pot, in a large nonstick skillet over medium-high heat, warm the remaining 1 tablespoon oil. Add the tofu in a single layer and cook without stirring for about 3 minutes, until lightly browned. 4. Using a spatula, turn the cubes over and cook for about 3 minutes more, until browned on the other side. Remove from the heat and set aside. 5. Add the ginger and garlic to the onion in the Instant Pot and sauté for about 2 minutes, until the garlic is bubbling but not browned. Add the sautéed tofu, salt, black pepper, and cayenne and stir gently to combine, taking care not to break up the tofu. Add the spinach and stir gently. Pour in the water and then pour the tomatoes and their liquid over the top in an even layer. Do not stir them in. 6. Secure the lid and set the Pressure Release to Sealing. Press the Cancel button to reset the cooking program, then select the Manual or Pressure Cook setting and set the cooking time for 10 minutes at low pressure. (The pot will take about 15 minutes to come up to pressure before the cooking program begins.) 7. When the cooking program ends, let the pressure release naturally for 10 minutes, then move the Pressure Release to Venting to release any remaining steam. Open the pot, add the coconut milk and garam masala, and stir to combine. 8. Ladle the tofu onto plates or into bowls. Serve piping hot, with the "rice" alongside.

Per Serving:
calories: 345 | fat: 24g | protein: 14g | carbs: 18g | sugars: 5g | fiber: 6g | sodium: 777mg

Edamame Falafel with Roasted Vegetables

Prep time: 10 minutes | Cook time: 55 minutes | Serves 2

For the roasted vegetables
1 cup broccoli florets
1 medium zucchini, sliced
½ cup cherry tomatoes, halved
1½ teaspoons extra-virgin olive oil
Salt, to season
Freshly ground black pepper, to season
Extra-virgin olive oil cooking spray
For the falafel
1 cup frozen shelled edamame, thawed
1 small onion, chopped
1 garlic clove, chopped
1 tablespoon freshly squeezed lemon juice
2 tablespoons hemp hearts
1 teaspoon ground cumin
2 tablespoons oat flour
¼ teaspoon salt
Pinch freshly ground black pepper
2 tablespoons extra-virgin olive oil, divided
Prepared hummus, for serving (optional)

To make the roasted vegetables 1. Preheat the oven to 425°F. 2. In a large bowl, toss together the broccoli, zucchini, tomatoes, and olive oil to coat. Season with salt and pepper. 3. Spray a baking sheet with cooking spray. 4. Spread the vegetables evenly atop the sheet. Place the sheet in the preheated oven. Roast for 35 to 40 minutes, stirring every 15 minutes, or until the vegetables are soft and cooked through. 5. Remove from the oven. Set aside. To make the falafel 1. In a food processor, pulse the edamame until coarsely ground. 2. Add the onion, garlic, lemon juice, and hemp hearts. Process until finely ground. Transfer the mixture to a medium bowl. 3. By hand, mix in the cumin, oat flour, salt, and pepper. 4. Roll the dough into 1-inch balls. Flatten slightly. You should have about 12 silver dollar–size patties. 5. In a large skillet set over medium heat, heat 1 tablespoon of olive oil. 6. Add 4 falafel patties to the pan at a time (or as many as will fit without crowding), and cook for about 3 minutes on each side, or until lightly browned. Remove from the pan. Repeat with the remaining 1 tablespoon of olive oil and falafel patties. 7. Serve immediately with the roasted vegetables and hummus (if using) and enjoy!

Per Serving:
calories: 316 | fat: 22g | protein: 12g | carbs: 21g | sugars: 4g | fiber: 6g | sodium: 649mg

Cheesy Zucchini Patties

Prep time: 10 minutes | Cook time: 20 minutes | Serves 2

1 cup grated zucchini	Salt, to season
1 cup chopped fresh mushrooms	Freshly ground black pepper, to season
½ cup grated carrot	
½ cup nonfat shredded mozzarella cheese	1 tablespoon extra-virgin olive oil
¼ cup finely ground flaxseed	4 cup mixed baby greens, divided
1 large egg, beaten	
1 garlic clove, minced	

1. In a medium bowl, stir together the zucchini, mushrooms, carrot, mozzarella cheese, flaxseed, egg, and garlic. Season with salt and pepper. Stir again to combine. 2. In a large skillet set over medium-high heat, heat the olive oil. 3. Drop 1 tablespoon of the zucchini mixture into the skillet. Continue dropping tablespoon-size portions in the pan until it is full, but not crowded. Cook for 2 to 3 minutes on each side, or until golden. Transfer to a serving plate. Repeat with the remaining mixture. 4. Place 2 cups of greens on each serving plate. Top each with zucchini patties. 5. Enjoy!

Per Serving:

calories: 252 | fat: 15g | protein: 19g | carbs: 14g | sugars: 4g | fiber: 9g | sodium: 644mg

Chile Relleno Casserole with Salsa Salad

Prep time: 10 minutes | Cook time: 55 minutes | Serves 4

Casserole	2 Roma tomatoes, seeded and diced
½ cup gluten-free flour (such as King Arthur)	1 green bell pepper, seeded and diced
1 teaspoon baking powder	
6 large eggs	½ small yellow onion, diced
½ cup nondairy milk or whole milk	1 jalapeño chile, seeded and diced (optional)
Three 4 ounces cans fire-roasted diced green chiles, drained	2 tablespoons chopped fresh cilantro
1 cup nondairy cheese shreds or shredded mozzarella cheese	4 teaspoons extra-virgin olive oil
Salad	4 teaspoons fresh lime juice
1 head green leaf lettuce, shredded	⅛ teaspoon fine sea salt

1. To make the casserole: Pour 1 cup water into the Instant Pot. Butter a 7-cup round heatproof glass dish or coat with nonstick cooking spray and place the dish on a long-handled silicone steam rack. (If you don't have the long-handled rack, use the wire metal steam rack and a homemade sling) 2. In a medium bowl, whisk together the flour and baking powder. Add the eggs and milk and whisk until well blended, forming a batter. Stir in the chiles and ¾ cup of the cheese. 3. Pour the batter into the prepared dish and cover tightly with aluminum foil. Holding the handles of the steam rack, lower the dish into the Instant Pot. 4. Secure the lid and set the Pressure Release to Sealing. Select the Pressure Cook or Manual setting and set the cooking time for 40 minutes at high pressure. (The pot will take about 10 minutes to come up to pressure before the cooking program begins.) 5. When the cooking program ends, let the pressure release naturally for at least 10 minutes, then move the Pressure Release to Venting to release any remaining steam. Open the pot and, wearing heat-resistant mitts, grasp the handles of the steam rack and lift it out of the pot. Uncover the dish, taking care not to get burned by the steam or to drip condensation onto the casserole. While the casserole is still piping hot, sprinkle the remaining ¼ cup cheese evenly on top. Let the cheese melt for 5 minutes. 6. To make the salad: While the cheese is melting, in a large bowl, combine the lettuce, tomatoes, bell pepper, onion, jalapeño (if using), cilantro, oil, lime juice, and salt. Toss until evenly combined. 7. Cut the casserole into wedges. Serve warm, with the salad on the side.

Per Serving:

calorie: 361 | fat: 22g | protein: 21g | carbs: 23g | sugars: 8g | fiber: 3g | sodium: 421mg

Gingered Tofu and Greens

Prep time: 15 minutes | Cook time: 20 minutes | Serves 2

For the marinade	oil, divided
2 tablespoons low-sodium soy sauce	1 tablespoon grated fresh ginger
¼ cup rice vinegar	2 cups coarsely shredded bok choy
⅓ cup water	2 cups coarsely shredded kale, thoroughly washed
1 tablespoon grated fresh ginger	
1 tablespoon coconut flour	½ cup fresh, or frozen, chopped green beans
1 teaspoon granulated stevia	
1 garlic clove, minced	1 tablespoon freshly squeezed lime juice
For the tofu and greens	
8 ounces extra-firm tofu, drained, cut into 1-inch cubes	1 tablespoon chopped fresh cilantro
3 teaspoons extra-virgin olive	2 tablespoons hemp hearts

To make the marinade 1. In a small bowl, whisk together the soy sauce, rice vinegar, water, ginger, coconut flour, stevia, and garlic until well combined. 2. Place a small saucepan set over high heat. Add the marinade. Bring to a boil. Cook for 1 minute. Remove from the heat. To make the tofu and greens 1. In a medium ovenproof pan, place the tofu in a single layer. Pour the marinade over. Drizzle with 1½ teaspoons of olive oil. Let sit for 5 minutes. 2. Preheat the broiler to high. 3. Place the pan under the broiler. Broil the tofu for 7 to 8 minutes, or until lightly browned. Using a spatula, turn the tofu over. Continue to broil for 7 to 8 minutes more, or until browned on this side. 4. In a large wok or skillet set over high heat, heat the remaining 1½ teaspoons of olive oil. 5. Stir in the ginger. 6. Add the bok choy, kale, and green beans. Cook for 2 to 3 minutes, stirring constantly, until the greens wilt. 7. Add the lime juice and cilantro. Remove from the heat. 8. Add the browned tofu with any remaining marinade in the pan to the bok choy, kale, and green beans. Toss gently to combine. 9. Top with the hemp hearts and serve immediately.

Per Serving:

calories: 252 | fat: 14g | protein: 15g | carbs: 20g | sugars: 4g | fiber: 3g | sodium: 679mg

Desserts

Oatmeal Chippers

Prep time: 10 minutes | Cook time: 11 minutes | Makes 20 chippers

3 to 3½ tablespoons almond butter (or tigernut butter, for nut-free)

¼ cup pure maple syrup

¼ cup brown rice syrup

2 teaspoons pure vanilla extract

1⅓ cups oat flour

1 cup + 2 tablespoons rolled oats

1½ teaspoons baking powder

½ teaspoon cinnamon

¼ teaspoon sea salt

2 to 3 tablespoons sugar-free nondairy chocolate chips

1. Preheat the oven to 350°F. Line a baking sheet with parchment paper. 2. In the bowl of a mixer, combine the almond butter, maple syrup, brown rice syrup, and vanilla. Using the paddle attachment, mix on low speed for a couple of minutes, until creamy. Turn off the mixer and add the flour, oats, baking powder, cinnamon, salt, and chocolate chips. Mix on low speed until incorporated. Place 1½-tablespoon mounds on the prepared baking sheet, spacing them 1" to 2" apart, and flatten slightly. Bake for 11 minutes, or until just set to the touch. Remove from the oven, let cool on the pan for just a minute, and then transfer the cookies to a cooling rack.

Per Serving:

calorie: 90 | fat: 2g | protein: 2g | carbs: 16g | sugars: 4g | fiber: 2g | sodium: 75mg

Banana N'Ice Cream with Cocoa Nuts

Prep time: 10 minutes | Cook time: 12 minutes | Serves 4 to 6

For the Cocoa Nuts:

¼ cup freshly squeezed orange juice

1 tablespoon coconut oil

2 teaspoons cocoa powder

½ teaspoon kosher salt

¼ teaspoon ground cinnamon

¼ teaspoon ground cardamom

½ teaspoon orange zest

1 cup raw almonds

For the Banana N'ice Cream:

2 frozen, diced bananas

Make the Cocoa Nuts: 1. Preheat the oven to 350°F. Line a baking sheet with parchment paper. 2. In a small saucepan, bring the orange juice to a boil over medium-high heat, reduce the heat to low, and simmer until the juice is reduced to about 2 tablespoons, 5 to 7 minutes. Add the coconut oil, stir until well combined, and remove from the heat. Whisk in the cocoa powder, salt, cinnamon, cardamom, and zest. Then add the almonds and stir to coat them. Spread the mixture onto the prepared baking sheet. 3. Bake the nuts for 10 to 12 minutes, stirring halfway through, until toasted. Allow to cool. 4. Store the nuts in an airtight container at room temperature for up to 2 weeks. Make the Banana N'ice Cream: 5. Put the frozen bananas in a food processor and pulse. Scrape down the sides, then pulse once more. Continue to do this for several minutes until the texture resembles ice cream. Serve immediately with the cooled nuts.

Per Serving:

calories: 199 | fat: 14g | protein: 6g | carbs: 16g | sugars: 7g | fiber: 4g | sodium: 195mg

Creamy Orange Cheesecake

Prep time: 35 minutes | Cook time: 35 minutes | Serves 10

Sauce:

¾ cup graham cracker crumbs

2 tablespoons sugar

3 tablespoons melted, light, soft tub margarine

Sauce:

2 (8 ounces) packages fat-free cream cheese, at room temperature

⅔ cup sugar

2 eggs

1 egg yolk

¼ cup frozen orange juice concentrate

1 teaspoon orange zest

1 tablespoon flour

½ teaspoon vanilla

1½ cups water

1. Combine crust ingredients. Pat into 7" springform pan. 2. Cream together cream cheese and sugar. Add eggs and yolk. Beat for 3 minutes. 3. Beat in juice, zest, flour, and vanilla. Beat 2 minutes. 4. Pour batter into crust. Cover with foil. 5. Place the trivet into your Instant Pot and pour in 1½ cups water. Place a foil sling on top of the trivet, then place the springform pan on top. 6. Secure the lid and make sure lid is set to sealing. Press Manual and set for 35 minutes. 7. When cook time is up, press Cancel and allow the pressure to release naturally for 7 minutes, then release the remaining pressure manually. 8. Carefully remove the springform pan by using hot pads to lift the pan up by the foil sling. Uncover and place on a cooling rack until cool, then refrigerate for 8 hours.

Per Serving:

calories: 159 | fat: 3g | protein: 9g | carbs: 25g | sugars: 19g | fiber: 0g | sodium: 300mg

Cream Cheese Swirl Brownies

Prep time: 10 minutes | Cook time: 20 minutes | Serves 12

2 eggs

¼ cup unsweetened applesauce

¼ cup coconut oil, melted

3 tablespoons pure maple syrup, divided

¼ cup unsweetened cocoa

powder

¼ cup coconut flour

¼ teaspoon salt

1 teaspoon baking powder

2 tablespoons low-fat cream cheese

1. Preheat the oven to 350°F. Grease an 8-by-8-inch baking dish. 2. In a large mixing bowl, beat the eggs with the applesauce, coconut oil, and 2 tablespoons of maple syrup. 3. Stir in the cocoa powder and coconut flour, and mix well. Sprinkle the salt and baking powder evenly over the surface and mix well to incorporate. Transfer the mixture to the prepared baking dish. 4. In a small, microwave-safe bowl, microwave the cream cheese for 10 to 20 seconds until softened. Add the remaining 1 tablespoon of maple syrup and mix to combine. 5. Drop the cream cheese onto the batter, and use a toothpick or chopstick to swirl it on the surface. Bake for 20 minutes, until a toothpick inserted in the center comes out clean. Cool and cut into 12 squares. 6. Store refrigerated in a covered container for up to 5 days.

Per Serving:

calories: 84 | fat: 6g | protein: 2g | carbs: 6g | sugars: 4g | fiber: 2g | sodium: 93mg

Spiced Pear Applesauce

Prep time: 15 minutes | Cook time: 5 minutes | Makes: 3½ cups

1 pound pears, peeled, cored, and sliced

2 teaspoons apple pie spice or

cinnamon

Pinch kosher salt

Juice of ½ small lemon

1. In the electric pressure cooker, combine the apples, pears, apple pie spice, salt, lemon juice, and ¼ cup of water. 2. Close and lock the lid of the pressure cooker. Set the valve to sealing. 3. Cook on high pressure for 5 minutes. 4. When the cooking is complete, hit Cancel and let the pressure release naturally. 5. Once the pin drops, unlock and remove the lid. 6. Mash the apples and pears with a potato masher to the consistency you like. 7. Serve warm, or cool to room temperature and refrigerate.

Per Serving:

(½ cup): calories: 108 | fat: 1g | protein: 1g | carbs: 29g | sugars: 20g | fiber: 6g | sodium: 15mg

Apple Cinnamon Bread Pudding

Prep time: 5 minutes | Cook time: 1 hour | Serves 10

9 slices whole-wheat bread, cubed (about 5–6 cups)

2 cups cubed apples (Granny Smith apples work well)

4 cups fat-free milk

1 cup egg substitute

2 teaspoon vanilla

2 teaspoon cinnamon

¼ cup agave nectar

½ cup raisins

1. Preheat the oven to 350 degrees. 2. In a large baking dish, combine the bread and apples. 3. In a bowl, whisk together the milk, egg substitute, vanilla, cinnamon, and agave nectar. Add the raisins. Pour the milk mixture over the bread, and let stand for 15 minutes so the bread can absorb some of the liquid. 4. Bake at 350 degrees for 40–45 minutes, until the bread pudding is set and firm. Cut into squares, and serve warm with whipped topping or low-fat ice cream.

Per Serving:

calories: 175 | fat: 1g | protein: 10g | carbs: 28g | sugars: 15g | fiber: 3g | sodium: 232mg

Mixed-Berry Cream Tart

Prep time: 20 minutes | Cook time: 0 minutes | Serves 8

2 cups sliced fresh strawberries

½ cup boiling water

1 box (4-serving size) sugar-free strawberry gelatin

3 pouches (1½ ounces each) roasted almond crunchy granola bars (from 8.9-oz box)

1 package (8 ounces) fat-free

cream cheese

¼ cup sugar

¼ teaspoon almond extract

1 cup fresh blueberries

1 cup fresh raspberries

Fat-free whipped topping, if desired

1. In small bowl, crush 1 cup of the strawberries with pastry blender or fork. Reserve remaining 1 cup strawberries. 2. In medium bowl, pour boiling water over gelatin; stir about 2 minutes or until gelatin is completely dissolved. Stir crushed strawberries into gelatin. Refrigerate 20 minutes. 3. Meanwhile, leaving granola bars in pouches, crush granola bars with rolling pin. Sprinkle crushed granola in bottom of 9-inch ungreased glass pie plate, pushing crumbs up side of plate to make crust. 4. In small bowl, beat cream cheese, sugar and almond extract with electric mixer on medium-high speed until smooth. Drop by spoonfuls over crushed granola; gently spread to cover bottom of crust. 5. Gently fold blueberries, raspberries and remaining 1 cup strawberries into gelatin mixture. Spoon over cream cheese mixture. Refrigerate about 3 hours or until firm. Serve topped with whipped topping.

Per Serving:

calorie: 170 | fat: 3g | protein: 8g | carbs: 27g | sugars: 17g | fiber: 3g | sodium: 340mg

Peach and Almond Meal Fritters

Prep time: 15 minutes | Cook time: 15 minutes | Serves 7

4 ripe bananas, peeled

2 cups chopped peaches

1 medium egg

2 medium egg whites

¾ cup almond meal

¼ teaspoon almond extract

1. In a large bowl, mash the bananas and peaches together with a fork or potato masher. 2. Blend in the egg and egg whites. 3. Stir in the almond meal and almond extract. 4. Working in batches, place ¼-cup portions of the batter into the basket of an air fryer. 5. Set the air fryer to 390°F, close, and cook for 12 minutes. 6. Once cooking is complete, transfer the fritters to a plate. Repeat until no batter remains.

Per Serving:

calories: 150 | fat: 6g | protein: 5g | carbs: 22g | sugars: 12g | fiber: 4g | sodium: 25mg

Chocolate Cupcakes

Prep time: 10 minutes | Cook time: 20 minutes | Serves 12

3 tablespoons canola oil

¼ cup agave nectar

¼ cup egg whites

1 teaspoon vanilla

1 teaspoon cold espresso or strong coffee

½ cup fat-free milk

1¼ cups quinoa flour

¼ cup ground walnuts

6 tablespoons cocoa powder

2 teaspoons baking powder

¼ teaspoon baking soda

1. Preheat the oven to 375 degrees. 2. In a medium bowl, beat the oil with the agave nectar, egg whites, vanilla, espresso, and milk. 3. In a separate bowl, combine the quinoa flour, walnuts, cocoa powder, baking powder, and baking soda. Add to the creamed mixture, and mix until smooth. 4. Spoon the batter into paper-lined muffin tins, and bake at 375 degrees for 20 minutes. Remove from the oven and let cool.

Per Serving:

calories: 113 | fat: 5g | protein: 3g | carbs: 15g | sugars: 4g | fiber: 2g | sodium: 43mg

Grilled Peach and Coconut Yogurt Bowls

Prep time: 5 minutes | Cook time: 10 minutes | Serves 4

2 peaches, halved and pitted

½ cup plain nonfat Greek yogurt

1 teaspoon pure vanilla extract

¼ cup unsweetened dried

coconut flakes

2 tablespoons unsalted pistachios, shelled and broken into pieces

1. Preheat the broiler to high. Arrange the rack in the closest position to the broiler. 2. In a shallow pan, arrange the peach halves, cut-side up. Broil for 6 to 8 minutes until browned, tender, and hot. 3. In a small bowl, mix the yogurt and vanilla. 4. Spoon the yogurt into the cavity of each peach half. 5. Sprinkle 1 tablespoon of coconut flakes and 1½ teaspoons of pistachios over each peach half. Serve warm.

Per Serving:

calories: 102 | fat: 5g | protein: 5g | carbs: 11g | sugars: 8g | fiber: 2g | sodium: 12mg

Banana Pineapple Freeze

Prep time: 30 minutes | Cook time: 0 minutes | Serves 12

2 cups mashed ripe bananas

2 cups unsweetened orange juice

2 tablespoon fresh lemon juice

1 cup unsweetened crushed pineapple, undrained

½ teaspoon ground cinnamon

1. In a food processor, combine all ingredients, and process until smooth and creamy. 2. Pour the mixture into a 9-x-9-x-2-inch baking dish, and freeze overnight or until firm. Serve chilled.

Per Serving:

calories: 60 | fat: 0g | protein: 1g | carbs: 15g | sugars: 9g | fiber: 1g | sodium: 1mg

Orange Praline with Yogurt

Prep time: 10 minutes | Cook time: 10 minutes | Serves 6

3 tablespoons sugar

4 teaspoons water

⅓ cup slivered almonds, toasted

½ teaspoon ground cinnamon

⅛ teaspoon ground cloves

1 tablespoon orange zest (optional)

Pinch kosher salt

3 cups plain Greek yogurt

1. Preheat the oven to 375°F. Line a baking sheet with parchment paper. 2. In a small saucepan, stir together the sugar and water and cook over high heat until light golden-brown in color, 3 to 4 minutes. Do not stir, but instead gently swirl to help the sugar dissolve. Add the almonds and cook for 1 minute. The goal is to coat the almonds with the heated sugar (think caramel here) without burning. Pour the mixture onto the prepared baking sheet and set aside to cool for about 5 minutes. 3. Meanwhile, in a medium bowl, stir together the cinnamon, cloves, orange zest (if using), and salt. 4. Break the praline into smaller pieces and toss them in the spices. 5. Evenly divide the yogurt among six bowls and serve topped with the spiced praline. Store the praline in a sealed container at room temperature for up to 2 weeks.

Per Serving:

calories: 126 | fat: 3g | protein: 8g | carbs: 16g | sugars: 15g | fiber: 1g | sodium: 250mg

Dark Chocolate–Cherry Multigrain Cookies

Prep time: 40 minutes | Cook time: 7 to 8 minutes | Makes 18 cookies

½ cup packed brown sugar

3 tablespoons granulated sugar

⅓ cup canola oil

1 egg or ¼ cup fat-free egg product

2 teaspoons vanilla

1 cup white whole wheat flour

¾ cup uncooked 5-grain rolled hot cereal

½ teaspoon baking soda

¼ teaspoon salt

½ cup dried cherries

⅓ cup bittersweet chocolate chips

1. Heat oven to 375°F. In medium bowl, mix sugars, oil, egg and vanilla. Stir in flour, cereal, baking soda and salt until blended (dough will be slightly soft). Stir in cherries and chocolate chips. 2. Onto ungreased cookie sheets, drop dough by rounded tablespoonfuls 2 inches apart. Bake 7 to 8 minutes or until light golden brown around edges (centers will look slightly underdone). Cool 1 minute; transfer from cookie sheets to cooling racks. Cool completely.

Per Serving:

1 Cookie: calorie: 160 | fat: 6g | protein: 2g | carbs: 23g | sugars: 13g | fiber: 2g | sodium: 110mg

Peach Shortcake

Prep time: 10 minutes | Cook time: 30 minutes | Serves 8

2½ cups sliced fresh peaches

½ cup slivered almonds

1½ tablespoons plus 1 teaspoon granulated sugar substitute (such as stevia), divided

½ teaspoon almond extract

½ teaspoon cinnamon

1 cup whole-wheat flour

2 teaspoons baking powder

2 tablespoons canola oil

¼ cup egg substitute

¼ cup fat-free milk

1. Preheat the oven to 400 degrees. 2. Lightly spray an 8-x-8-x-2-inch baking pan with nonstick cooking spray. Arrange the peaches and almonds in the bottom of the dish. 3. In a small bowl, mix together 1 teaspoon of the sugar substitute, the almond extract, and the cinnamon; sprinkle over the peaches, and set aside. 4. In a medium bowl, combine the flour, baking powder, and the remaining 1½ tablespoons of sugar substitute; mix well. 5. Add the oil, egg substitute, and milk to the dry ingredients; mix until smooth. Spread evenly over the peaches, and bake for 25–30 minutes or until the top is golden brown. Remove from the oven, invert onto a serving plate, and serve.

Per Serving:

calories: 110 | fat: 4g | protein: 3g | carbs: 16g | sugars: 5g | fiber: 3g | sodium: 22mg

Pineapple Pear Medley

Prep time: 10 minutes | Cook time: 10 minutes | Serves 12

1 large orange
15 ounces canned unsweetened pineapple chunks, undrained
32 ounces canned unsweetened pear halves, drained
16 ounces canned unsweetened apricot halves, drained
6 whole cloves
2 cinnamon sticks

1. Peel the orange, and reserve the rind. Divide the orange into sections, and remove the membrane. 2. Drain the pineapple, reserve the juice, and set aside. 3. In a large bowl, combine the orange sections, pineapple, pears, and apricots. Toss, and set aside. 4. In a small saucepan over medium heat, combine the orange rind, pineapple juice, cloves, and cinnamon. Let simmer for 5–10 minutes; then strain the juices, and pour over the fruit. 5. Cover, and refrigerate for at least 2–3 hours. Toss before serving.

Per Serving:

calories: 67 | fat: 0g | protein: 1g | carbs: 67g | sugars: 11g | fiber: 4g | sodium: 2mg

Fudgy Walnut Brownies

Prep time: 10 minutes | Cook time: 1 hour | Serves 12

¾ cup walnut halves and pieces
½ cup unsalted butter, melted and cooled
4 large eggs
1½ teaspoons instant coffee crystals
1½ teaspoons vanilla extract
1 cup Lakanto Monkfruit Sweetener Golden
¼ teaspoon fine sea salt
¾ cup almond flour
¾ cup natural cocoa powder
¾ cup stevia-sweetened chocolate chips

1. In a dry small skillet over medium heat, toast the walnuts, stirring often, for about 5 minutes, until golden. Transfer the walnuts to a bowl to cool. 2. Pour 1 cup water into the Instant Pot. Line the base of a 7 by 3-inch round cake pan with a circle of parchment paper. Butter the sides of the pan and the parchment or coat with nonstick cooking spray. 3. Pour the butter into a medium bowl. One at a time, whisk in the eggs, then whisk in the coffee crystals, vanilla, sweetener, and salt. Finally, whisk in the flour and cocoa powder just until combined. Using a rubber spatula, fold in the chocolate chips and walnuts. 4. Transfer the batter to the prepared pan and, using the spatula, spread it in an even layer. Cover the pan tightly with aluminum foil. Place the pan on a long-handled silicone steam rack, then, holding the handles of the steam rack, lower it into the Instant Pot. 5. Secure the lid and set the Pressure Release to Sealing. Select the Cake, Pressure Cook, or Manual setting and set the cooking time for 45 minutes at high pressure. (The pot will take about 10 minutes to come up to pressure before the cooking program begins.) 6. When the cooking program ends, let the pressure release naturally for 10 minutes, then move the Pressure Release to Venting to release any remaining steam. Open the pot and, wearing heat-resistant mitts, grasp the handles of the steam rack and lift it out of the pot.

Uncover the pan, taking care not to get burned by the steam or to drip condensation onto the brownies. Let the brownies cool in the pan on a cooling rack for about 2 hours, to room temperature. 7. Run a butter knife around the edge of the pan to make sure the brownies are not sticking to the pan sides. Invert the brownies onto the rack, lift off the pan, and peel off the parchment paper. Invert the brownies onto a serving plate and cut into twelve wedges. The brownies will keep, stored in an airtight container in the refrigerator for up to 5 days, or in the freezer for up to 4 months.

Per Serving:

calories: 199 | fat: 19g | protein: 5g | carbs: 26g | sugars: 10g | fiber: 20g | sodium: 56mg

Apple Crunch

Prep time: 13 minutes | Cook time: 2 minutes | Serves 4

3 apples, peeled, cored, and sliced (about 1½ pounds)
1 teaspoon pure maple syrup
1 teaspoon apple pie spice or
ground cinnamon
¼ cup unsweetened apple juice, apple cider, or water
¼ cup low-sugar granola

1. In the electric pressure cooker, combine the apples, maple syrup, apple pie spice, and apple juice. 2. Close and lock the lid of the pressure cooker. Set the valve to sealing. 3. Cook on high pressure for 2 minutes. 4. When the cooking is complete, hit Cancel and quick release the pressure. 5. Once the pin drops, unlock and remove the lid. 6. Spoon the apples into 4 serving bowls and sprinkle each with 1 tablespoon of granola.

Per Serving:

calories: 103 | fat: 1g | protein: 1g | carbs: 26g | sugars: 18g | fiber: 4g | sodium: 13mg

Superfood Brownie Bites

Prep time: 15 minutes | Cook time: 0 minutes | Makes 30

1 cup raw nuts (walnuts, pecans, or cashews)
½ cup hulled hemp seeds
⅓ cup raw pepitas
½ cup raw cacao powder
1 cup pitted dates
2 tablespoons coconut oil
1 teaspoon vanilla extract

1. Line a baking sheet with parchment paper. 2. Place the nuts, hemp seeds, and pepitas in a food processor and pulse until the ingredients are a meal consistency. Add the cacao powder, dates, coconut oil, and vanilla extract and pulse until the mixture holds together if you pinch it with your fingers. The dough should ball up and appear glossy, and not be too sticky and wet. If it doesn't stick together enough to form a dough consistency, add water in drops until the correct consistency is reached. Be careful not to add too much liquid. If you do, add more cacao to balance the texture. 3. Scoop out the brownie bite mixture in 1-tablespoon amounts and roll the mixture into balls. Set the balls on the baking sheet and then chill them in the refrigerator for at least 10 minutes to hold their shape. 4. Transfer the balls to a container with a lid and store in the refrigerator until ready to eat. You could eat these immediately, but they are more likely to

crumble. 5. Store brownies in an airtight container in the refrigerator for 5 to 7 days.

Per Serving:

calories: 145 | fat: 11g | protein: 4g | carbs: 11g | sugars: 7g | fiber: 3g | sodium: 2mg

Chewy Chocolate-Oat Bars

Prep time: 20 minutes | Cook time: 30 minutes | Makes 16 bars

¾ cup semisweet chocolate chips	¼ cup fat-free egg product or 1 egg
⅓ cup fat-free sweetened condensed milk (from 14-oz can)	¾ cup packed brown sugar
	¼ cup canola oil
1 cup whole wheat flour	1 teaspoon vanilla
½ cup quick-cooking oats	2 tablespoons quick-cooking oats
½ teaspoon baking powder	
½ teaspoon baking soda	2 teaspoons butter or margarine, softened
¼ teaspoon salt	

1. Heat oven to 350°F. Spray 8-inch or 9-inch square pan with cooking spray. 2. In 1-quart saucepan, heat chocolate chips and milk over low heat, stirring frequently, until chocolate is melted and mixture is smooth. Remove from heat. 3. In large bowl, mix flour, ½ cup oats, the baking powder, baking soda and salt; set aside. In medium bowl, stir egg product, brown sugar, oil and vanilla with fork until smooth. Stir into flour mixture until blended. Reserve ½ cup dough in small bowl for topping. 4. Pat remaining dough in pan (if dough is sticky, spray fingers with cooking spray or dust with flour). Spread chocolate mixture over dough. Add 2 tablespoons oats and the butter to reserved ½ cup dough; mix with pastry blender or fork until well mixed. Place small pieces of mixture evenly over chocolate mixture. 5. Bake 20 to 25 minutes or until top is golden and firm. Cool completely, about 1 hour 30 minutes. For bars, cut into 4 rows by 4 rows.

Per Serving:

1 Bar: calorie: 180 | fat: 7g | protein: 3g | carbs: 27g | sugars: 18g | fiber: 1g | sodium: 115mg

Banana Pudding

Prep time: 30 minutes | Cook time: 20 minutes | Serves 10

For The Pudding	2 (8 ounces) containers sugar-free spelt hazelnut biscuits, crushed
¾ cup erythritol or other sugar replacement	
5 teaspoons almond flour	5 medium bananas, sliced
¼ teaspoon salt	For The Meringue
2½ cups fat-free milk	5 medium egg whites (1 cup)
6 tablespoons prepared egg replacement	¼ cup erythritol or other sugar replacement
½ teaspoon vanilla extract	½ teaspoon vanilla extract

Make The Pudding: 1. In a saucepan, whisk the erythritol, almond flour, salt, and milk together. Cook over medium heat until the sugar is dissolved. 2. Whisk in the egg replacement and cook for about 10 minutes, or until thickened. 3. Remove from the heat and stir in the vanilla. 4. Spread the thickened pudding onto the bottom of a 3 × 6-inch casserole dish. 5. Arrange a layer of crushed biscuits on top of the pudding. 6. Place a layer of sliced bananas on top of the biscuits. Make The Meringue: 1. Preheat the oven to 350°F. 2. In a medium bowl, beat the egg whites for about 5 minutes, or until stiff. 3. Add the erythritol and vanilla while continuing to beat for about 3 more minutes. 4. Spread the meringue on top of the banana pudding. 5. Transfer the casserole dish to the oven, and bake for 7 to 10 minutes, or until the top is lightly browned.

Per Serving:

calories: 323 | fat: 14g | protein: 12g | carbs: 42g | sugars: 11g | fiber: 3g | sodium: 148mg

Broiled Pineapple

Prep time: 5 minutes | Cook time: 5 minutes | Serves 4

4 large slices fresh pineapple	2 tablespoons unsweetened shredded coconut
2 tablespoons canned coconut milk	
	¼ teaspoon sea salt

1. Preheat the oven broiler on high. 2. On a rimmed baking sheet, arrange the pineapple in a single layer. Brush lightly with the coconut milk and sprinkle with the coconut. 3. Broil until the pineapple begins to brown, 3 to 5 minutes. 4. Sprinkle with the sea salt.

Per Serving:

calories: 110 | fat: 3g | protein: 1g | carbs: 23g | sugars: 15g | fiber: 3g | sodium: 16mg

Classic Crêpes

Prep time: 30 minutes | Cook time: 10 minutes | Serves 10

¾ cup egg substitute	1½ cups fat-free milk
1⅓ cups buckwheat flour	2 teaspoons canola oil
½ teaspoon salt	

1. In a food processor or blender, combine all ingredients. Process for 30 seconds, scraping down the sides of the container. Continue to process until the mixture is smooth; refrigerate for 1 hour. 2. Coat the bottom of a 6-inch crêpe pan or small skillet with nonstick cooking spray. Place the pan over medium heat until hot but not smoking. 3. Pour 2 tablespoons of the batter into the pan, and quickly tilt it in all directions so the batter covers the pan in a thin film. Cook for about 1 minute, lifting the edge of the crêpe to test for doneness. The crêpe is ready to be flipped when it can be shaken loose from the pan. 4. Flip the crêpe, and continue to cook for 30 seconds on the other side. (This side usually has brownish spots on it, so place the filling on this side.) 5. Stack the cooked crêpes between layers of wax paper to avoid sticking, and repeat the process with the remaining batter.

Per Serving:

calories: 83 | fat: 1g | protein: 5g | carbs: 13g | sugars: 3g | fiber: 2g | sodium: 173mg

Avocado Chocolate Mousse

Prep time: 5 minutes | Cook time: 0 minutes | Serves 4

2 avocados, mashed
¼ cup canned coconut milk
2 tablespoons unsweetened cocoa powder

2 tablespoons pure maple syrup
½ teaspoon espresso powder
½ teaspoon vanilla extract

1. In a blender, combine all of the ingredients. Blend until smooth. 2. Pour the mixture into 4 small bowls and serve.

Per Serving:

calories: 222 | fat: 18g | protein: 3g | carbs: 17g | sugars: 7g | fiber: 8g | sodium: 11mg

Double-Ginger Cookies

Prep time: 45 minutes | Cook time: 8 to 10 minutes | Makes 5 dozen cookies

¾ cup sugar
¼ cup butter or margarine, softened
1 egg or ¼ cup fat-free egg product
¼ cup molasses
1¾ cups all-purpose flour
1 teaspoon baking soda

½ teaspoon ground cinnamon
½ teaspoon ground ginger
¼ teaspoon ground cloves
¼ teaspoon salt
¼ cup sugar
¼ cup orange marmalade
2 tablespoons finely chopped crystallized ginger

1. In medium bowl, beat ¾ cup sugar, the butter, egg and molasses with electric mixer on medium speed, or mix with spoon. Stir in flour, baking soda, cinnamon, ground ginger, cloves and salt. Cover and refrigerate at least 2 hours, until firm. 2. Heat oven to 350°F. Lightly spray cookie sheets with cooking spray. Place ¼ cup sugar in small bowl. Shape dough into ¾-inch balls; roll in sugar. Place balls about 2 inches apart on cookie sheet. Make indentation in center of each ball, using finger. Fill each indentation with slightly less than ¼ teaspoon of the marmalade. Sprinkle with crystallized ginger. 3. Bake 8 to 10 minutes or until set. Immediately transfer from cookie sheets to cooling racks. Cool completely, about 30 minutes.

Per Serving:

1 Cookie: calorie: 45 | fat: 1g | protein: 0g | carbs: 9g | sugars: 5g | fiber: 0g | sodium: 40mg

Low-Fat Cream Cheese Frosting

Prep time: 5 minutes | Cook time: 0 minutes | Serves 8

3 cups fat-free ricotta cheese
1⅓ cups plain fat-free yogurt, strained overnight in cheesecloth over a bowl set in the refrigerator

2 cups low-fat cottage cheese
⅓ cup fructose
3 tablespoons evaporated fat-free milk

1. In a large bowl, combine all the ingredients; beat well with electric beaters until slightly stiff. 2. Place frosting in a covered container, and refrigerate until ready to use (this frosting can be refrigerated

for up to 1 week).

Per Serving:

calories: 209 | fat: 7g | protein: 24g | carbs: 9g | sugars: 7g | fiber: 1g | sodium: 594mg

Berry Smoothie Pops

Prep time: 5 minutes | Cook time: 0 minutes | Serves 6

2 cups frozen mixed berries
½ cup unsweetened plain almond milk

1 cup plain nonfat Greek yogurt
2 tablespoons hemp seeds

1. Place all the ingredients in a blender and process until finely blended. 2. Pour into 6 clean ice pop molds and insert sticks. 3. Freeze for 3 to 4 hours until firm.

Per Serving:

calorie: 70 | fat: 2g | protein: 5g | carbs: 9g | sugars: 2g | fiber: 3g | sodium: 28mg

Ambrosia

Prep time: 10 minutes | Cook time: 0 minutes | Serves 8

3 oranges, peeled, sectioned, and quartered
2 (4 ounces) cups diced peaches in water, drained

1 cup shredded, unsweetened coconut
1 (8 ounces) container fat-free crème fraîche

1. In a large mixing bowl, combine the oranges, peaches, coconut, and crème fraîche. Gently toss until well mixed. Cover and refrigerate overnight.

Per Serving:

calories: 111 | fat: 5g | protein: 2g | carbs: 12g | sugars: 8g | fiber: 3g | sodium: 7mg

Baked Pumpkin Pudding

Prep time: 5 minutes | Cook time: 20 minutes | Serves 4

1½ cups mashed pumpkin
1 egg
2½ tablespoons agave nectar
½ teaspoon vanilla extract

1 teaspoon pumpkin pie spice
¼ cup slivered almonds
¼ cup raisins

1. Preheat the oven to 350 degrees. 2. In a large bowl, combine the pumpkin, egg, agave nectar, vanilla, and pumpkin pie spice, and mix well. Stir in the almonds and raisins, leaving a few for garnish. 3. Spoon the mixture into 4 ramekins, and garnish with the remaining almonds and raisins. 4. Bake at 350 degrees for approximately 20 minutes, or until golden on top. 5. Serve warm or at room temperature.

Per Serving:

calories: 130 | fat: 5g | protein: 4g | carbs: 20g | sugars: 13g | fiber: 2g | sodium: 18mg

5-Ingredient Chunky Cherry and Peanut Butter Cookies

Prep time: 5 minutes | Cook time: 10 to 12 minutes | Makes 12 cookies

1 cup (240 g) all-natural peanut butter

¼ cup (60 ml) pure maple syrup

1 large egg, beaten

1 cup (80 g) gluten-free rolled or quick oats

½ cup (80 g) dried cherries

1. Preheat the oven to 350°F (177°C). Line a large baking sheet with parchment paper. 2. In a large bowl, whisk together the peanut butter, maple syrup, and egg. Add the oats and cherries, and mix until the ingredients are combined. 3. Chill the dough for 10 to 15 minutes. 4. Use a cookie scoop to scoop balls of the dough onto the prepared baking sheet. 5. Using a fork, gently flatten the dough balls into your desired shape (the cookies will not change shape much during baking). Bake the cookies for 10 to 12 minutes, until they are lightly golden on top. 6. Remove the cookies from the oven and let them cool for 5 minutes before transferring them to a wire rack.

Per Serving:

calorie: 198 | fat: 12g | protein: 7g | carbs: 19g | sugars: 11g | fiber: 3g | sodium: 13mg

Chocolate Tahini Bombs

Prep time: 20 minutes | Cook time: 8 minutes | Makes 15 each

15 whole dates, pits removed (date intact, not split in half completely)

2½ tablespoons tahini, divided

½ cup canned coconut milk

4 ounces dark chocolate, chopped

1 tablespoon toasted sesame seeds

1. Line a baking sheet with parchment paper. 2. Fill each date with a small amount of the tahini, roughly ¼ teaspoon, and place them on the prepared baking sheet. Put the filled dates in the freezer for 10 to 15 minutes. 3. Meanwhile, heat the coconut milk in a small saucepan over medium-low until simmering. 4. Place the chocolate in a medium heatproof bowl, and when the milk is simmering, pour it into the bowl and let stand for 3 minutes to soften the chocolate. 5. Stir the mixture until it is smooth and the chocolate is completely melted. 6. Remove the dates from the freezer and dip one date at a time into the chocolate. Coat evenly using a fork and place them back on the baking sheet. Sprinkle the dates with the sesame seeds and repeat until all dates are coated in chocolate. 7. Allow to cool completely for the chocolate to harden, or eat immediately.

Per Serving:

calories: 98 | fat: 6g | protein: 1g | carbs: 9g | sugars: 6g | fiber: 2g | sodium: 6mg

Chocolate Chip and Cranberry Cookies

Prep time: 15 minutes | Cook time: 10 minutes | Serves 15

¼ cup canola oil

¼ cup granulated sugar substitute (such as stevia)

1 egg white

1 teaspoon vanilla

1 cup almond flour

¼ teaspoon baking soda

¼ teaspoon salt

4 tablespoons semisweet chocolate mini morsels

½ cup dried cranberries

½ cup chopped walnuts

1. Preheat the oven to 375 degrees. 2. In a medium bowl, cream the oil and sugar substitute, Beat in the egg white and vanilla; mix thoroughly. 3. In a sifter, combine the flour, baking soda, and salt. Sift the dry ingredients into the creamed mixture, and mix well. Stir in the chocolate mini morsels, cranberries, and walnuts. 4. Lightly spray cookie sheets with nonstick cooking spray. Drop teaspoonfuls of dough onto the cookie sheet. Place in the freezer for 10 minutes to chill. 5. Bake at 375 degrees for 8–10 minutes. Remove the cookies from the oven, and cool them on racks.

Per Serving:

calories: 119 | fat: 10g | protein: 2g | carbs: 5g | sugars: 3g | fiber: 2g | sodium: 45mg

Strawberry Cream Cheese Crepes

Prep time: 10 minutes | Cook time: 10 minutes | Serves 4

½ cup old-fashioned oats

1 cup unsweetened plain almond milk

1 egg

3 teaspoons honey, divided

Nonstick cooking spray

2 ounces low-fat cream cheese

¼ cup low-fat cottage cheese

2 cups sliced strawberries

1. In a blender jar, process the oats until they resemble flour. Add the almond milk, egg, and 1½ teaspoons honey, and process until smooth. 2. Heat a large skillet over medium heat. Spray with nonstick cooking spray to coat. 3. Add ¼ cup of oat batter to the pan and quickly swirl around to coat the bottom of the pan and let cook for 2 to 3 minutes. When the edges begin to turn brown, flip the crepe with a spatula and cook until lightly browned and firm, about 1 minute. Transfer to a plate. Continue with the remaining batter, spraying the skillet with nonstick cooking spray before adding more batter. Set the cooked crepes aside, loosely covered with aluminum foil, while you make the filling. 4. Clean the blender jar, then combine the cream cheese, cottage cheese, and remaining 1½ teaspoons honey, and process until smooth. 5. Fill each crepe with 2 tablespoons of the cream cheese mixture, topped with ¼ cup of strawberries. Serve.

Per Serving:

calories: 149 | fat: 6g | protein: 6g | carbs: 20g | sugars: 10g | fiber: 3g | sodium: 177mg

Stews and Soups

Eggplant Stew

Prep time: 5 minutes | Cook time: 1 hour | Serves 2

1 tablespoon extra-virgin olive oil	1 medium tomato, diced with juice
1 small Vidalia onion, chopped	2 teaspoons dried basil
2 garlic cloves, chopped	2 teaspoons dried oregano
1 small red bell pepper, chopped	⅛ teaspoon salt
1 small eggplant, chopped	3 cups water
1 cup black-eyed peas, fresh or frozen	1 tablespoon red wine vinegar

1. To a large saucepan set over medium heat, and the olive oil and onion. Sauté for about 5 minutes. 2. Add the garlic and bell pepper. Sauté for 5 minutes more, or until the vegetables just begin to soften. 3. Add the eggplant, black-eyed peas, tomato, basil, oregano, salt, and water. Increase the heat to high. Bring to a boil. Reduce the heat to medium-low. Simmer for about 1 hour, or until the eggplant is completely cooked and tender. 4. Stir in the red wine vinegar. Cook for 2 minutes more. 5. Serve immediately and enjoy!

Per Serving:

calories: 156 | fat: 5g | protein: 4g | carbs: 26g | sugars: 14g | fiber: 11g | sodium: 176mg

Chicken Noodle Soup

Prep time: 15 minutes | Cook time: 20 minutes | Serves 12

2 tablespoons avocado oil	3 pounds bone-in chicken breasts (about 3)
1 medium onion, chopped	4 cups Chicken Bone Broth or low-sodium store-bought chicken broth
3 celery stalks, chopped	
1 teaspoon kosher salt	
¼ teaspoon freshly ground black pepper	4 cups water
2 teaspoons minced garlic	2 tablespoons soy sauce
5 large carrots, peeled and cut into ¼-inch-thick rounds	6 ounces whole grain wide egg noodles

1. Set the electric pressure cooker to the Sauté setting. When the pot is hot, pour in the avocado oil. 2. Sauté the onion, celery, salt, and pepper for 3 to 5 minutes or until the vegetables begin to soften. 3. Add the garlic and carrots, and stir to mix well. Hit Cancel. 4. Add the chicken to the pot, meat-side down. Add the broth, water, and soy sauce. Close and lock the lid of the pressure cooker. Set the valve to sealing. 5. Cook on high pressure for 20 minutes. 6. When the cooking is complete, hit Cancel and quick release the pressure. Unlock and remove the lid. 7. Using tongs, remove the chicken breasts to a cutting board. Hit Sauté/More and bring the soup to a boil. 8. Add the noodles and cook for 4 to 5 minutes or until the noodles are al dente. 9. While the noodles are cooking, use two forks to shred the chicken. Add the meat back to the pot and save the bones to make more bone broth. 10. Season with additional pepper, if desired, and serve.

Per Serving:

calories: 294 | fat: 14g | protein: 27g | carbs: 15g | sugars: 3g | fiber:

3g | sodium: 640mg

Tomato and Kale Soup

Prep time: 10 minutes | Cook time: 15 minutes | Serves 4

1 tablespoon extra-virgin olive oil	1 (28 ounces) can crushed tomatoes
1 medium onion, chopped	½ teaspoon dried oregano
2 carrots, finely chopped	¼ teaspoon dried basil
3 garlic cloves, minced	4 cups chopped baby kale leaves
4 cups low-sodium vegetable broth	¼ teaspoon salt

1. In a large pot, heat the oil over medium heat. Add the onion and carrots to the pan. Sauté for 3 to 5 minutes until they begin to soften. Add the garlic and sauté for 30 seconds more, until fragrant. 2. Add the vegetable broth, tomatoes, oregano, and basil to the pot and bring to a boil. Reduce the heat to low and simmer for 5 minutes. 3. Using an immersion blender, purée the soup. 4. Add the kale and simmer for 3 more minutes. Season with the salt. Serve immediately.

Per Serving:

calories: 170 | fat: 5g | protein: 6g | carbs: 31g | sugars: 13g | fiber: 9g | sodium: 600mg

Jamaican Stew

Prep time: 10 minutes | Cook time: 20 minutes | Serves 4

1½ cups chopped onions	3½ cups water
3–4 cups cubed plantains (see Note; can substitute sweet potatoes)	2 cans (15 ounces each) black beans or adzuki beans, rinsed and drained
1¼ teaspoons sea salt	3 cups cauliflower florets
1½ teaspoons ground coriander	2 tablespoons freshly grated ginger
½ teaspoon ground cumin	
½ teaspoon ground turmeric	3 tablespoons freshly squeezed lime juice
1 teaspoon dried thyme	
½ teaspoon ground allspice	3 cups baby spinach leaves
¼ teaspoon crushed red-pepper flakes (or to taste)	¼ cup freshly chopped cilantro (optional)
1 small can (5.5 ounces) light coconut milk	Lime wedges for serving

1. In a large pot over medium or medium-high heat, combine the onion, plantains, salt, coriander, cumin, turmeric, thyme, allspice, red-pepper flakes, and a few tablespoons of the coconut milk. Cook for 6 to 7 minutes, stirring occasionally. Add the water, beans, cauliflower, ginger, and remaining coconut milk. Increase the heat to high to bring to a boil, then reduce the heat to low, cover, and cook for 12 to 15 minutes, or until the plantains are cooked through. Add the lime juice, spinach, and cilantro (if using), and stir just until the spinach wilts. Serve immediately, with the lime wedges.

Per Serving:

calorie: 426 | fat: 5g | protein: 16g | carbs: 88g | sugars: 22g | fiber: 22g | sodium: 1053mg

Favorite Chili

Prep time: 10 minutes | Cook time: 35 minutes | Serves 5

1 pound extra-lean ground beef	2 tablespoons chili powder
1 teaspoon salt	½ teaspoons cumin
½ teaspoons black pepper	1 cup water
1 tablespoon olive oil	16 ounces can chili beans
1 small onion, chopped	15 ounces can low-sodium
2 cloves garlic, minced	crushed tomatoes
1 green pepper, chopped	

1. Press Sauté button and adjust once to Sauté More function. Wait until indicator says "hot." 2. Season the ground beef with salt and black pepper. 3. Add the olive oil into the inner pot. Coat the whole bottom of the pot with the oil. 4. Add ground beef into the inner pot. The ground beef will start to release moisture. Allow the ground beef to brown and crisp slightly, stirring occasionally to break it up. Taste and adjust the seasoning with more salt and ground black pepper. 5. Add diced onion, minced garlic, chopped pepper, chili powder, and cumin. Sauté for about 5 minutes, until the spices start to release their fragrance. Stir frequently. 6. Add water and 1 can of chili beans, not drained. Mix well. Pour in 1 can of crushed tomatoes. 7. Close and secure lid, making sure vent is set to sealing, and pressure cook on Manual at high pressure for 10 minutes. 8. Let the pressure release naturally when cooking time is up. Open the lid carefully.

Per Serving:

calories: 213 | fat: 10g | protein: 18g | carbs: 11g | sugars: 4g | fiber: 4g | sodium: 385mg

African Peanut Stew

Prep time: 10 minutes | Cook time: 35 minutes | Serves 2

3 cups low-sodium vegetable broth	½ cup unsalted natural peanut butter
1 small onion, chopped	2 tablespoons tomato paste
1 small red bell pepper, chopped	1 bunch kale, thoroughly washed, deveined, and chopped (about 2½ cups)
1 medium carrot, chopped	
1 tablespoon minced fresh ginger	Freshly ground black pepper, to season
2 garlic cloves, minced	
¼ teaspoon salt, plus more to season	2 scallions, chopped

1. In a medium pot set over medium-low heat, bring the vegetable broth to a boil. 2. Add the onion, bell pepper, carrot, ginger, garlic, and salt. Cook for 20 minutes. 3. In a medium, heat-safe mixing bowl, stir together the peanut butter and tomato paste. 4. Transfer 1 cup of the hot vegetable broth to the bowl. Whisk until smooth. Pour the peanut butter mixture back into the soup. Mix well to combine. 5. Stir in the kale. Season with salt and pepper. Simmer for about 15 minutes more, stirring frequently. 6. Top with the scallions and enjoy!

Per Serving:

calories: 565 | fat: 36g | protein: 24g | carbs: 51g | sugars: 26g | fiber:

12g | sodium: 580mg

Italian Meatball-Zucchini "Noodle" Soup

Prep time: 15 minutes | Cook time: 30 minutes | Serves 2

1 large egg, lightly beaten	1 medium carrot, thinly sliced
1 tablespoon chia seeds	1 celery stalk, chopped
¼ cup minced fresh parsley	1 small onion, chopped
Salt, to season	1 tablespoon tomato paste
Freshly ground black pepper, to season	2 teaspoons Italian seasoning
	1 teaspoon dried oregano
¼ pound (93 percent) lean ground beef	2 cups diced tomatoes
	2 cups low-sodium beef broth
Extra-virgin olive oil cooking spray	1 medium zucchini, spiral-sliced

1. In a small bowl, blend together the egg, chia seeds, and parsley. Season with salt and pepper. 2. Crumble the beef into the bowl. Mix well. Shape into 1-inch balls. 3. In a large saucepan set over medium heat, brown the meatballs for about 5 minutes per side, turning frequently. Drain and set aside. 4. Lightly spray a large soup pot with cooking spray. 5. Add the carrot, celery, and onion. Cook for 4 to 5 minutes, stirring occasionally, or until the vegetables begin to brown. Push the vegetables to one side of the pot. 6. Add the tomato paste to the side of the pot without the vegetables. Cook for 1 to 2 minutes, or until the paste begins to caramelize. 7. Add the Italian seasoning and oregano. Mix well. 8. Stir in the tomatoes and beef broth. Mix the ingredients together. Bring to a simmer. 9. Add the meatballs and zucchini "noodles." Simmer for 10 to 12 minutes more. 10. Season the soup with salt and pepper. 11. Serve hot.

Per Serving:

calories: 410 | fat: 16g | protein: 32g | carbs: 40g | sugars: 9g | fiber: 5g | sodium: 846mg

Lentil Soup

Prep time: 10 minutes | Cook time: 55 minutes | Serves 8

1 large onion, diced	or beef broth
1 large carrot, peeled and diced	2 medium russet or white potatoes, peeled and diced
2 stalks celery, diced	
2 tablespoons extra-virgin olive oil	1 tablespoon finely chopped fresh oregano
1 pound lentils	1 teaspoon finely chopped fresh thyme
1½ quarts low-sodium chicken	

1. In a stockpot or Dutch oven, sauté the onion, carrot, and celery in the olive oil for 10 minutes. Add the lentils, broth, and potatoes. 2. Continue to cook for 30–45 minutes, adding the oregano and thyme 15 minutes before serving. Soup will keep for 3 days in the refrigerator or can be frozen for 3 months.

Per Serving:

calories: 174 | fat: 2g | protein: 8g | carbs: 36g | sugars: 2g | fiber: 3g | sodium: 81mg

Golden Chicken Soup

Prep time: 10 minutes | Cook time: 20 minutes | Serves 4 to 6

1 tablespoon extra-virgin olive oil

1 yellow onion, chopped

2 teaspoons garlic powder

1 tablespoon ginger powder

2 teaspoons turmeric

½ teaspoon freshly ground black pepper

6 cups low-sodium chicken broth

3 (5 to 6 ounces) boneless, skinless chicken breasts

4 celery stalks, cut into ¼-inch-thick slices

1 fennel bulb, thinly sliced

1. Heat the extra-virgin olive oil in a large stockpot over medium heat. Sauté the onion until translucent, about 3 minutes. Add the garlic powder, ginger powder, turmeric, black pepper, and chicken broth. 2. Bring to a boil, then carefully add the chicken, celery, and fennel. Reduce the heat to medium-low, cover, and simmer until the internal temperature of the chicken is 160°F, 5 to 10 minutes. 3. Remove the chicken breasts and allow them to cool for 5 minutes while the soup keeps simmering. 4. Shred the chicken using two forks and return it to the stockpot. Heat the soup for about 1 minute and adjust the seasonings as desired. 5. Store the cooled soup in an airtight container in the refrigerator for 3 to 5 days.

Per Serving:

calories: 107 | fat: 4g | protein: 10g | carbs: 10g | sugars: 3g | fiber: 2g | sodium: 370mg

West African–Inspired Peanut Soup

Prep time: 10 minutes | Cook time: 20 minutes | Serves 4 to 6

6 garlic cloves, minced

1½-inch piece ginger, grated

1 jalapeño pepper, stemmed, halved, and minced, divided

Kosher salt

2 (14 ounces) cans coconut milk, divided

2 tablespoons vegetable oil, divided

1 teaspoon turmeric

½ cup unsweetened peanut butter

8 cups vegetable broth

2 sweet potatoes, cut into ½-inch cubes

1 bunch collard greens, chopped

Juice of 1 lime

Freshly ground black pepper

½ cup chopped cilantro

1. Place the garlic, ginger, half the jalapeño, and a pinch of salt in a mound on a cutting board. Use the flat of your knife to create a paste. The paste can also be made in a food processor or with a mortar and pestle. 2. Scoop 3 tablespoons of the solid white coconut fat off the top of one can of coconut milk and place it in a large Dutch oven or stockpot. Add 1 tablespoon of vegetable oil to the coconut fat and heat over medium-high heat, stirring frequently, until the coconut fat separates and the solids start to sizzle, about 2 minutes. Continue cooking, stirring constantly, until the solids turn pale golden brown, about 1 minute longer. Add the garlic paste, turmeric, and peanut butter. Cook, stirring, until aromatic, about 30 seconds. 3. Add the remaining coconut milk from both cans, the broth, and sweet potatoes. Bring the soup to a boil, reduce the heat to low, and simmer until the sweet potatoes are tender, about 15 minutes. 4. When the potatoes are cooked through, use a large spoon to smash about half of the sweet potatoes against the side of the stockpot to help thicken the stew. Add the collard greens and lime juice. 5. Season the soup to taste with salt and pepper and serve topped with cilantro and the remaining minced jalapeños. 6. Store the cooled soup in an airtight container in the refrigerator for 3 to 5 days.

Per Serving:

calories: 312 | fat: 12g | protein: 11g | carbs: 45g | sugars: 15g | fiber: 9g | sodium: 866mg

Turkey and Pinto Chili

Prep time: 0 minutes | Cook time: 60 minutes | Serves 8

2 tablespoons cold-pressed avocado oil

4 garlic cloves, diced

1 large yellow onion, diced

4 jalapeño chiles, seeded and diced

2 carrots, diced

4 celery stalks, diced

2 teaspoons fine sea salt

2 pounds 93 percent lean ground turkey

Two 4 ounces cans fire-roasted diced green chiles

4 tablespoons chili powder

2 teaspoons ground cumin

2 teaspoons ground coriander

1 teaspoon dried oregano

1 teaspoon dried sage

1 cup low-sodium chicken broth

3 cups drained cooked pinto beans, or two 15 ounces cans pinto beans, drained and rinsed

Two 14½-ounce cans no-salt petite diced tomatoes and their liquid

¼ cup tomato paste

1. Select the Sauté setting on the Instant Pot and heat the oil and garlic for 3 minutes, until the garlic is bubbling but not browned. Add the onion, jalapeños, carrots, celery, and salt and sauté for 5 minutes, until the onion begins to soften. Add the turkey and sauté, using a wooden spoon or spatula to break up the meat as it cooks, for 6 minutes, until cooked through and no streaks of pink remain. Stir in the green chiles, chili powder, cumin, coriander, oregano, sage, and broth, using a wooden spoon or spatula to nudge any browned bits from the bottom of the pot. 2. Pour in the beans in a layer on top of the turkey. Pour in the tomatoes and their liquid and add the tomato paste in a dollop on top. Do not stir in the beans, tomatoes, or tomato paste. 3. Secure the lid and set the Pressure Release to Sealing. Press the Cancel button to reset the cooking program, then select the Pressure Cook or Manual setting and set the cooking time for 15 minutes at high pressure. (The pot will take about 15 minutes to come up to pressure before the cooking program begins.) 4. When the cooking program ends, let the pressure release naturally for at least 20 minutes, then move the Pressure Release to Venting to release any remaining steam. Open the pot and stir the chili to mix all of the ingredients. 5. Press the Cancel button to reset the cooking program, then select the Sauté setting and set the cooking time for 10 minutes. Allow the chili to reduce and thicken. Do not stir the chili while it is cooking, as this will cause it to sputter more. 6. When the cooking program ends, the pot will turn off. Wearing heat-resistant mitts, remove the inner pot from the housing. Wait for about 2 minutes to allow the chili to stop simmering, then give it a final stir. 7. Ladle the chili into bowls and serve hot.

Per Serving:

calories: 354 | fat: 14g | protein: 30g | carbs: 28g | sugars: 6g | fiber: 9g | sodium: 819mg

Comforting Summer Squash Soup with Crispy Chickpeas

Prep time: 10 minutes | Cook time: 20 minutes | Serves 4

1 (15 ounces) can low-sodium chickpeas, drained and rinsed
1 teaspoon extra-virgin olive oil, plus 1 tablespoon
¼ teaspoon smoked paprika
Pinch salt, plus ½ teaspoon
3 medium zucchini, coarsely chopped

3 cups low-sodium vegetable broth
½ onion, diced
3 garlic cloves, minced
2 tablespoons plain low-fat Greek yogurt
Freshly ground black pepper

1. Preheat the oven to 425°F. Line a baking sheet with parchment paper. 2. In a medium mixing bowl, toss the chickpeas with 1 teaspoon of olive oil, the smoked paprika, and a pinch salt. Transfer to the prepared baking sheet and roast until crispy, about 20 minutes, stirring once. Set aside. 3. Meanwhile, in a medium pot, heat the remaining 1 tablespoon of oil over medium heat. 4. Add the zucchini, broth, onion, and garlic to the pot, and bring to a boil. Reduce the heat to a simmer, and cook until the zucchini and onion are tender, about 20 minutes. 5. In a blender jar, or using an immersion blender, purée the soup. Return to the pot. 6. Add the yogurt, remaining ½ teaspoon of salt, and pepper, and stir well. Serve topped with the roasted chickpeas.

Per Serving:
calories: 188 | fat: 7g | protein: 8g | carbs: 24g | sugars: 7g | fiber: 7g | sodium: 528mg

Tasty Tomato Soup

Prep time: 10 minutes | Cook time: 1 hour 25 minutes | Serves 2

3 cups chopped tomatoes
1 red bell pepper, cut into chunks
2 tablespoons extra-virgin olive oil, divided
Salt, to season
Freshly ground black pepper, to season

1 medium onion, chopped
1 garlic clove, minced
2 cups low-sodium vegetable broth
1 cup sliced fresh button mushrooms
½ cup fresh chopped basil

1. Preheat the oven to 400°F. 2. On a baking sheet, spread out the tomatoes and red bell pepper. 3. Drizzle with 1 tablespoon of olive oil. Toss to coat. Season with salt and pepper. Place the sheet in the preheated oven. Roast for 45 minutes. 4. In a large stockpot set over medium heat, heat the remaining 1 tablespoon of olive oil. 5. Add the onion. Cook for 2 to 3 minutes, or until tender. 6. Stir in the garlic. Cook for 2 minutes more. 7. Add the vegetable broth, mushrooms, and basil. 8. Stir in the roasted tomatoes and peppers. Reduce the heat to medium-low. Cook for 30 minutes. 9. To a blender or food processor, carefully transfer the soup in batches, blending until smooth. Return the processed soup to the pot. Simmer for 5 minutes. 10. Serve warm and enjoy!

Per Serving:

calories: 255 | fat: 15g | protein: 6g | carbs: 29g | sugars: 18g | fiber: 7g | sodium: 738mg

White Bean Soup

Prep time: 15 minutes | Cook time: 20 minutes | Serves 2

1 teaspoon extra-virgin olive oil
⅓ cup chopped yellow onion
1 garlic clove, minced
1 teaspoon dried rosemary
½ cup sliced fresh mushrooms
½ cup jarred roasted red peppers, chopped
1 teaspoon freshly squeezed

lemon juice
1 teaspoon white wine vinegar
1 cup water
1 (15 ounces) can white beans, drained and rinsed
½ cup diced tomatoes, with juice
1½ cups fresh spinach

1. In a large pot set over medium heat, heat the olive oil. 2. Add the onion and garlic. Sauté for about 5 minutes, or until tender. 3. Add the rosemary, mushrooms, red peppers, lemon juice, white wine vinegar, and water. Cook for 5 minutes more, or until the mushrooms are soft. 4. Stir in the white beans, tomatoes, and spinach. Cook for 10 minutes more, or until the spinach is wilted. 5. Serve immediately and enjoy!

Per Serving:
calories: 96 | fat: 5g | protein: 3g | carbs: 13g | sugars: 4g | fiber: 4g | sodium: 28mg

Cauliflower Chili

Prep time: 10 minutes | Cook time: 35 minutes | Serves 5

2 cups thickly sliced carrot
½ large or 1 full small head cauliflower
4 or 5 cloves garlic, minced
1 tablespoon balsamic vinegar
1½ cups diced onion
1 teaspoon sea salt
1½ tablespoons mild chili powder
1 tablespoon cocoa powder
2 teaspoons ground cumin
2 teaspoons dried oregano

⅛ teaspoon allspice
¼ teaspoon crushed red-pepper flakes (or to taste)
1 can (28 ounces) crushed tomatoes
1 can (15 ounces) pinto beans, rinsed and drained
1 can (15 ounces) kidney beans or black beans, rinsed and drained
½ cup water
Lime wedges

1. In a food processor, combine the carrot, cauliflower, and garlic, and pulse until finely minced. (Alternatively, you could mince by hand.) In a large pot over medium heat, combine the vinegar, onion, salt, chili powder, cocoa, cumin, oregano, allspice, and red-pepper flakes. Cook for 3 to 4 minutes, stirring occasionally. Add the minced carrot, cauliflower, and garlic, and cook for 5 to 6 minutes, stirring occasionally. Add the tomatoes, pinto and kidney beans, and water, and stir to combine. Increase the heat to high to bring to a boil. Reduce the heat to low, cover, and simmer for 25 minutes. Taste, and season as desired. Serve with lime wedges.

Per Serving:
calorie: 237 | fat: 3g | protein: 13g | carbs: 45g | sugars: 13g | fiber: 15g | sodium: 1036mg

Roasted Tomato and Sweet Potato Soup

Prep time: 10 minutes | Cook time: 40 to 50 minutes | Serves 4

1½ cups onions, finely chopped

2 cups cubed red or yellow potatoes (not russet)

2 cups cubed sweet potatoes (can use frozen)

3–4 large cloves garlic, minced

1¼ teaspoons sea salt

1½ cups peeled, quartered onion (roughly 1 large onion)

4 cups cubed sweet potato (roughly 1–1¼ pounds before peeling)

4 cups (about 1½ pounds) quartered Roma or other tomatoes, juices squeezed out

1½ teaspoons dried basil

1½ teaspoons dried oregano

1 tablespoon balsamic vinegar

1 teaspoon blackstrap molasses

Freshly ground black pepper to taste

1⅛ teaspoons sea salt

2¼ to 2½ cups water

¼ cup chopped fresh basil (optional)

1. Preheat the oven to 450°F. 2. In a large baking dish, combine the onion, sweet potato, tomatoes, basil, oregano, vinegar, molasses, pepper, and 1 teaspoon of the salt. Cook for 40 to 50 minutes, stirring a couple of times, until the sweet potatoes are softened and the mixture is becoming caramelized. Transfer the vegetables and any juices they've released in the pan to a medium soup pot, add 2¼ cups of the water and the remaining ⅛ teaspoon salt, and use an immersion blender to puree. (Alternatively, you can transfer everything to a blender to puree.) Blend to the desired smoothness, using the additional ¼ cup water if needed. Stir in fresh basil, if using, and serve.

Per Serving:

calorie: 152 | fat: 0.4g | protein: 4g | carbs: 35g | sugars: 14g | fiber: 5g | sodium: 648mg

Chicken Brunswick Stew

Prep time: 0 minutes | Cook time: 30 minutes | Serves 6

2 tablespoons extra-virgin olive oil

2 garlic cloves, chopped

1 large yellow onion, diced

2 pounds boneless, skinless chicken (breasts, tenders, or thighs), cut into bite-size pieces

1 teaspoon dried thyme

1 teaspoon smoked paprika

1 teaspoon fine sea salt

½ teaspoon freshly ground black pepper

1 cup low-sodium chicken broth

1 tablespoon hot sauce (such as Tabasco or Crystal)

1 tablespoon raw apple cider vinegar

1½ cups frozen corn

1½ cups frozen baby lima beans

One 14½ ounces can fire-roasted diced tomatoes and their liquid

2 tablespoons tomato paste

Cornbread, for serving

1. Select the Sauté setting on the Instant Pot and heat the oil and garlic for 2 minutes, until the garlic is bubbling but not browned. Add the onion and sauté for 3 minutes, until it begins to soften. Add the chicken and sauté for 3 minutes more, until mostly opaque. The chicken does not have to be cooked through. Add the thyme, paprika, salt, and pepper and sauté for 1 minute more. 2. Stir in the broth, hot sauce, vinegar, corn, and lima beans. Add the diced tomatoes and their liquid in an even layer and dollop the tomato paste on top. Do not stir them in. 3. Secure the lid and set the Pressure Release to Sealing. Press the Cancel button to reset the cooking program, then select the Pressure Cook or Manual setting and set the cooking time for 5 minutes at high pressure. (The pot will take about 15 minutes to come up to pressure before the cooking program begins.) 4. When the cooking program ends, let the pressure release naturally for at least 10 minutes, then move the Pressure Release to Venting to release any remaining steam. Open the pot and stir the stew to mix all of the ingredients. 5. Ladle the stew into bowls and serve hot, with cornbread alongside.

Per Serving:

calories: 349 | fat: 7g | protein: 40g | carbs: 17g | sugars: 7g | fiber: 7g | sodium: 535mg

Ground Turkey Stew

Prep time: 5 minutes | Cook time: 25 minutes | Serves 5

1 tablespoon olive oil

1 onion, chopped

1 pound ground turkey

½ teaspoon garlic powder

1 teaspoon chili powder

¾ teaspoon cumin

2 teaspoons coriander

1 teaspoon dried oregano

½ teaspoon salt

1 green pepper, chopped

1 red pepper, chopped

1 tomato, chopped

1½ cups reduced-sodium tomato sauce

1 tablespoon low-sodium soy sauce

1 cup water

2 handfuls cilantro, chopped

15 ounces can reduced-salt black beans

1. Press the Sauté function on the control panel of the Instant Pot. 2. Add the olive oil to the inner pot and let it get hot. Add onion and sauté for a few minutes, or until light golden. 3. Add ground turkey. Break the ground meat using a wooden spoon to avoid formation of lumps. Sauté for a few minutes, until the pink color has faded. 4. Add garlic powder, chili powder, cumin, coriander, dried oregano, and salt. Combine well. Add green pepper, red pepper, and chopped tomato. Combine well. 5. Add tomato sauce, soy sauce, and water; combine well. 6. Close and secure the lid. Click on the Cancel key to cancel the Sauté mode. Make sure the pressure release valve on the lid is in the sealing position. 7. Click on Manual function first and then select high pressure. Click the + button and set the time to 15 minutes. 8. You can either have the steam release naturally (it will take around 20 minutes) or, after 10 minutes, turn the pressure release valve on the lid to venting and release steam. Be careful as the steam is very hot. After the pressure has released completely, open the lid. 9. If the stew is watery, turn on the Sauté function and let it cook for a few more minutes with the lid off. 10. Add cilantro and can of black beans, combine well, and let cook for a few minutes.

Per Serving:

calories: 209 | fat: 3g | protein: 24g | carbs: 21g | sugars: 8g | fiber: 6g | sodium: 609mg

Italian Vegetable Soup

Prep time: 20 minutes | Cook time: 5 to 9 hours | Serves 6

3 small carrots, sliced

1 small onion, chopped

2 small potatoes, diced

2 tablespoons chopped parsley

1 garlic clove, minced

3 teaspoons sodium-free beef bouillon powder

1¼ teaspoons dried basil

¼ teaspoon pepper

16 ounces can red kidney beans, undrained

3 cups water

14½-ounce can stewed tomatoes, with juice

1 cup diced, extra-lean, lower-sodium cooked ham

1. In the inner pot of the Instant Pot, layer the carrots, onion, potatoes, parsley, garlic, beef bouillon, basil, pepper, and kidney beans. Do not stir. Add water. 2. Secure the lid and cook on the Low Slow Cook mode for 8–9 hours, or on high 4½–5½ hours, until vegetables are tender. 3. Remove the lid and stir in the tomatoes and ham. Secure the lid again and cook on high Slow Cook mode for 10–15 minutes more.

Per Serving:

calories: 156 | fat: 1g | protein: 9g | carbs: 29g | sugars: 8g | fiber: 5g | sodium: 614mg

Tomato-Basil Soup with Grilled Cheese Croutons

Prep time: 10 minutes | Cook time: 20 minutes | Serves 4 to 6

For the tomato soup

2 tablespoons extra-virgin olive oil

1 onion, chopped

1 tablespoon minced garlic

3 pounds fresh tomatoes, cored and chopped, or canned diced tomatoes

8 cups low-sodium vegetable broth

4 tablespoons tomato paste

½ cup coconut milk

½ teaspoon garlic powder

Pinch kosher salt

Pinch freshly ground black pepper

⅓ cup fresh basil, chopped

For the grilled cheese croutons

1 tablespoon butter or cooking spray

4 slices whole-wheat bread

4 ounces cheese (cheddar or Gruyère), shredded

Freshly ground black pepper (optional)

To make the tomato soup: 1. Heat the extra-virgin olive oil in a medium stockpot over medium heat. Sauté the onion and minced garlic until translucent, about 3 minutes. 2. Add the tomatoes and vegetable broth, increase the heat to medium-high, cover, and simmer until the tomato skin wrinkles and pulls back from the tomato flesh, 8 to 10 minutes. 3. Add the tomato paste, coconut milk, garlic powder, salt, and pepper and simmer for 3 to 5 minutes. 4. Transfer the soup to a blender and blend until smooth, in batches if necessary. Leave the center piece out of the lid and cover the lid with a clean kitchen towel while blending to allow the steam to escape. 5. Pour the soup back into the stockpot. 6. Serve the soup topped with basil and the grilled cheese croutons (if using). 7. Store the cooled soup in an airtight container in the refrigerator for 3 to 5 days.

Keep the garnishes separate. To make the grilled cheese croutons 8. Meanwhile, apply the butter on one side of each slice of bread. 9. Put a small nonstick skillet over medium heat, and place 1 slice of bread in the skillet, buttered-side down. Top with half of the cheese and season with pepper (if using). Then top with the second slice of bread, buttered-side up. When the underside is golden brown, 3 to 4 minutes, turn the sandwich. Cook until the second side of the bread is golden and crispy. 10. Repeat with the remaining ingredients. 11. Cut each sandwich into 1-inch squares and use them to garnish the soup.

Per Serving:

calories: 307 | fat: 15g | protein: 12g | carbs: 38g | sugars: 14g | fiber: 7g | sodium: 931mg

Quick Shrimp Gumbo

Prep time: 10 minutes | Cook time: 40 minutes | Serves 4

2 cups low-sodium canned tomatoes, undrained

¼ cup chopped green bell pepper

1 medium onion, chopped

1 cup cooked brown rice

½ cup low-sodium chicken

broth

1 medium garlic clove, minced

Dash hot pepper sauce

Freshly ground black pepper

12 ounces precooked fresh (never frozen) jumbo shrimp

1. Place all the ingredients except the shrimp in a large stockpot and bring to a boil. Reduce the heat, cover, and let simmer for 25 to 30 minutes. 2. Add the shrimp, cover, and simmer for 5 to 10 minutes or until the shrimp is thoroughly heated. Serve hot.

Per Serving:

calories: 195 | fat: 2g | protein: 21g | carbs: 23g | sugars: 6g | fiber: 2g | sodium: 889mg

French Market Soup

Prep time: 20 minutes | Cook time: 1 hour | Serves 8

2 cups mixed dry beans, washed with stones removed

7 cups water

1 ham hock, all visible fat removed

1 teaspoon salt

¼ teaspoon pepper

16 ounces can low-sodium tomatoes

1 large onion, chopped

1 garlic clove, minced

1 chile, chopped, or 1 teaspoon chili powder

¼ cup lemon juice

1. Combine all ingredients in the inner pot of the Instant Pot. 2. Secure the lid and make sure vent is set to sealing. Using Manual, set the Instant Pot to cook for 60 minutes. 3. When cooking time is over, let the pressure release naturally. When the Instant Pot is ready, unlock the lid, then remove the bone and any hard or fatty pieces. Pull the meat off the bone and chop into small pieces. Add the ham back into the Instant Pot.

Per Serving:

calories: 191 | fat: 4g | protein: 12g | carbs: 29g | sugars: 5g | fiber: 7g | sodium: 488mg

Beef and Mushroom Barley Soup

Prep time: 10 minutes | Cook time: 1 hour 20 minutes | Serves 6

1 pound beef stew meat, cubed
¼ teaspoon salt
¼ teaspoon freshly ground black pepper
1 tablespoon extra-virgin olive oil
8 ounces sliced mushrooms
1 onion, chopped
2 carrots, chopped
3 celery stalks, chopped
6 garlic cloves, minced
½ teaspoon dried thyme
4 cups low-sodium beef broth
1 cup water
½ cup pearl barley

1. Season the meat with the salt and pepper. 2. In an Instant Pot, heat the oil over high heat. Add the meat and brown on all sides. Remove the meat from the pot and set aside. 3. Add the mushrooms to the pot and cook for 1 to 2 minutes, until they begin to soften. Remove the mushrooms and set aside with the meat. 4. Add the onion, carrots, and celery to the pot. Sauté for 3 to 4 minutes until the vegetables begin to soften. Add the garlic and continue to cook until fragrant, about 30 seconds longer. 5. Return the meat and mushrooms to the pot, then add the thyme, beef broth, and water. Set the pressure to high and cook for 15 minutes. Let the pressure release naturally. 6. Open the Instant Pot and add the barley. Use the slow cooker function on the Instant Pot, affix the lid (vent open), and continue to cook for 1 hour until the barley is cooked through and tender. Serve.

Per Serving:

calories: 245 | fat: 9g | protein: 21g | carbs: 19g | sugars: 3g | fiber: 4g | sodium: 516mg

Chickpea Spinach Soup

Prep time: 5 minutes | Cook time: 25 minutes | Serves 4

4 medium carrots, cut into ¼-inch pieces
3 tablespoons extra-virgin olive oil, divided
1 teaspoon ground cumin
1 teaspoon paprika
½ teaspoon ground coriander
½ teaspoon ground cinnamon
2 (15 ounces) cans chickpeas,
drained and rinsed
1 onion, thinly sliced
2 tablespoons minced fresh ginger
5 cups low-sodium vegetable broth
1 pound fresh baby spinach
1 cup Greek yogurt (optional)

1. Preheat the oven to 425°F. Line a baking sheet with parchment paper. 2. In a medium bowl, toss the carrots with 2 tablespoons of extra-virgin olive oil, the cumin, paprika, coriander, and cinnamon. Spread the carrots evenly on the baking sheet and roast for 8 to 10 minutes. Add half the chickpeas to the carrots, place the baking sheet back in the oven, and roast until the carrots are tender, about 10 minutes more. Set aside. 3. Meanwhile, heat the remaining 1 tablespoon of extra-virgin olive oil in a large stockpot over medium-high heat. Sauté the onion in the oil until translucent, about 3 minutes, then add the ginger, remaining chickpeas, broth, and spinach. Bring the soup to a boil, reduce the heat to low, and simmer until the greens begin to wilt, 2 to 3 minutes. 4. Transfer the soup to a blender and puree until smooth. Leave the center piece out of the lid and cover the lid with a clean dish towel to allow the steam to escape. Adjust the seasonings as desired and thin the soup with water or additional broth if you prefer a thinner soup. 5. Divide the soup among four bowls and serve topped with yogurt (if using) and the carrot and chickpea topping. 6. Store the cooled soup in an airtight container in the refrigerator for 3 to 5 days.

Per Serving:

calories: 372 | fat: 11g | protein: 18g | carbs: 56g | sugars: 20g | fiber: 14g | sodium: 696mg

Easy Southern Brunswick Stew

Prep time: 20 minutes | Cook time: 8 minutes | Serves 12

2 pounds pork butt, visible fat removed
17 ounces can white corn
1¼ cups ketchup
2 cups diced, cooked potatoes
10 ounces package frozen peas
Two 10¾ ounces cans reduced-sodium tomato soup
Hot sauce to taste, optional

1. Place pork in the Instant Pot and secure the lid. 2. Press the Slow Cook setting and cook on low 6 to 8 hours. 3. When cook time is over, remove the meat from the bone and shred, removing and discarding all visible fat. 4. Combine all the meat and remaining ingredients (except the hot sauce) in the inner pot of the Instant Pot. 5. Secure the lid once more and cook in Slow Cook mode on low for 30 minutes more. Add hot sauce if you wish.

Per Serving:

calories: 213 | fat: 7g | protein: 13g | carbs: 27g | sugars: 9g | fiber: 3g | sodium: 584mg

Hearty Italian Minestrone

Prep time: 10 minutes | Cook time: 50 minutes | Serves 8

½ cup sliced onion
1 tablespoon extra-virgin olive oil
4 cups low-sodium chicken broth
¾ cup diced carrot
½ cup diced potato (with skin)
2 cups sliced cabbage or coarsely chopped spinach
1 cup diced zucchini
½ cup cooked garbanzo beans (drained and rinsed, if canned)
½ cup cooked navy beans (drained and rinsed, if canned)
One 14.5 ounces can low-sodium tomatoes, with liquid
½ cup diced celery
2 tablespoons fresh basil, finely chopped
½ cup uncooked whole-wheat rotini or other shaped pasta
2 tablespoons fresh parsley, finely chopped, for garnish

1. In a large stockpot over medium heat, sauté the onion in oil until the onion is slightly browned. Add the chicken broth, carrot, and potato. Cover and cook over medium heat for 30 minutes. 2. Add the remaining ingredients and cook for an additional 15 to 20 minutes, until the pasta is cooked through. Garnish with parsley and serve hot.

Per Serving:

calories: 101 | fat: 2g | protein: 6g | carbs: 17g | sugars: 4g | fiber: 4g | sodium: 108mg

Cauli-Curry Bean Soup

Prep time: 10 minutes | Cook time: 25 minutes | Serves 8

2 cups chopped onion
1½ cups chopped carrot or sweet potato
1½ tablespoons curry powder (or to taste; use more if you really love curry)
1¼ teaspoons sea salt
Freshly ground black pepper to taste
1 teaspoon mustard seeds
1 teaspoon ground cumin
1 teaspoon ground turmeric
¼ teaspoon ground cardamom
⅛ teaspoon ground cinnamon

4 to 5 tablespoons + 4 cups water
3 to 4 cups cauliflower florets
1 can (15 ounces) chickpeas, rinsed and drained
1 can (15 ounces) adzuki or black beans, rinsed and drained
1 cup dried red lentils
1 can (28 ounces) crushed tomatoes
1 tablespoon grated fresh ginger
1 to 2 teaspoons pure maple syrup (optional)

1. In a large pot over medium-high heat, combine the onion, carrot or sweet potato, curry powder, salt, pepper, mustard seeds, cumin, turmeric, cardamom, cinnamon, and 3 tablespoons of the water. Stir, cover, and cook for 4 to 5 minutes, stirring occasionally. (Add another 1 to 2 tablespoons of water if needed to keep the vegetables and spices from sticking.) Add the cauliflower, chickpeas, beans, lentils, tomatoes, and remaining 4 cups water. Stir and increase the heat to high to bring to a boil. Reduce the heat to low, cover, and simmer for 15 to 20 minutes. Stir in the ginger and syrup (if using). Season to taste, and serve.

Per Serving:

calorie: 226 | fat: 2g | protein: 14g | carbs: 42g | sugars: 7g | fiber: 13g | sodium: 577mg

Four-Bean Field Stew

Prep time: 10 minutes | Cook time: 40 minutes | Serves 8 to 10

6 cups store-bought low-sodium vegetable broth
1 cup dried lima beans
1 cup dried black beans
1 cup dried pinto beans
1 cup dried kidney beans
1 cup roughly chopped tomato
2 carrots, peeled and roughly chopped

1 zucchini, chopped
½ cup chopped white onion
1 celery stalk, roughly chopped
2 garlic cloves, minced
1 teaspoon dried oregano
1 teaspoon dried thyme
¼ teaspoon freshly ground black pepper

1. In an electric pressure cooker, combine the broth, lima beans, black beans, pinto beans, kidney beans, tomato, carrots, zucchini, onion, celery, garlic, oregano, thyme, and pepper. 2. Close and lock the lid, and set the pressure valve to sealing. 3. Select the Manual/Pressure Cook setting, and cook for 40 minutes. 4. Once cooking is complete, quick-release the pressure. Carefully remove the lid. 5. Serve.

Per Serving:

calories: 262 | fat: 3g | protein: 15g | carbs: 47g | sugars: 8g | fiber:

10g | sodium: 143mg

Gazpacho

Prep time: 15 minutes | Cook time: 0 minutes | Serves 4

3 pounds ripe tomatoes, chopped
1 cup low-sodium tomato juice
½ red onion, chopped
1 cucumber, peeled, seeded, and chopped
1 red bell pepper, seeded and chopped
2 celery stalks, chopped
2 tablespoons chopped fresh

parsley
2 garlic cloves, chopped
2 tablespoons extra-virgin olive oil
2 tablespoons red wine vinegar
1 teaspoon honey
½ teaspoon salt
¼ teaspoon freshly ground black pepper

1. In a blender jar, combine the tomatoes, tomato juice, onion, cucumber, bell pepper, celery, parsley, garlic, olive oil, vinegar, honey, salt, and pepper. Pulse until blended but still slightly chunky. 2. Adjust the seasonings as needed and serve. 3. To store, transfer to a nonreactive, airtight container and refrigerate for up to 3 days.

Per Serving:

calories: 170 | fat: 8g | protein: 5g | carbs: 24g | sugars: 16g | fiber: 6g | sodium: 332mg

Buttercup Squash Soup

Prep time: 15 minutes | Cook time: 10 minutes | Serves 6

2 tablespoons extra-virgin olive oil
1 medium onion, chopped
4 to 5 cups Vegetable Broth or Chicken Bone Broth
1½ pounds buttercup squash,

peeled, seeded, and cut into 1-inch chunks
½ teaspoon kosher salt
¼ teaspoon ground white pepper
Whole nutmeg, for grating

1. Set the electric pressure cooker to the Sauté setting. When the pot is hot, pour in the olive oil. 2. Add the onion and sauté for 3 to 5 minutes, until it begins to soften. Hit Cancel. 3. Add the broth, squash, salt, and pepper to the pot and stir. (If you want a thicker soup, use 4 cups of broth. If you want a thinner, drinkable soup, use 5 cups.) 4. Close and lock the lid of the pressure cooker. Set the valve to sealing. 5. Cook on high pressure for 10 minutes. 6. When the cooking is complete, hit Cancel and allow the pressure to release naturally. 7. Once the pin drops, unlock and remove the lid. 8. Use an immersion blender to purée the soup right in the pot. If you don't have an immersion blender, transfer the soup to a blender or food processor and purée. (Follow the instructions that came with your machine for blending hot foods.) 9. Pour the soup into serving bowls and grate nutmeg on top.

Per Serving:

calories: 320 | fat: 16g | protein: 36g | carbs: 7g | sugars: 3g | fiber: 2g | sodium: 856mg

Chapter 14

Salads

Grilled Hearts of Romaine with Buttermilk Dressing

Prep time: 5 minutes | Cook time: 5 minutes | Serves 4

For The Romaine
2 heads romaine lettuce, halved lengthwise
2 tablespoons extra-virgin olive oil
For The Dressing
½ cup low-fat buttermilk

1 tablespoon extra-virgin olive oil
1 garlic clove, pressed
¼ bunch fresh chives, thinly chopped
1 pinch red pepper flakes

To Make The Romaine 1. Heat a grill pan over medium heat. 2. Brush each lettuce half with the olive oil, and place flat-side down on the grill. Grill for 3 to 5 minutes, or until the lettuce slightly wilts and develops light grill marks. To Make The Dressing 1. In a small bowl, whisk the buttermilk, olive oil, garlic, chives, and red pepper flakes together. 2. Drizzle 2 tablespoons of dressing over each romaine half, and serve.

Per Serving:
calorie: 157 | fat: 11g | protein: 5g | carbs: 12g | sugars: 5g | fiber: 7g | sodium: 84mg

Carrot and Cashew Chicken Salad

Prep time: 20 minutes | Cook time: 25 minutes | Serves 2

Extra-virgin olive oil cooking spray
1 cup carrots rounds
1 red bell pepper, thinly sliced
1½ teaspoons granulated stevia
1 tablespoon extra-virgin olive oil, divided
¼ teaspoon salt, divided
⅜ teaspoon freshly ground black pepper, divided

1 (6 ounces) boneless skinless chicken breast, thinly sliced across the grain
2 tablespoons chopped scallions
1 tablespoon apple cider vinegar
1 cup sugar snap peas
4 cups baby spinach
4 tablespoons chopped cashews, divided

1. Preheat the oven to 425°F. 2. Coat an 8-by-8-inch baking pan and a rimmed baking sheet with cooking spray. 3. In the prepared baking pan, add the carrots and red bell pepper. Sprinkle with the stevia, 1 teaspoon of olive oil, ⅛ teaspoon of salt, and ⅛ teaspoon of pepper. Toss to coat. 4. Place the pan in the preheated oven. Roast for about 25 minutes, stirring several times, or until tender. 5. About 5 minutes before the vegetables are done, place the sliced chicken in a medium bowl and drizzle with 1 teaspoon of olive oil. Sprinkle with the scallions. Season with the remaining ⅛ teaspoon of salt and ⅛ teaspoon of pepper. Toss to mix. Arrange in a single layer on the prepared baking sheet. 6. Place the sheet in the preheated oven. Roast for 5 to 7 minutes, turning once, or until cooked through. 7. Remove the pan with the vegetables and the baking sheet from the oven. Cool for about 3 minutes. 8. In a large salad bowl, mix together the apple cider vinegar, the remaining 1 teaspoon of olive oil, the sugar snap peas, and remaining ⅛ teaspoon of pepper. Let stand 5 minutes to blend the flavors. 9. To finish, add the spinach to the bowl with the dressing and peas. Toss to mix well. 10. Evenly divide between 2 serving plates. Top each with half of the roasted carrots, half of the roasted red bell peppers, and half of the cooked chicken. 11. Sprinkle each with about 2 tablespoons of cashews. Serve warm.

Per Serving:
calorie: 335 | fat: 17g | protein: 26g | carbs: 21g | sugars: 8g | fiber: 6g | sodium: 422mg

Winter Chicken and Citrus Salad

Prep time: 10 minutes | Cook time: 0 minutes | Serves 4

4 cups baby spinach
2 tablespoons extra-virgin olive oil
1 tablespoon freshly squeezed lemon juice
⅛ teaspoon salt

Freshly ground black pepper
2 cups chopped cooked chicken
2 mandarin oranges, peeled and sectioned
½ peeled grapefruit, sectioned
¼ cup sliced almonds

1. In a large mixing bowl, toss the spinach with the olive oil, lemon juice, salt, and pepper. 2. Add the chicken, oranges, grapefruit, and almonds to the bowl. Toss gently. 3. Arrange on 4 plates and serve.

Per Serving:
calories: 249 | fat: 12g | protein: 24g | carbs: 11g | sugars: 7g | fiber: 3g | sodium: 135mg

Sesame Chicken-Almond Slaw

Prep time: 20 minutes | Cook time: 40 minutes | Serves 2

For the dressing
1 tablespoon rice vinegar
1 teaspoon granulated stevia
2 teaspoons extra-virgin olive oil
1 teaspoon water
½ teaspoon sesame oil
¼ teaspoon reduced-sodium soy sauce
Pinch salt
Pinch freshly ground black

pepper
For the salad
8 ounces chicken breast, rinsed and drained
4 cups angel hair cabbage
1 cup shredded romaine lettuce
2 tablespoons sliced scallions
2 tablespoons toasted slivered almonds
2 teaspoons toasted sesame seeds

To make the dressing: 1. In a jar with a tight-fitting lid, add the rice vinegar, stevia, olive oil, water, sesame oil, soy sauce, salt, and pepper. Shake well to combine. Set aside. To make the salad: 2. Preheat the oven to 400°F. 3. To a medium baking dish, add the chicken. Place the dish in the preheated oven. Bake for 30 to 40 minutes, or until completely opaque and the temperature registers 165°F on an instant-read thermometer. 4. Remove from the oven. Slice into strips. Set aside. 5. In a large bowl, toss together the cabbage, romaine, scallions, almonds, sesame seeds, and chicken strips. Add the dressing. Toss again to coat the ingredients evenly. 6. Serve immediately.

Per Serving:
calorie: 318 | fat: 15g | protein: 31g | carbs: 17g | sugars: 8g | fiber: 6g | sodium: 125mg

Summer Salad

Prep time: 5 minutes | Cook time: 0 minutes | Serves 4

For The Salad

8 cups mixed greens or preferred lettuce, loosely packed

4 cups arugula, loosely packed

2 peaches, sliced ½ cup thinly sliced red onion

½ cup chopped walnuts or pecans

½ cup crumbled feta

For The Dressing

4 teaspoons extra-virgin olive oil

4 teaspoons honey

Make The Salad 1. Combine the mixed greens, arugula, peaches, red onion, walnuts, and feta in a large bowl. Divide the salad into four portions. 2. Drizzle the dressing over each individual serving of salad. Make The Dressing 3. In a small bowl, whisk together the olive oil and honey.

Per Serving:

calorie: 261 | fat: 19g | protein: 8g | carbs: 20g | sugars: 15g | fiber: 4g | sodium: 184mg

Chicken Salad with Apricots

Prep time: 10 minutes | Cook time: 0 minutes | Makes 4 cups

1 cup plain Greek yogurt

2 tablespoons minced shallots

1 teaspoon ground coriander

1 teaspoon Dijon mustard (optional)

1 tablespoon freshly squeezed lemon juice

¼ teaspoon cayenne pepper

12 ounces cooked rotisserie chicken, shredded

2 cups chopped celery with the leaves

¼ cup slivered almonds, toasted

¼ cup thinly sliced dried apricots

1 bunch fresh parsley, chopped

1. In a medium bowl, mix together the Greek yogurt, shallots, coriander, mustard (if using), lemon juice, and cayenne until well combined. 2. Add the chicken, celery, almonds, apricots, and parsley. 3. Serve on your food of choice (lettuce, crackers, jicama slices, radish slices—you name it). 4. Store any leftovers in an airtight container in the refrigerator for up to 3 days.

Per Serving:

calorie: 232 | fat: 7g | protein: 31g | carbs: 11g | sugars: 7g | fiber: 3g | sodium: 152mg

Nutty Deconstructed Salad

Prep time: 10 minutes | Cook time: 0 minutes | Serves 1

6 ounces (170 g) grilled or baked chicken, sliced or cubed to the desired size

½ cup (75 g) red seedless grapes

¼ cup (32 g) crumbled feta

cheese

¼ cup (30 g) raw walnuts

2 tablespoon (10 g) raw pumpkin seeds

1 small apple, thinly sliced

1. In a salad bowl, combine the chicken, grapes, feta cheese, walnuts, pumpkin seeds, and apple. Toss to combine the ingredients and serve.

Per Serving:

calorie: 613 | fat: 33g | protein: 42g | carbs: 42g | sugars: 30g | fiber: 6g | sodium: 501mg

Pasta Salad–Stuffed Tomatoes

Prep time: 10 minutes | Cook time: 0 minutes | Serves 4

1 cup uncooked whole-wheat fusilli

2 small carrots, sliced

2 scallions, chopped

¼ cup chopped pimiento

1 cup cooked kidney beans

½ cup sliced celery

¼ cup cooked peas

2 tablespoons chopped fresh

parsley

¼ cup calorie-free, fat-free Italian salad dressing

2 tablespoons low-fat mayonnaise

¼ teaspoon dried marjoram

¼ teaspoon freshly ground black pepper

4 medium tomatoes

1. Cook the fusilli in boiling water until cooked, about 7 to 8 minutes; drain. 2. In a large bowl, combine the macaroni with the remaining salad ingredients (except the tomatoes), and toss well. Cover, and chill in the refrigerator 1 hour or more. 3. With the stem end down, cut each tomato into 6 wedges, cutting to, but not through, the base of the tomato. Spread the wedges slightly apart, and spoon the pasta mixture into the tomatoes. Chill until ready to serve.

Per Serving:

calorie: 214 | fat: 3g | protein: 10g | carbs: 40g | sugars: 6g | fiber: 8g | sodium: 164mg

Mediterranean Pasta Salad with Goat Cheese

Prep time: 25 minutes | Cook time: 0 minutes | Serves 4

½ cup (75 g) grape tomatoes, sliced in half lengthwise

1 medium red bell pepper, coarsely chopped

½ medium red onion, sliced into thin strips

1 medium zucchini, coarsely chopped

1 cup (175 g) broccoli florets

½ cup (110 g) oil-packed artichoke hearts, drained

¼ cup (60 ml) olive oil

sea salt

½ teaspoon black pepper

1 tablespoon (3 g) dried oregano

½ teaspoon garlic powder

4 ounces (113 g) crumbled goat cheese

½ cup (50 g) shaved Parmesan cheese

8 ounces (227 g) lentil or chickpea penne pasta, cooked, rinsed, and drained

1. In a large bowl, combine the tomatoes, bell pepper, onion, zucchini, broccoli, artichoke hearts, oil, sea salt, black pepper, oregano, garlic powder, goat cheese, and Parmesan cheese. Gently mix everything together to combine and coat all of the ingredients with the oil. 2. Add the pasta to the bowl and stir to combine. 3. Let the pasta salad rest for 1 to 2 hours in the refrigerator to marinate it, or serve the pasta salad immediately if desired.

Per Serving:

calorie: 477 | fat: 24g | protein: 23g | carbs: 41g | sugars: 6g | fiber: 6g | sodium: 706mg

Italian Potato Salad

Prep time: 10 minutes | Cook time: 25 minutes | Serves 8

12 new red potatoes, 3–4 ounces each, washed and skins left on
3 celery stalks, chopped
1 red bell pepper, minced
¼ cup chopped scallions
2 tablespoons olive oil

1 tablespoon balsamic vinegar
½ tablespoon red vinegar
1 teaspoon chopped fresh parsley
⅛ teaspoon freshly ground black pepper

1. Boil the potatoes for 20 minutes in a large pot of boiling water. Drain, and let cool for 30 minutes. 2. Cut the potatoes into large chunks, and toss the potatoes with the celery, bell pepper, and scallions. 3. In a medium bowl, combine the olive oil, balsamic vinegar, red vinegar, parsley, and pepper; pour the dressing over the potato salad. Serve at room temperature.

Per Serving:

calorie: 128 | fat: 4g | protein: 3g | carbs: 22g | sugars: 3g | fiber: 3g | sodium: 30mg

Blueberry and Chicken Salad on a Bed of Greens

Prep time: 10 minutes | Cook time: 0 minutes | Serves 4

2 cups chopped cooked chicken
1 cup fresh blueberries
¼ cup finely chopped almonds
1 celery stalk, finely chopped
¼ cup finely chopped red onion
1 tablespoon chopped fresh basil
1 tablespoon chopped fresh

cilantro
½ cup plain, nonfat Greek yogurt or vegan mayonnaise
¼ teaspoon salt
¼ teaspoon freshly ground black pepper
8 cups salad greens (baby spinach, spicy greens, romaine)

1. In a large mixing bowl, combine the chicken, blueberries, almonds, celery, onion, basil, and cilantro. Toss gently to mix. 2. In a small bowl, combine the yogurt, salt, and pepper. Add to the chicken salad and stir to combine. 3. Arrange 2 cups of salad greens on each of 4 plates and divide the chicken salad among the plates to serve.

Per Serving:

calories: 207 | fat: 6g | protein: 28g | carbs: 11g | sugars: 6g | fiber: 3g | sodium: 235mg

Three-Bean Salad with Black Bean Crumbles

Prep time: 15 minutes | Cook time: 0 minutes | Serves 4

½ cup bottled Italian dressing
2 cups frozen black bean crumbles, microwaved per package instructions
1 cup cherry tomatoes, halved
1 (16 ounces) can or jar three-

bean salad mix, drained
1 medium onion, quartered and thinly sliced
4 cups romaine salad greens
1 cup shredded reduced-fat cheddar cheese, divided

1. Pour the Italian dressing into a large bowl. Add the black bean crumbles, cherry tomatoes, three-bean salad, and onion and mix until everything is well coated. 2. Divide the greens into 4 bowls and top each with the bean mixture. 3. Sprinkle ¼ cup of shredded cheddar cheese on each portion.

Per Serving:

calorie: 357 | fat: 10g | protein: 22g | carbs: 48g | sugars: 6g | fiber: 9g | sodium: 478mg

Celery and Apple Salad with Cider Vinaigrette

Prep time: 20 minutes | Cook time: 0 minutes | Serves 4

Dressing
2 tablespoons apple cider or apple juice
1 tablespoon cider vinegar
2 teaspoons canola oil
2 teaspoons finely chopped shallots
½ teaspoon Dijon mustard
½ teaspoon honey
½ teaspoon salt

Salad
2 cups chopped romaine lettuce
2 cups diagonally sliced celery
½ medium apple, unpeeled, sliced very thin (about 1 cup)
⅓ cup sweetened dried cranberries
2 tablespoons chopped walnuts
2 tablespoons crumbled blue cheese

1. In small bowl, beat all dressing ingredients with whisk until blended; set aside. 2. In medium bowl, place lettuce, celery, apple and cranberries; toss with dressing. To serve, arrange salad on 4 plates. Sprinkle with walnuts and blue cheese. Serve immediately.

Per Serving:

calorie: 130 | fat: 6g | protein: 2g | carbs: 17g | sugars: 13g | fiber: 3g | sodium: 410mg

Wild Rice Salad

Prep time: 5 minutes | Cook time: 45 minutes | Serves 6

1 cup raw wild rice (rinsed)
4 cups cold water
1 cup mandarin oranges, packed in their own juice (drain and reserve 2 tablespoons of liquid)
½ cup chopped celery

¼ cup minced red bell pepper
1 shallot, minced
1 teaspoon minced thyme
2 tablespoons raspberry vinegar
1 tablespoon extra-virgin olive oil

1. Place the rinsed, raw rice and the water in a saucepan. Bring to a boil, lower the heat, cover the pan, and cook for 45 to 50 minutes until the rice has absorbed the water. Set the rice aside to cool. 2. In a large bowl, combine the mandarin oranges, celery, red pepper, and shallot. 3. In a small bowl, combine the reserved juice, thyme, vinegar, and oil. 4. Add the rice to the mandarin oranges and vegetables. Pour the dressing over the salad, toss, and serve.

Per Serving:

calorie: 134 | fat: 3g | protein: 4g | carbs: 24g | sugars: 4g | fiber: 3g | sodium: 12mg

Mozzarella-Tomato Salad

Prep time: 15 minutes | Cook time: 0 minutes | Serves 2

Fresh mozzarella cheese (2 ounces), cut into ¾-inch cubes
½ cup cherry tomatoes, halved
½ cup cannellini beans, drained and rinsed
½ cup artichoke hearts, drained
¼ cup jarred roasted red peppers
¼ cup chopped scallions
1 tablespoon minced fresh basil
1 tablespoon extra-virgin olive oil
2 teaspoons balsamic vinegar
⅛ teaspoon salt
4 cups baby spinach, divided

1. In a small bowl, stir together the mozzarella cheese, tomatoes, beans, artichoke hearts, red peppers, and scallions. 2. In another small bowl, whisk the basil, olive oil, balsamic vinegar, and salt until combined. 3. Drizzle the dressing over the cheese and vegetables. Toss to coat. Chill for 15 minutes. 4. Using 2 plates, arrange 2 cups of spinach on each. Top with half of the cheese and vegetable mixture. 5. Serve immediately.

Per Serving:
calorie: 199 | fat: 8g | protein: 9g | carbs: 26g | sugars: 6g | fiber: 10g | sodium: 387mg

Herbed Spring Peas

Prep time: 10 minutes | Cook time: 15 minutes | Serves 6

1 tablespoon unsalted non-hydrogenated plant-based butter
½ Vidalia onion, thinly sliced
1 cup store-bought low-sodium
vegetable broth
3 cups fresh shelled peas
1 tablespoon minced fresh tarragon

1. In a skillet, melt the butter over medium heat. 2. Add the onion and sauté for 2 to 3 minutes, or until the onion is translucent. 3. Add the broth, and reduce the heat to low. 4. Add the peas and tarragon, cover, and cook for 7 to 10 minutes, or until the peas soften. 5. Serve.

Per Serving:
calorie: 43 | fat: 2g | protein: 2g | carbs: 6g | sugars: 3g | fiber: 2g | sodium: 159mg

Kidney Bean Salad

Prep time: 10 minutes | Cook time: 0 minutes | Serves 4

3 cups diced cucumber
1 (15 ounces) can low-sodium dark red kidney beans, drained and rinsed
2 avocados, diced
1½ cups diced tomatoes
1 cup cooked corn
¾ cup sliced red onion
1 tablespoon extra-virgin olive oil
1 tablespoon apple cider vinegar

1. In a large bowl, combine the cucumber, kidney beans, avocados, tomatoes, corn, onion, olive oil, and vinegar.

Per Serving:
calorie: 394 | fat: 20g | protein: 13g | carbs: 47g | sugars: 10g | fiber: 16g | sodium: 261mg

Warm Barley and Squash Salad with Balsamic Vinaigrette

Prep time: 20 minutes | Cook time: 40 minutes | Serves 8

1 small butternut squash
3 teaspoons plus 2 tablespoons extra-virgin olive oil, divided
2 cups broccoli florets
1 cup pearl barley
1 cup toasted chopped walnuts
2 cups baby kale
½ red onion, sliced
2 tablespoons balsamic vinegar
2 garlic cloves, minced
½ teaspoon salt
¼ teaspoon freshly ground black pepper

1. Preheat the oven to 400°F. Line a baking sheet with parchment paper. 2. Peel and seed the squash, and cut it into dice. In a large bowl, toss the squash with 2 teaspoons of olive oil. Transfer to the prepared baking sheet and roast for 20 minutes. 3. While the squash is roasting, toss the broccoli in the same bowl with 1 teaspoon of olive oil. After 20 minutes, flip the squash and push it to one side of the baking sheet. Add the broccoli to the other side and continue to roast for 20 more minutes until tender. 4. While the veggies are roasting, in a medium pot, cover the barley with several inches of water. Bring to a boil, then reduce the heat, cover, and simmer for 30 minutes until tender. Drain and rinse. 5. Transfer the barley to a large bowl, and toss with the cooked squash and broccoli, walnuts, kale, and onion. 6. In a small bowl, mix the remaining 2 tablespoons of olive oil, balsamic vinegar, garlic, salt, and pepper. Toss the salad with the dressing and serve.

Per Serving:
calories: 274 | fat: 15g | protein: 6g | carbs: 32g | sugars: 3g | fiber: 7g | sodium: 144mg

Three Bean and Basil Salad

Prep time: 10 minutes | Cook time: 0 minutes | Serves 8

1 (15 ounces) can low-sodium chickpeas, drained and rinsed
1 (15 ounces) can low-sodium kidney beans, drained and rinsed
1 (15 ounces) can low-sodium white beans, drained and rinsed
1 red bell pepper, seeded and finely chopped
¼ cup chopped scallions, both
white and green parts
¼ cup finely chopped fresh basil
3 garlic cloves, minced
2 tablespoons extra-virgin olive oil
1 tablespoon red wine vinegar
1 teaspoon Dijon mustard
¼ teaspoon freshly ground black pepper

1. In a large mixing bowl, combine the chickpeas, kidney beans, white beans, bell pepper, scallions, basil, and garlic. Toss gently to combine. 2. In a small bowl, combine the olive oil, vinegar, mustard, and pepper. Toss with the salad. 3. Cover and refrigerate for an hour before serving, to allow the flavors to mix.

Per Serving:
Calorie: 193 | fat: 5g | protein: 10g | carbs: 29g | sugars: 3g | fiber: 8g | sodium: 246mg

Edamame and Walnut Salad

Prep time: 10 minutes | Cook time: 0 minutes | Serves 2

For the vinaigrette
2 tablespoons balsamic vinegar
1 tablespoon extra-virgin olive oil
1 teaspoon grated fresh ginger
½ teaspoon Dijon mustard
Pinch salt
Freshly ground black pepper, to season

For the salad
1 cup shelled edamame
½ cup shredded carrots
½ cup shredded red cabbage
½ cup walnut halves
6 cups prewashed baby spinach, divided

To make the vinaigrette In a small bowl, whisk together the balsamic vinegar, olive oil, ginger, Dijon mustard, and salt. Season with pepper. Set aside. To make the salad 1. In a medium bowl, mix together the edamame, carrots, red cabbage, and walnuts. 2. Add the vinaigrette. Toss to coat. 3. Place 3 cups of spinach on each of 2 serving plates. 4. Top each serving with half of the dressed vegetables. 5. Enjoy immediately!

Per Serving:
calorie: 341 | fat: 26g | protein: 13g | carbs: 19g | sugars: 7g | fiber: 8g | sodium: 117mg

Garden-Fresh Greek Salad

Prep time: 20 minutes | Cook time: 0 minutes | Serves 6

Dressing
3 tablespoons fresh lemon juice
1 tablespoon chopped fresh or 1 teaspoon dried oregano leaves
½ teaspoon salt
½ teaspoon sugar
½ teaspoon Dijon mustard
¼ teaspoon pepper
1 clove garlic, finely chopped
Salad

1 bag (10 ounces) ready-to-eat romaine lettuce
¾ cup chopped seeded peeled cucumber
½ cup sliced red onion
¼ cup sliced kalamata olives
2 medium tomatoes, seeded, chopped (1½ cups)
¼ cup reduced-fat feta cheese

1. In small bowl, beat all dressing ingredients with whisk. 2. In large bowl, toss all salad ingredients except cheese. Stir in dressing until salad is well coated. Sprinkle with cheese.

Per Serving:
calorie: 45 | fat: 2g | protein: 3g | carbs: 6g | sugars: 3g | fiber: 2g | sodium: 340mg

Sunflower-Tuna-Cauliflower Salad

Prep time: 30 minutes | Cook time: 0 minutes | Serves 2

1 (5 ounces) can tuna packed in water, drained
½ cup plain nonfat Greek yogurt
1 teaspoon freshly squeezed lemon juice
1 teaspoon dried dill

1 scallion, chopped
¼ cup sunflower seeds
2 cups fresh chopped cauliflower florets
4 cups mixed salad greens, divided

1. In a medium bowl, mix together the tuna, yogurt, lemon juice, dill, scallion, and sunflower seeds. 2. Add the cauliflower. Toss gently to coat. 3. Cover and refrigerate for at least 2 hours before serving, stirring occasionally. 4. Serve half of the tuna mixture atop 2 cups of salad greens.

Per Serving:
calorie: 251 | fat: 11g | protein: 24g | carbs: 18g | sugars: 8g | fiber: 7g | sodium: 288mg

Triple-Berry and Jicama Spinach Salad

Prep time: 30 minutes | Cook time: 0 minutes | Serves 6

Dressing
¼ cup fresh raspberries
3 tablespoons hot pepper jelly
2 tablespoons canola oil
2 tablespoons raspberry vinegar or red wine vinegar
2 medium jalapeño chiles, seeded, finely chopped (2 tablespoons)
2 teaspoons finely chopped shallot

¼ teaspoon salt
1 small clove garlic, crushed
Salad
1 bag (6 ounces) fresh baby spinach leaves
1 cup bite-size strips (1x¼x¼ inch) peeled jicama
1 cup fresh blackberries
1 cup fresh raspberries
1 cup sliced fresh strawberries

1. In small food processor or blender, combine all dressing ingredients; process until smooth. 2. In large bowl, toss spinach and ¼ cup of the dressing. On 6 serving plates, arrange salad. To serve, top each salad with jicama, blackberries, raspberries, strawberries and drizzle with scant 1 tablespoon of remaining dressing.

Per Serving:
calorie: 120 | fat: 5g | protein: 2g | carbs: 18g | sugars: 9g | fiber: 5g | sodium: 125mg

Young Kale and Cabbage Salad with Toasted Peanuts

Prep time: 15 minutes | Cook time: 0 minutes | Serves 6

2 bunches baby kale, thinly sliced
½ head green savoy cabbage, cored and thinly sliced
¼ cup apple cider vinegar
Juice of 1 lemon

1 teaspoon ground cumin
¼ teaspoon smoked paprika
1 medium red bell pepper, thinly sliced
1 cup toasted peanuts
1 garlic clove, thinly sliced

1. In a large salad bowl, toss the kale and cabbage together. 2. In a small bowl, to make the dressing, whisk the vinegar, lemon juice, cumin, and paprika together. 3. Pour the dressing over the greens, and gently massage with your hands. 4. Add the pepper, peanuts, and garlic, and toss to combine.

Per Serving:
calorie: 177 | fat: 12g | protein: 8g | carbs: 13g | sugars: 5g | fiber: 5g | sodium: 31mg

Greek Rice Salad

Prep time: 10 minutes | Cook time: 0 minutes | Serves 4

3 tablespoons fresh lemon juice

1½ tablespoons coconut nectar or pure maple syrup

1 tablespoon red wine vinegar

1 teaspoon sea salt

1 teaspoon Dijon mustard

¼ teaspoon allspice

½ to 1 teaspoon grated fresh garlic

Freshly ground black pepper to taste (optional)

4 cups cooked brown rice

1 cup chopped cucumber (seeds removed, if you prefer)

1 cup sliced grape or cherry tomatoes or chopped tomatoes (can substitute chopped red pepper)

½ cup sliced kalamata olives

½ tablespoon chopped fresh oregano

2 tablespoons chopped fresh dill

1. In a large bowl, whisk together the lemon juice, nectar or syrup, vinegar, salt, mustard, allspice, garlic, and pepper (if using). Add the rice, cucumber, tomatoes, olives, oregano, and dill, and stir to combine. Taste, and add extra salt or lemon juice, if desired. Serve as a side or as a hearty lunch over greens.

Per Serving:

calorie: 306 | fat: 4g | protein: 6g | carbs: 62g | sugars: 7g | fiber: 5g | sodium: 751mg

Quinoa, Beet, and Greens Salad

Prep time: 15 minutes | Cook time: 25 minutes | Serves 2

For the vinaigrette

1 tablespoon extra-virgin olive oil

2 tablespoons red wine vinegar

1 garlic clove, chopped

Freshly ground black pepper, to season

For the salad

2 medium beets

1 small bunch fresh kale leaves, thoroughly washed, deveined, and dried

Extra-virgin olive oil cooking spray

⅓ cup dry quinoa

⅔ cup water

¼ cup chopped scallions

½ cup unsalted soy nuts

To make the vinaigrette: 1. In a large bowl, whisk together the olive oil, red wine vinegar, and garlic. Season with pepper. Set aside. To make the salad: 1. Into a medium saucepan set over high heat, insert a steamer basket. Fill the pan with water to just below the bottom of the steamer. Cover and bring to a boil. 2. Add the beets. Cover and steam for 7 to 10 minutes, or until just tender. Remove from the steamer. Let sit until cool enough to handle. Peel and slice. Set aside. 3. Spray the kale leaves with cooking spray. Massage the leaves, breaking down the fibers so they're easier to chew. Chop finely. You should have 1 cup. 4. In a small saucepan set over high heat, mix together the quinoa and water. Bring to a boil. Reduce the heat to medium-low. Cover and simmer for about 15 minutes, or until the quinoa is tender and the liquid has been absorbed. Remove from the heat. 5. Immediately add half of the vinaigrette to the saucepan while fluffing the quinoa with a fork. Cover and refrigerate for at least 1 hour, or until completely cooled. Set aside the remaining vinaigrette. 6. Into the cooled quinoa, stir the chopped kale, scallions, soy nuts,

sliced beets, and remaining vinaigrette. Toss lightly before serving.

Per Serving:

calorie: 461 | fat: 29g | protein: 14g | carbs: 41g | sugars: 7g | fiber: 9g | sodium: 100mg

Rainbow Quinoa Salad

Prep time: 10 minutes | Cook time: 0 minutes | Serves 3

Dressing

3½ tablespoons orange juice

1 tablespoon apple cider vinegar

1 tablespoon pure maple syrup

1½ teaspoons yellow mustard

Couple pinches of cloves

Rounded ½ teaspoon sea salt

Freshly ground black pepper to taste

Salad

2 cups cooked quinoa, cooled

½ cup corn kernels

½ cup diced apple tossed in ½ teaspoon lemon juice

¼ cup diced red pepper

¼ cup sliced green onions or chives

1 can (15 ounces) black beans, rinsed and drained

Sea salt to taste

Freshly ground black pepper to taste

To make the dressing: 1. In a large bowl, whisk together the orange juice, vinegar, syrup, mustard, cloves, salt, and pepper. To make the salad: 1. Add the quinoa, corn, apple, red pepper, green onion or chives, and black beans, and stir to combine well. Season with the salt and black pepper to taste. Serve, or store in an airtight container in the fridge.

Per Serving:

calorie: 355 | fat: 4g | protein: 15g | carbs: 68g | sugars: 12g | fiber: 15g | sodium: 955mg

Power Salad

Prep time: 15 minutes | Cook time: 0 minutes | Serves 2

For the dressing

1 tablespoon extra-virgin olive oil

1 tablespoon freshly squeezed lemon juice

1 tablespoon balsamic vinegar

1 tablespoon chia seeds

1 teaspoon liquid stevia

Pinch salt

Freshly ground black pepper

For the salad

6 cups mixed baby greens

1 cup shelled edamame

1 cup chopped red cabbage

1 cup chopped red bell pepper

1 cup sliced fresh button mushrooms

½ cup sliced avocado

¼ cup sliced almonds

1 cup pea shoots, divided

Make The Dressing: 1. In a small bowl, whisk together the olive oil, lemon juice, balsamic vinegar, chia seeds, and stevia until well combined. Season with salt and pepper. Make The Salad: 2. In a large bowl, toss together the mixed greens, edamame, red cabbage, red bell pepper, mushrooms, avocado, and almonds. Drizzle the dressing over the salad. Toss again to coat well. 3. Divide the salad between 2 plates. Top each with ½ cup of pea shoots and serve.

Per Serving:

calorie: 449 | fat: 24g | protein: 22g | carbs: 47g | sugars: 11g | fiber: 16g | sodium: 86mg

Mediterranean Chicken Salad

Prep time: 5 minutes | Cook time: 0 minutes | Serves 3

8 ounces boneless, skinless, cooked chicken breast	pepper
2 tablespoons extra-virgin olive oil	1 cup cooked green beans, cut into 2-inch pieces
2 tablespoons balsamic vinegar	1 cup cooked artichokes
¼ teaspoon dried basil	¼ cup pine nuts, toasted
2 small garlic cloves, minced	¼ cup sliced black olives
¼ teaspoon freshly ground black	3 cherry tomatoes, halved
	Tomato wedges (optional)

1. Cut the cooked chicken into bite-sized chunks, and set aside. 2. In a medium bowl, whisk together the oil, vinegar, basil, garlic, and pepper. Add the chicken, and toss with the dressing. 3. Add the green beans, artichokes, pine nuts, olives, and cherry tomatoes; toss well. Chill in the refrigerator for several hours. Garnish the salad with tomato wedges, and serve.

Per Serving:

calorie: 307 | fat: 19g | protein: 21g | carbs: 14g | sugars: 4g | fiber: 7g | sodium: 73mg

Tu-No Salad

Prep time: 10 minutes | Cook time: 0 minutes | Serves 2

1 can (15 ounces) chickpeas, rinsed and drained	Worcestershire sauce (optional)
1 tablespoon tahini	½ teaspoon Dijon mustard
2 tablespoons water	½ teaspoon coconut nectar
1 tablespoon red wine vinegar (can substitute apple cider vinegar)	2 tablespoons minced celery
	2 tablespoons minced cucumber
1 tablespoon chickpea miso (or other mild-flavored miso)	2 tablespoons minced apple
	⅛ teaspoon sea salt
1 teaspoon vegan	Freshly ground black pepper to taste

1. In a small food processor, pulse the chickpeas until fairly crumbly but not finely ground. (Alternatively, you can mash by hand.) In a large bowl, combine the chickpeas, tahini, water, vinegar, miso, Worcestershire sauce, mustard, nectar, celery, cucumber, apple, and salt. Mix together well. Season with additional salt and pepper to taste, and serve!

Per Serving:

calorie: 264 | fat: 8g | protein: 12g | carbs: 37g | sugars: 8g | fiber: 10g | sodium: 800mg

Roasted Asparagus–Berry Salad

Prep time: 10 minutes | Cook time: 18 minutes | Serves 4

1 pound fresh asparagus spears	4 cups mixed salad greens
Cooking spray	¼ cup fat-free balsamic vinaigrette dressing
2 tablespoons chopped pecans	
1 cup sliced fresh strawberries	Cracked pepper, if desired

1. Heat oven to 400°F. Line 15x10x1-inch pan with foil; spray with cooking spray. Break off tough ends of asparagus as far down as stalks snap easily. Cut into 1-inch pieces. 2. Place asparagus in single layer in pan; spray with cooking spray. Place pecans in another shallow pan. 3. Bake pecans 5 to 6 minutes or until golden brown, stirring occasionally. Bake asparagus 10 to 12 minutes or until crisp-tender. Cool pecans and asparagus 8 to 10 minutes or until room temperature. 4. In medium bowl, mix asparagus, pecans, strawberries, greens and dressing. Sprinkle with pepper.

Per Serving:

calorie: 90 | fat: 3g | protein: 4g | carbs: 11g | sugars: 6g | fiber: 4g | sodium: 180mg

Cabbage Slaw Salad

Prep time: 15 minutes | Cook time: 0 minutes | Serves 6

2 cups finely chopped green cabbage	2 tablespoons extra-virgin olive oil
2 cups finely chopped red cabbage	2 tablespoons rice vinegar
	1 teaspoon honey
2 cups grated carrots	1 garlic clove, minced
3 scallions, both white and green parts, sliced	¼ teaspoon salt

1. In a large bowl, toss together the green and red cabbage, carrots, and scallions. 2. In a small bowl, whisk together the oil, vinegar, honey, garlic, and salt. 3. Pour the dressing over the veggies and mix to thoroughly combine. 4. Serve immediately, or cover and chill for several hours before serving.

Per Serving:

calories: 80 | fat: 5g | protein: 1g | carbs: 10g | sugars: 6g | fiber: 3g | sodium: 126mg

Raw Corn Salad with Black-Eyed Peas

Prep time: 15 minutes | Cook time: 0 minutes | Serves 8

2 ears fresh corn, kernels cut off	vinegar
2 cups cooked black-eyed peas	2 tablespoons extra-virgin olive oil
1 green bell pepper, chopped	
½ red onion, chopped	1 garlic clove, minced
2 celery stalks, finely chopped	¼ teaspoon smoked paprika
½ pint cherry tomatoes, halved	¼ teaspoon ground cumin
3 tablespoons white balsamic	¼ teaspoon red pepper flakes

1. In a large salad bowl, combine the corn, black-eyed peas, bell pepper, onion, celery, and tomatoes. 2. In a small bowl, to make the dressing, whisk the vinegar, olive oil, garlic, paprika, cumin, and red pepper flakes together. 3. Pour the dressing over the salad, and toss gently to coat. Serve and enjoy.

Per Serving:

calorie: 127 | fat: 4g | protein: 5g | carbs: 19g | sugars: 5g | fiber: 5g | sodium: 16mg

Mediterranean Chef Salad

Prep time: 20 minutes | Cook time: 0 minutes | Serves 4

½ cup extra-virgin olive oil

½ cup red wine vinegar

2 tablespoons grated Parmesan cheese

1 teaspoon dried Italian herb blend

1 (15 ounces) can chickpeas, rinsed and drained

1 medium cucumber, peeled and diced

½ cup diced roasted red peppers

½ cup pitted and sliced kalamata olives

½ cup crumbled feta cheese

4 cups spinach, romaine, and arugula salad mix, divided

1. In large bowl, whisk together the olive oil, red wine vinegar, Parmesan cheese, and Italian herbs. 2. Add the chickpeas, cucumber, red peppers, olives, and feta cheese and mix until everything is coated well. 3. Divide the greens into 4 bowls and top each with 1 cup of the salad mix.

Per Serving:

calorie: 318 | fat: 22g | protein: 10g | carbs: 20g | sugars: 5g | fiber: 7g | sodium: 510mg

Lentil Salad

Prep time: 10 minutes | Cook time: 45 minutes | Serves 8

1 pound dried lentils, washed (rinse with cold water in a colander)

3 cups water

2 tablespoons extra-virgin olive oil

2 teaspoons cumin

1 teaspoon minced fresh oregano

3 tablespoons fresh lemon juice

¼ teaspoon freshly ground black pepper

2 large green bell peppers, cored, seeded, and diced

2 large red bell peppers, cored, seeded, and diced

3 stalks celery, diced

1 red onion, minced

1. In a large saucepan over high heat, bring lentils and water to a boil. Reduce the heat to low, cover, and simmer for 35 to 45 minutes. Drain, and set aside. 2. In a large bowl, mix together the oil, cumin, oregano, lemon juice, and pepper until well blended. Add the lentils and the prepared vegetables. Cover, and chill in the refrigerator before serving.

Per Serving:

calorie: 261 | fat: 4g | protein: 15g | carbs: 43g | sugars: 5g | fiber: 8g | sodium: 15mg

Cucumber-Mango Salad

Prep time: 20 minutes | Cook time: 0 minutes | Serves 4

1 small cucumber

1 medium mango

¼ teaspoon grated lime peel

1 tablespoon lime juice

1 teaspoon honey

¼ teaspoon ground cumin

Pinch salt

4 leaves Bibb lettuce

1. Cut cucumber lengthwise in half; scoop out seeds. Chop cucumber

(about 1 cup). 2. Score skin of mango lengthwise into fourths with knife; peel skin. Cut peeled mango lengthwise close to both sides of pit. Chop mango into ½-inch cubes. 3. In small bowl, mix lime peel, lime juice, honey, cumin and salt. Stir in cucumber and mango. Place lettuce leaves on serving plates. Spoon mango mixture onto lettuce leaves.

Per Serving:

calorie: 50 | fat: 0g | protein: 0g | carbs: 12g | sugars: 9g | fiber: 1g | sodium: 40mg

Couscous Salad

Prep time: 10 minutes | Cook time: 6 minutes | Serves ½ cup

1 cup whole-wheat couscous

2 cups boiling water

¼ cup finely chopped red or yellow bell pepper

¼ cup chopped carrots

¼ cup finely chopped celery

2 tablespoons minced Italian parsley

1 tablespoon extra-virgin olive

oil

4 tablespoons rice vinegar

2 garlic cloves, minced

3 tablespoons finely minced scallions

¼ cup slivered almonds

¼ teaspoon freshly ground black pepper

1. Place dry couscous in a heat-proof bowl. Pour boiling water over it, and let sit for 5 to 10 minutes until all the water is absorbed. 2. In a large bowl, combine the couscous, bell pepper, carrots, celery, and parsley together. 3. In a blender or food processor, combine the olive oil, vinegar, garlic, and scallions, and process for 1 minute. Pour over the couscous and vegetables, toss well, garnish with almonds, and season with the pepper. Serve.

Per Serving:

calorie: 373 | fat: 15g | protein: 12g | carbs: 51g | sugars: 3g | fiber: 10g | sodium: 34mg

Thai Broccoli Slaw

Prep time: 20 minutes | Cook time: 0 minutes | Serves 8

Dressing

2 tablespoons reduced-fat creamy peanut butter

1 tablespoon grated gingerroot

1 tablespoon rice vinegar

1 tablespoon orange marmalade

1½ teaspoons reduced-sodium soy sauce

¼ to ½ teaspoon chili garlic sauce

Slaw

3 cups broccoli slaw mix (from 10-oz bag)

½ cup bite-size thin strips red bell pepper

½ cup julienne (matchstick-cut) carrots

½ cup shredded red cabbage

2 tablespoons chopped fresh cilantro

1. In small bowl, combine all dressing ingredients. Beat with whisk, until blended. 2. In large bowl, toss all slaw ingredients. Pour dressing over slaw mixture; toss until coated. Cover and refrigerate at least 1 hour to blend flavors but no longer than 6 hours, tossing occasionally to blend dressing from bottom of bowl back into slaw mixture.

Per Serving:

calorie: 50 | fat: 1.5g | protein: 2g | carbs: 7g | sugars: 3g | fiber: 1g | sodium: 75mg

Appendix 1:
Measurement Conversion Chart

VOLUME EQUIVALENTS(DRY)

US STANDARD	METRIC (APPROXIMATE)
1/8 teaspoon	0.5 mL
1/4 teaspoon	1 mL
1/2 teaspoon	2 mL
3/4 teaspoon	4 mL
1 teaspoon	5 mL
1 tablespoon	15 mL
1/4 cup	59 mL
1/2 cup	118 mL
3/4 cup	177 mL
1 cup	235 mL
2 cups	475 mL
3 cups	700 mL
4 cups	1 L

WEIGHT EQUIVALENTS

US STANDARD	METRIC (APPROXIMATE)
1 ounce	28 g
2 ounces	57 g
5 ounces	142 g
10 ounces	284 g
15 ounces	425 g
16 ounces (1 pound)	455 g
1.5 pounds	680 g
2 pounds	907 g

VOLUME EQUIVALENTS(LIQUID)

US STANDARD	US STANDARD (OUNCES)	METRIC (APPROXIMATE)
2 tablespoons	1 fl.oz.	30 mL
1/4 cup	2 fl.oz.	60 mL
1/2 cup	4 fl.oz.	120 mL
1 cup	8 fl.oz.	240 mL
1 1/2 cup	12 fl.oz.	355 mL
2 cups or 1 pint	16 fl.oz.	475 mL
4 cups or 1 quart	32 fl.oz.	1 L
1 gallon	128 fl.oz.	4 L

TEMPERATURES EQUIVALENTS

FAHRENHEIT(F)	CELSIUS(C) (APPROXIMATE)
225 °F	107 °C
250 °F	120 °C
275 °F	135 °C
300 °F	150 °C
325 °F	160 °C
350 °F	180 °C
375 °F	190 °C
400 °F	205 °C
425 °F	220 °C
450 °F	235 °C
475 °F	245 °C
500 °F	260 °C

Appendix 2:

The Dirty Dozen and Clean Fifteen

The Environmental Working Group (EWG) is a nonprofit, nonpartisan organization dedicated to protecting human health and the environment Its mission is to empower people to live healthier lives in a healthier environment. This organization publishes an annual list of the twelve kinds of produce, in sequence, that have the highest amount of pesticide residue-the Dirty Dozen-as well as a list of the fifteen kinds ofproduce that have the least amount of pesticide residue-the Clean Fifteen.

THE DIRTY DOZEN	THE CLEAN FIFTEEN
• The 2016 Dirty Dozen includes the following produce. These are considered among the year's most important produce to buy organic:	• The least critical to buy organically are the Clean Fifteen list. The following are on the 2016 list:

THE DIRTY DOZEN

Strawberries	Spinach
Apples	Tomatoes
Nectarines	Bell peppers
Peaches	Cherry tomatoes
Celery	Cucumbers
Grapes	Kale/collard greens
Cherries	Hot peppers

THE CLEAN FIFTEEN

Avocados	Papayas
Corn	Kiw
Pineapples	Eggplant
Cabbage	Honeydew
Sweet peas	Grapefruit
Onions	Cantaloupe
Asparagus	Cauliflower
Mangos	

• The Dirty Dozen list contains two additional itemskale/collard greens and hot peppers-because they tend to contain trace levels of highly hazardous pesticides.

• Some of the sweet corn sold in the United States are made from genetically engineered (GE) seedstock. Buy organic varieties of these crops to avoid GE produce.

Appendix 3:
Recipe Index

A

African Peanut Stew · 99
Ambrosia · 95
Apple Cinnamon Bread Pudding · 91
Apple Crunch · 93
Artichokes Parmesan · 74
Asian Cod with Brown Rice, Asparagus, and Mushrooms · 62
Asian Fried Rice · 30
Asian Mushroom-Chicken Soup · 43
Asparagus with Cashews · 77
Asparagus, Sun-Dried Tomato, and Green Pea Sauté · 83
Autumn Pork Chops with Red Cabbage and Apples · 59
Avo-Tuna with Croutons · 64
Avocado Chocolate Mousse · 95

B

Bacon-Wrapped Vegetable Kebabs · 55
Baked Avocado and Egg · 19
Baked Eggs · 19
Baked Oysters · 68
Baked Pumpkin Pudding · 95
Baked Turkey Spaghetti · 41
Balsamic Green Beans and Fennel · 75
Banana N'Ice Cream with Cocoa Nuts · 90
Banana Pineapple Freeze · 92
Banana Protein Pancakes · 17
Banana Pudding · 94
BBQ Ribs and Broccoli Slaw · 51
BBQ Turkey Meat Loaf · 48
Beef and Mushroom Barley Soup · 104
Beef and Pepper Fajita Bowls · 52
Berry Smoothie Pops · 95
Biscuits · 22
Blackened Pollock · 65
Blooming Onion · 72
BLT Breakfast Wrap · 21
Blueberry and Chicken Salad on a Bed of Greens · 109
Blueberry Oat Mini Muffins · 21
Braised Kale with Ginger and Sesame Seeds · 77
Bran Apple Muffins · 22
Breakfast Banana Barley · 21
Breakfast Meatballs · 17
Broccoli Beef Stir-Fry · 60
Broiled Pineapple · 94
Broiled Shrimp with Garlic · 37
Broiled Sole with Mustard Sauce · 68
Brussels Sprout Hash and Eggs · 21

Buttercup Squash Soup · 105

C

Cabbage Slaw Salad · 113
Callaloo Redux · 74
Candied Pecans · 37
Caprese Eggplant Stacks · 86
Caramelized Onion–Shrimp Spread · 34
Caribbean Haddock in a Packet · 67
Carnitas Burrito Bowls · 51
Carrot and Cashew Chicken Salad · 107
Cashew-Kale and Chickpeas · 81
Cast Iron Hot Chicken · 48
Catfish with Corn and Pepper Relish · 69
Cauli-Curry Bean Soup · 105
Cauliflower Chili · 101
Cauliflower Rice · 76
Celery and Apple Salad with Cider Vinaigrette · 109
Charcuterie Dinner For One · 65
Cheesy Broiled Tomatoes · 76
Cheesy Quinoa-Crusted Spinach Frittata · 20
Cheesy Zucchini Patties · 88
Cherry, Chocolate, and Almond Shake · 20
Chewy Chocolate-Oat Bars · 94
Chicken and Vegetables with Quinoa · 29
Chicken Brunswick Stew · 102
Chicken Casablanca · 47
Chicken Enchilada Spaghetti Squash · 46
Chicken in Mushroom Gravy · 39
Chicken in Wine · 49
Chicken Kabobs · 34
Chicken Noodle Soup · 98
Chicken Provençal · 40
Chicken Reuben Bake · 47
Chicken Salad with Apricots · 108
Chicken Satay Stir-Fry · 41
Chicken with Lemon Caper Pan Sauce · 45
Chickpea and Tofu Bolognese · 82
Chickpea Coconut Curry · 83
Chickpea Spinach Soup · 104
Chickpea-Spinach Curry · 84
Chile Relleno Casserole with Salsa Salad · 88
Chilled Shrimp · 33
Chocolate Chip and Cranberry Cookies · 96
Chocolate Cupcakes · 91
Chocolate Tahini Bombs · 96
Cinnamon Bun Oatmeal · 24
Cinnamon Overnight Oats · 19
Cinnamon Toasted Pumpkin Seeds · 32

Citrus-Glazed Salmon · 66
Classic Crêpes · 94
Cocoa Carrot Muffins · 16
Coconut Chicken Curry · 44
Coconut Lime Chicken · 45
Coconut-Ginger Rice · 28
Coddled Huevos Rancheros · 18
Colorful Rice Casserole · 30
Comforting Summer Squash Soup with Crispy Chickpeas · 101
Corn, Egg and Potato Bake · 18
Couscous Salad · 114
Crab-Filled Mushrooms · 36
Cream Cheese Swirl Brownies · 90
Creamy Apple-Cinnamon Quesadilla · 34
Creamy Cheese Dip · 33
Creamy Cod with Asparagus · 64
Creamy Garlic Chicken with Broccoli · 47
Creamy Jalapeño Chicken Dip · 35
Creamy Orange Cheesecake · 90
Creamy Spinach Dip · 35
Crispy Eggplant Rounds · 85
Cucumber Roll-Ups · 37
Cucumber-Mango Salad · 114

D

Dandelion Greens with Sweet Onion · 75
Dark Chocolate–Cherry Multigrain Cookies · 92
Double-Ginger Cookies · 95
Dry-Rubbed Sirloin · 53
Dutch Oven Apple Pork Chops · 56

E

Easy Lentil Burgers · 30
Easy Southern Brunswick Stew · 104
Easy Tuna Patties · 62
Edamame and Walnut Salad · 111
Edamame Falafel with Roasted Vegetables · 87
Edamame-Tabbouleh Salad · 26
Egg Bites with Sausage and Peppers · 19
Eggplant Stew · 98

F

Farmers' Market Barley Risotto · 27
Faux Conch Fritters · 65
Favorite Chili · 99
Fennel and Chickpeas · 78
Fish Tacos · 70
Four-Bean Field Stew · 105
French Market Soup · 103
Fresh Dill Dip · 32
Fudgy Walnut Brownies · 93

G

Garden-Fresh Greek Salad · 111
Garlic Dill Wings · 47
Garlic Herb Radishes · 78
Garlic Roasted Radishes · 74

Gazpacho · 105
Gingered Tofu and Greens · 88
Gluten-Free Carrot and Oat Pancakes · 18
Golden Chicken Soup · 100
Grain-Free Parmesan Chicken · 42
Greek Rice Salad · 112
Greek Yogurt Cinnamon Pancakes · 24
Green Chickpea Falafel · 29
Griddle Corn Cakes · 17
Grilled Hearts of Romaine with Buttermilk Dressing · 107
Grilled Lemon Mustard Chicken · 48
Grilled Peach and Coconut Yogurt Bowls · 92
Grilled Pork Loin Chops · 59
Grilled Salmon with Dill Sauce · 65
Grilled Scallop Kabobs · 62
Grilled Steak and Vegetables · 52
Ground Turkey Stew · 102
Gruyere Apple Spread · 34
Guacamole with Jicama · 36

H

Haddock with Creamy Cucumber Sauce · 67
Hearty Italian Minestrone · 104
Herb-Roasted Turkey and Vegetables · 45
Herbed Beans and Brown Rice · 28
Herbed Buttermilk Chicken · 40
Herbed Cornish Hens · 40
Herbed Spring Peas · 110
Herbed Whole Turkey Breast · 49
High-Protein Oatmeal · 17
Homemade Sun-Dried Tomato Salsa · 35
Hoppin' John · 26
Hummus · 33

I

5-Ingredient Chunky Cherry and Peanut Butter Cookies · 96
5-Ingredient Mexican Lasagna · 57
Instant Popcorn · 34
Instant Pot Hard-Boiled Eggs · 15
Instant Pot Hoppin' John with Skillet Cauli "Rice" · 82
Italian Bean Burgers · 28
Italian Meatball-Zucchini "Noodle" Soup · 99
Italian Potato Salad · 109
Italian Sausages with Peppers and Onions · 52
Italian Tofu with Mushrooms and Peppers · 87
Italian Vegetable Soup · 103
Italian Wild Mushrooms · 73
Italian Zucchini Boats · 84

J

Jalapeño Popper Pork Chops · 53
Jamaican Stew · 98
Jerk Chicken Casserole · 45
Juicy Turkey Burgers · 43

K

Kidney Bean Salad · 110

Kielbasa and Cabbage ⋯⋯⋯⋯⋯⋯ 52
Kung Pao Chicken and Zucchini Noodles ⋯⋯⋯ 42

L

Lamb Kofta Meatballs with Cucumber Quick-Pickled Salad ⋯ 57
Lean Green Avocado Mashed Potatoes ⋯⋯⋯ 72
Lemon Artichokes ⋯⋯⋯⋯⋯⋯⋯ 33
Lemon Cream Fruit Dip ⋯⋯⋯⋯⋯ 33
Lemon-Pineapple Muffins ⋯⋯⋯⋯⋯ 23
Lemony Brussels Sprouts with Poppy Seeds ⋯⋯ 75
Lentil Salad ⋯⋯⋯⋯⋯⋯⋯⋯ 114
Lentil Soup ⋯⋯⋯⋯⋯⋯⋯⋯ 99
Loaded Cottage Pie ⋯⋯⋯⋯⋯⋯ 58
Lobster Fricassee ⋯⋯⋯⋯⋯⋯⋯ 69
Low-Fat Cream Cheese Frosting ⋯⋯⋯⋯ 95
Low-Sugar Blueberry Muffins ⋯⋯⋯⋯ 35

M

Marjoram-Pepper Steaks ⋯⋯⋯⋯⋯ 57
Mashed Sweet Potatoes ⋯⋯⋯⋯⋯ 77
Mediterranean Chef Salad ⋯⋯⋯⋯⋯ 114
Mediterranean Chicken Salad ⋯⋯⋯⋯ 113
Mediterranean Pasta Salad with Goat Cheese ⋯⋯ 108
Mediterranean Steak Sandwiches ⋯⋯⋯⋯ 59
Mediterranean-Style Chicken Scaloppine ⋯⋯⋯ 41
Mexican Turkey Tenderloin ⋯⋯⋯⋯⋯ 49
30-Minute Garlic Lamb Lollipops ⋯⋯⋯⋯ 58
Mixed-Berry Cream Tart ⋯⋯⋯⋯⋯ 91
Mozzarella-Tomato Salad ⋯⋯⋯⋯⋯ 110
Mushroom "Bacon" Topper ⋯⋯⋯⋯⋯ 77
Mustard Herb Pork Tenderloin ⋯⋯⋯⋯ 53
Mustard-Glazed Pork Chops ⋯⋯⋯⋯ 60

N

No-Bake Coconut and Cashew Energy Bars ⋯⋯ 37
No-Tuna Lettuce Wraps ⋯⋯⋯⋯⋯ 84
Nutty Deconstructed Salad ⋯⋯⋯⋯⋯ 108

O

Oat and Walnut Granola ⋯⋯⋯⋯⋯ 20
Oatmeal Chippers ⋯⋯⋯⋯⋯⋯⋯ 90
One-Pan Chicken Dinner ⋯⋯⋯⋯⋯ 46
Open-Faced Philly Cheesesteak Sandwiches ⋯⋯ 58
Orange Chicken Thighs with Bell Peppers ⋯⋯⋯ 46
Orange Muffins ⋯⋯⋯⋯⋯⋯⋯ 24
Orange Praline with Yogurt ⋯⋯⋯⋯⋯ 92
Orange Tofu ⋯⋯⋯⋯⋯⋯⋯⋯ 85
Orange-Marinated Pork Tenderloin ⋯⋯⋯⋯ 55

P

Palak Tofu ⋯⋯⋯⋯⋯⋯⋯⋯ 87
Pasta Salad–Stuffed Tomatoes ⋯⋯⋯⋯ 108
Peach and Almond Meal Fritters ⋯⋯⋯⋯ 91
Peach Shortcake ⋯⋯⋯⋯⋯⋯⋯ 92
Peach-Glazed Chicken over Dandelion Greens ⋯⋯ 49
Peanut Butter Protein Bites ⋯⋯⋯⋯⋯ 32

Peas with Mushrooms and Thyme ⋯⋯⋯⋯ 72
Peppercorn-Crusted Baked Salmon ⋯⋯⋯⋯ 62
Peppered Chicken with Balsamic Kale ⋯⋯⋯ 39
Perfect Sweet Potatoes ⋯⋯⋯⋯⋯⋯ 79
Pineapple Pear Medley ⋯⋯⋯⋯⋯⋯ 93
Pizza in a Pot ⋯⋯⋯⋯⋯⋯⋯⋯ 39
Pork Chop Diane ⋯⋯⋯⋯⋯⋯⋯ 60
Pork Chops with Raspberry-Chipotle Sauce and Herbed Rice ⋯ 56
Pork Tenderloin Stir-Fry ⋯⋯⋯⋯⋯⋯ 60
Pot Roast with Gravy and Vegetables ⋯⋯⋯ 53
Potato-Bacon Gratin ⋯⋯⋯⋯⋯⋯ 17
Power Salad ⋯⋯⋯⋯⋯⋯⋯⋯ 112
Pra Ram Vegetables and Peanut Sauce with Seared Tofu ⋯ 81
Pumpkin–Peanut Butter Single-Serve Muffins ⋯⋯ 24

Q

Quick Shrimp Gumbo ⋯⋯⋯⋯⋯⋯ 103
Quinoa Breakfast Bake with Pistachios and Plums ⋯ 23
Quinoa Pilaf with Salmon and Asparagus ⋯⋯⋯ 69
Quinoa–White Bean Loaf ⋯⋯⋯⋯⋯ 83
Quinoa, Beet, and Greens Salad ⋯⋯⋯⋯ 112

R

Radish Chips ⋯⋯⋯⋯⋯⋯⋯⋯ 79
Rainbow Quinoa Salad ⋯⋯⋯⋯⋯⋯ 112
Raw Corn Salad with Black-Eyed Peas ⋯⋯⋯ 113
Red Beans ⋯⋯⋯⋯⋯⋯⋯⋯ 29
Ribboned Squash with Bacon ⋯⋯⋯⋯⋯ 72
Rice Breakfast Bake ⋯⋯⋯⋯⋯⋯ 22
Rice with Spinach and Feta ⋯⋯⋯⋯⋯ 26
Roast Chicken with Pine Nuts and Fennel ⋯⋯⋯ 40
Roasted Asparagus–Berry Salad ⋯⋯⋯⋯ 113
Roasted Beef with Peppercorn Sauce ⋯⋯⋯ 54
Roasted Carrot and Chickpea Dip ⋯⋯⋯⋯ 32
Roasted Carrot and Herb Spread ⋯⋯⋯⋯ 35
Roasted Eggplant ⋯⋯⋯⋯⋯⋯⋯ 75
Roasted Halibut with Red Peppers, Green Beans, and Onions ⋯ 63
Roasted Lemon and Garlic Broccoli ⋯⋯⋯⋯ 72
Roasted Red Snapper and Shrimp in Parchment ⋯⋯ 66
Roasted Salmon with Salsa Verde ⋯⋯⋯⋯ 67
Roasted Tomato and Sweet Potato Soup ⋯⋯⋯ 102
Roasted Veggie Bowl ⋯⋯⋯⋯⋯⋯ 86
Rosemary Lamb Chops ⋯⋯⋯⋯⋯⋯ 54

S

Saffron-Spiced Chicken Breasts ⋯⋯⋯⋯ 44
Salmon en Papillote ⋯⋯⋯⋯⋯⋯ 68
Salmon Florentine ⋯⋯⋯⋯⋯⋯⋯ 66
Salmon with Brussels Sprouts ⋯⋯⋯⋯⋯ 64
Sausage, Sweet Potato, and Kale Hash ⋯⋯⋯ 20
Sautéed Garlicky Mushrooms ⋯⋯⋯⋯⋯ 76
Sautéed Spinach and Lima Beans ⋯⋯⋯⋯ 82
Sautéed Spinach with Parmesan and Almonds ⋯⋯ 74
Sautéed Sweet Peppers ⋯⋯⋯⋯⋯⋯ 75
Savory Shrimp ⋯⋯⋯⋯⋯⋯⋯⋯ 64
Scallops and Asparagus Skillet ⋯⋯⋯⋯⋯ 70
Seedy Muesli ⋯⋯⋯⋯⋯⋯⋯⋯ 15
Sesame Bok Choy with Almonds ⋯⋯⋯⋯ 78

Sesame Chicken-Almond Slaw ·········· 107
Sesame-Crusted Halibut ·········· 66
Shakshuka ·········· 16
Shepherd's Pie with Cauliflower-Carrot Mash ·········· 54
Sherried Peppers with Bean Sprouts ·········· 78
Shredded Potato Omelet ·········· 23
Shrimp Creole ·········· 65
Shrimp with Tomatoes and Feta ·········· 63
Simple Bibimbap ·········· 76
Simple Grain-Free Biscuits ·········· 21
Sirloin Steaks with Cilantro Chimichurri ·········· 58
Slow-Cooked Pork Burrito Bowls ·········· 55
Smashed Cucumber Salad ·········· 73
Smoked Salmon and Asparagus Quiche Cups ·········· 23
Smoky Spinach Hummus with Popcorn Chips ·········· 36
"Smothered" Steak ·········· 53
Snow Peas with Sesame Seeds ·········· 74
Sole Piccata ·········· 64
Southwestern Egg Casserole ·········· 15
Southwestern Quinoa Salad ·········· 29
Spaghetti Squash ·········· 78
Speedy Chicken Cacciatore ·········· 44
Spice-Infused Roast Beef ·········· 60
Spiced Pear Applesauce ·········· 91
Spicy Beef Stew with Butternut Squash ·········· 55
Spicy Chicken Drumsticks ·········· 47
Spicy Couscous and Chickpea Salad ·········· 27
Spicy Roasted Cauliflower with Lime ·········· 73
Spinach Salad with Eggs, Tempeh Bacon, and Strawberries ·········· 86
Squash and Tomato Cassoulet ·········· 73
Steak Stroganoff ·········· 57
Steaks with Walnut-Blue Cheese Butter ·········· 56
Stewed Green Beans ·········· 28
Strawberry Cream Cheese Crepes ·········· 96
Stuffed Acorn Squash ·········· 84
Stuffed Flounder Florentine ·········· 70
Stuffed Portobello Mushrooms ·········· 86
Stuffed Portobellos ·········· 85
Summer Salad ·········· 108
Summer Squash Casserole ·········· 76
Sunflower-Tuna-Cauliflower Salad ·········· 111
Sunshine Burgers ·········· 27
Superfood Brownie Bites ·········· 93
Sweet Potato Fennel Bake ·········· 26
Sweet-and-Sour Cabbage Slaw ·········· 73

T

Tangy Barbecue Strawberry-Peach Chicken ·········· 42
Tantalizing Jerked Chicken ·········· 41
Tasty Tomato Soup ·········· 101
Tenderloin with Crispy Shallots ·········· 56
Teriyaki Salmon ·········· 67
Texas Caviar ·········· 30
Thai Broccoli Slaw ·········· 114
Thai Red Lentils ·········· 30
Thai Yellow Curry with Chicken Meatballs ·········· 39

Three Bean and Basil Salad ·········· 110
Three-Bean Salad with Black Bean Crumbles ·········· 109
Three-Berry Dutch Pancake ·········· 15
Tofu and Bean Chili ·········· 81
Tomato and Chive Waffles ·········· 18
Tomato and Kale Soup ·········· 98
Tomato Tuna Melts ·········· 68
Tomato-Basil Soup with Grilled Cheese Croutons ·········· 103
Triple-Berry and Jicama Spinach Salad ·········· 111
Tu-No Salad ·········· 113
Tuna Poke with Riced Broccoli ·········· 69
Turkey and Pinto Chili ·········· 100
Turkey Bolognese with Chickpea Pasta ·········· 48
Turkey Cabbage Soup ·········· 44
Turkey Chili ·········· 46
Turkey Rollups with Veggie Cream Cheese ·········· 33
Turkey with Almond Duxelles ·········· 43
Vanilla Steel-Cut Oatmeal ·········· 20
Vegan Dal Makhani ·········· 85

V

Vegetable Burgers ·········· 84
Vegetable Frittata ·········· 16
Vegetable Kabobs with Mustard Dip ·········· 36
Veggie Fajitas ·········· 83
Veggie Unfried Rice ·········· 27
Veggie-Stuffed Omelet ·········· 22
Veggies with Cottage Cheese Ranch Dip ·········· 36
Vietnamese Meatball Lollipops with Dipping Sauce ·········· 32

W

Walnut-Crusted Halibut with Pear Salad ·········· 63
Warm Barley and Squash Salad with Balsamic Vinaigrette ·········· 110
West African–Inspired Peanut Soup ·········· 100
Western Omelet ·········· 16
White Bean Soup ·········· 101
Whole Veggie-Stuffed Trout ·········· 63
Whole Wheat Waffles with Honey–Peanut Butter Drizzle ·········· 15
Whole-Wheat Linguine with Kale Pesto ·········· 26
Wild Rice Salad ·········· 109
Wild Rice with Blueberries and Pumpkin Seeds ·········· 28
Wilted Kale and Chard ·········· 79
Wine-Poached Chicken with Herbs and Vegetables ·········· 43
Winter Chicken and Citrus Salad ·········· 107

Y

Young Kale and Cabbage Salad with Toasted Peanuts ·········· 111

Z

Zesty Swiss Steak ·········· 59
Zucchini on the Half Shell ·········· 77
Zucchini Sauté ·········· 78

Made in the USA
Coppell, TX
01 February 2024